THE GIRLS ‘TIL DEATH DO US PART

Also by Lisa Moreno

Ungodly Intent

THE GIRLS 'TIL DEATH DO US PART

Lisa Moreno

This book is a work of fiction. The names, characters, places, and incidents portrayed in the story are the product of the author's imagination or have been used fictitiously. Any resemblance to actual persons, living or dead, businesses, companies, events, or locales, is purely coincidental.

Second Edition: January 2017

Printed in the United States of America

ISBN: 978-1-48359-450-7

Acknowledgments

To my amazing editor, Betsy Smith, who never wearied or complained through long editing sessions. My husband, Richard Moreno, who gets to hear every chapter repeated ad nauseam. And to my readers, always stay engaged.

Table of Contents

Chapter

PROLOGUE

EVERYONE'S GOT A SECRET cloaked by a deceptive story most want to forget. Then there are those who fear if their deception ever surfaces, lives will be indelibly altered. People have all kinds of moral dilemmas tucked away. Often, the passage of time allows them to become irrelevant, fading into passing shadows tracking the back of our minds. Then again, secrets that char our souls buried so deep smolder quietly waiting their turn to escape and their contents purged. These secrets obsess and abscess in our minds feeding the flames of self-destruction. Though life has changed immensely in the past 20 years Natalie Grant's recollections marooned within her psyche since 1988, assault her fragmented memories leaving her a blind victim to their haunts. Finally able to grip the reality of the past, resonating voices have assigned her the task of revealing the truth about the girls. After all, she was their leader.

This story is not only about conquering one's inner demons, but also exposing something far more sinister than any of the girls could ever have imagined; a reality so deviant, so twisted, it defies comprehension and transcends the unimaginable. It is about surviving a destructive phantom of malevolence that parades as the voice of primal truth.

CHAPTER 1
THE FUNERAL

COLD, MUSTY AIR filled the modest chapel that served as the memorial site for Caitlin "KT" O'Neill's funeral. Here, just beyond the quiet, lay the forgotten town of Heaven's Door, in the rural farming community of Macon County, Illinois.

In the back pew is Natalie Grant, a forty-year-old attractive brunette, flanked by her mother and younger brother. Natalie sits trancelike. Underneath, deep in thought, she is trying to make sense of KT's suicide. The decision to unearth the past was not an option anymore.

Natalie is convinced two unsolved murders from her youth are connected to KT's suicide. But the pages of her younger self were erased after a serious car accident in 1988 put her life in a tailspin. Only frightening, unexplained nightmares remained.

She glanced around the chapel taking in the mix of predominately Irish people, then locked eyes with KT's visibly aged mom. Siobhan O'Neill, the matriarch, is sitting in the front right pew tucked between her three sons and surviving daughter.

Widowed only two months, she must now bury a child. Yet, the expression on Siobhan's face is peculiar, not the expected look of a grieving mother. Seeing Natalie for the first time in years, her hands tighten around a sealed envelope.

Meanwhile, Maggie Grant tried her best to comfort her only daughter. But Natalie never felt Maggie's reassuring hand, nor her brother Kevin's. She couldn't sense beyond her own internal isolation.

Yet, somehow, Natalie knew if she could unscramble the baffling nightmares she'd not only figure out the tie between those past murders and KT's suicide, but find desperately needed salvation.

CHAPTER 2

AND SO IT BEGINS

MAYBE IT WAS the stillness in the air or the specter of death that propelled her thoughts through the conundrum of time. It really didn't matter. Hell graciously opened its arms beckoning her in.

Natalie's mind flashed back in time to when she and her girlfriends were teenagers and she was about to leave for a sleepover at KT's. In spite of her arresting amnesia, certain memories are crystal clear.

Natalie could still remember that heavy, suffocating day vividly. The time was early July, 1986. She caught a ride with one of KT's neighbors, Betty McCloud. Her daughter Annie shared ballet classes with Natalie in Decatur. Mrs. McCloud assured Natalie it wasn't an imposition to drop her off.

The scenery to KT's family farm seemed to change abruptly once they left the township of Decatur and entered the rural area of Macon County. They drove through an old, rundown, sleepy town. The place looked deserted, except for a few rusted cars parked along the curb.

Natalie recalled a strange eerie feeling creep over her. An old, distressed greeting sign placed mid-block had some odd symbol she didn't recognize with words beneath stating…

"Welcome to Heaven's Door
Enjoy your stay"

Up ahead was an old army surplus store with a decaying wooden statue of an Indian Chief standing guard out front. The dull crumbling paint had peeled away from the face leaving its eyes vacant and haunting. There was a narrow, shrine-like building set back a bit next to the surplus store. It had the same odd symbol carved above the doorway.

Brought up a Protestant, Sundays were always spent in reverence. Natalie's mom felt worshiping together kept families united. Natalie had her own thoughts about the spiritual world; however, she held her feelings very private, deep inside. All she knew of God was abandonment.

KT was an Irish Catholic, yet went to public school as far back as Natalie could remember. Natalie wondered why she didn't attend St. Teresa's Catholic School but decided better to leave it alone. There were, after all, some secrets they just couldn't share.

At the end of town was a small airfield where retired single-engine prop planes and crop-dusters sat as relics beaten down by the elements waiting to be salvaged. Natalie remembered the scene with a sense of foreboding.

There was an active war going on here and the elements were clearly winning. Once they passed the airstrip, another curious sign placed again in the center of the block read…

"Leaving Heaven's Door
Watch your step"

Natalie felt relieved when she was on the other side of the sign. That place gave her the willies. Reliving it now was no different.

KT said her ancestors had built the original settlement, church and cemetery when they arrived from Ireland, adding that the Irish clans who migrated to Macon County were hard working farmers who made their own rules and rarely ventured out of their community. She did mention that her father and his friends were involved in some kind of pagan mysticism.

Driving up the private road to KT's farmhouse were unusual circular patterns of white river rocks placed on both sides of the driveway. Further up was a wrought iron gate with the O'Neill family name embellished with that odd symbol she had seen in town on the signs.

The two-story farmhouse loomed out at her. It looked to be at least 100 years old. The place was surrounded by endless rows of tall reaching cornfields. Multitudes of blackbirds squawked in a frenzy, circling above. Natalie sensed inexplicable dread.

Mrs. McCloud pulled up to the house and Natalie got out of the car thanking her for the ride. Siobhan O'Neill greeted her at the front door. She was a hard-edged woman dressed in a plain Irish linen frock. Dark, foreboding eyes branded her face. Her black hair was pulled back in a severe twist. She seemed pleasant enough, but Natalie still felt an uneasy chill run through her veins.

"Natalie, please come in."

"Hello, Mrs. O'Neill."

"KT will be down shortly. Can I offer you some lemonade?"

"That would be wonderful," realizing her mouth was parched.

"I'll be right back. Make yourself at home."

"Thank you," Natalie said politely.

Natalie took the time to look at her surroundings. Their living room held a collection of family photos on the mantle. There was a picture of Darcy who was three years younger than KT. Natalie recalled thinking things just weren't right with her mentally. Once Natalie asked KT about her sister, but it was clear she didn't want to discuss it. Her three brothers were away at college.

The sleepover haunted Natalie all these years leaving baffling, disconnected images. Waking that night to hot, stagnant air, she stumbled out of bed to open the window and thought she saw someone being chased out in the cornfields. Natalie strained to see into the night but only saw blackbirds fluttering about. She didn't want to arouse KT. Accepting her eyes were playing tricks, she crawled back into bed. At 15, she was terrified. Now, at 40, she still was.

CHAPTER 3

GRADUATION DAY

AS THE FUNERAL PROCEEDED, Natalie's mind raced like a locomotive trying hard to find the proper track that would take her home, back through the empty corridors that held her prisoner and threatened her very existence. She challenged herself to persevere and reconnect the memories that were so fractured in her mind.

Natalie's thoughts spooled forward to graduation day. The day her life changed forever. It was June 17, 1988, and high school graduation ceremony had just ended. The graduates were all smiles.

A younger, vivacious Natalie offered to have a graduation slumber party at her home with her five best friends. KT, Melanie and Deidra Stuart, Emily Martin and Jennifer Lawson made up the group. With more pictures surely to come, Natalie made a quick stop in the restroom to freshen up. After lots of good-byes and promises to keep in touch, Natalie and her family left.

Back at home, she thought about the plans KT connived with her oldest brother, Patrick. All the girls would show up at Natalie's home, then they'd secretly meet the boys at Whispering Lake to have a private party and go skinny dipping.

Patrick had invited two college friends, Colin Sullivan and Dylan Maguire, from South Bend to come along and celebrate. Even though they couldn't get home in time to attend graduation, they'd make it in time for KT's celebration dinner. The O'Neills would be caravanning with their friends. Natalie replayed her telephone conversation with KT. Their young voices echoed in her head.

"KT, can I borrow those sexy tight pants and tank top of yours to wear tonight?"

"Sure. I'm giving you a heads up now, I have dibs on Colin. His friend Dylan is no slouch either. Plus, you'll finally get to meet my brothers. I bet you'll like Aidan, and I think you're his type, too.

"My mom still thinks I'm staying at your place for a sleepover party with the girls following my celebration dinner tonight. After my dad bowed out from coming to graduation, she hasn't questioned me about anything. Why shouldn't we celebrate at Whispering Lake? It's on our property and so remote no one will have a clue we're there. The night is ours for the taking!" KT's words were haunting.

"The lake is a great idea, KT. Make sure to remind your brothers to keep quiet. We don't need any parents getting wind of our plans. They better not pick us up at my home. It'll be too obvious. We have very nosy neighbors."

"Then how are we getting out to the lake?" KT asked.

Natalie told her not to worry and cut the conversation short. She needed to concentrate on getting a viable plan together. She'd figure out an alternative means of transportation and decide who would bring the necessary items, food and such. After working things out with the other girls, Natalie called KT back.

"Hello, hello. Is anybody there? Darcy, if that's you, just say hello, it's Natalie."

"Hello, Natalie. The blackbirds watch me everywhere."

"Give me the phone now, Darcy! I'm sorry, Natalie. Never mind her."

"KT, is she okay?"

"Okay as she'll ever be. What's up?"

"Everything's set." Natalie went on to tell KT the intricacies of her plan.

"Deidra and Melanie told their mom that there's a school sponsored party in the gymnasium so she's dropping them off at school at 8:45 p.m. Mrs. Stuart thinks they're coming back to my house for the sleepover. They're packing a duffel bag with extra clothes. Emily is walking over after her family dinner celebration is finished. Jen's mom offered to drop her over here after dinner so that's fine. I guess we're all a go and the party is on. The way I see it everyone should arrive here by 9 p.m. Now all I have to figure out is how to get us over to Whispering Lake without attracting suspicion."

THE DARK LABYRINTH that has defined Natalie Grant's mind all these years has now illuminated a corridor she's able to access. Like a blind person being led by a firm hand, she ventured on. It is a chance to let her courage strengthen her resolve while defeating the icy fear that has kept her memory frozen.

CHAPTER 4
REMEMBERING BACK

NATALIE HEARD THE SOUND of her mother's voice calling her from the kitchen.

"Natalie, would you please come downstairs? I need to talk with you."

"Sure, Mom, be down in a minute."

After losing her husband, Bernard Grant, to a freakish boating accident, Maggie Grant took on the role of both parents. She worked as a full-time secretary at Caterpillar and did part-time bookkeeping for the Callaghans.

John Callaghan, of a neighboring clan and a close friend of the O'Neills, purchased Bernard's business after the tragedy. He asked Maggie to continue the bookkeeping. It only required one night a week.

Maggie and Amanda Martin, Emily's mother, were best friends through college at Columbia. It's because of this friendship that the Grants moved to Illinois from Minnesota years back when Natalie was eight and Kevin was five. Emily and Natalie were close in age so their friendship naturally blossomed.

Natalie visualized Em's curly red hair and piercing green eyes. Unfortunately, her pretty friend harbored many phobias. Something happened to Emily when she was very young that left her scarred with panic attacks, but Emily didn't remember what it was. Natalie tried to protect her from the paralyzing fears whenever she could. Emily, in turn, always tried to please her girlfriend. Natalie loved Rocky Road ice cream and Em knew it. Emily surprised her often with a double scoop cone.

To solve the transportation issue, Natalie planned on asking her mom to borrow the family car. She had cleared the path earlier inferring that the girls had a surprise in store for her. This would cover for them leaving the house. She came downstairs.

"Natalie, I just heard a message from Mr. Callaghan on the answering machine asking me to come over this evening and help him with a financial statement he needs to give the bank on Monday morning. You're fine to stay here alone with your girlfriends, right?"

"Sure, Mom."

"Need any money for refreshments?"

"No. The girls are bringing snacks. We're good, Mom."

"Kevin's spending the night at his friend Gary's so you girls will have the house all to yourselves. I'll be home rather late. I kind of remember you saying something to me about having some surprise plans for tonight?" Maggie cocked an inquisitive eyebrow.

"Yes, we do, but everyone's being so secretive about it. I guess I'm out of the loop. Regardless, you know you can trust me. If we're not here when you get back, please don't worry."

"Fine, Natalie, but whatever you do keep your wits about you. I don't want to hear any gossip from the neighbors or get a phone call from the police and keep the music down past curfew."

"You've got my word, Mom."

"I'm going to have to leave right away. The roads are a complete mess out on the expressway due to a terrible accident." Maggie grabbed a stack of papers and her purse.

"Did anyone die?"

"Unfortunately, yes. It sounds like a dreadful situation. I just heard about it on the radio so I need to get going. Have a wonderful time tonight. Love you."

Natalie kissed her mom and smiled. Underneath, she mused, *Mr. Callaghan, you and your financial worries are the answer to my prayer.* Natalie didn't know how she was going to tell her mom the party had shifted locations and they wouldn't be there most of the night. Fortunately, Maggie didn't question Natalie's phony story. It was perfect--no argument, no debate.

LIKE AN ASCENDING staircase, each step revealed a lost memory. The transportation answer was sitting right in the garage--her father's car! She remembered that nice mechanic installing a disconnect to prevent the battery from draining since the car wasn't in use. He showed Natalie and her mother how to flip the switch to reconnect it so the car would turn over. It would only need fresh gas. The station was close to the convenience store. It was foolproof.

The time had arrived to call Em and share the good news, adding that it would be more efficient to meet at Miller's Convenience Store, pick up the food, gas up and drive them both back to her home.

Then a flush came over Natalie's face as her dad filled her thoughts. *I guess this was meant to be, Dad. You'll be celebrating my high school graduation with me, after all. It's a little weird that you died down at the same lake where we'll be partying. You called it our own, quiet, little sanctuary. Maybe, that's why I'm so happy I get to spend tonight down there. Whispering Lake was, after all, the last place we were together.*

CHAPTER 5

PUTTING IT ALL TOGETHER

AT EMILY MARTIN'S home not far away, the anxious graduate was busy planning what she was going to wear to the party. Natalie phoned and got Mrs. Martin who called up to Emily to grab the extension. Natalie heard their voices echoing in her head.

"Hi, Nat. What's up?"

"I figured out how we're getting over to Whispering Lake. My mom has to work tonight at the Callaghans so she took the car. I think between work and traffic she'll be home really late. I checked my dad's car out and it still has some gas in it. The car sputtered a bit but finally started. I'll bring jumper cables along anyway. We'll need to add fresh gas and take a hose to it, but other than that it's good to go."

"Natalie, would you mind if I skip tonight?"

"What? Are you kidding?" Natalie was taken.

"That place really scares me. I have this terrible feeling. Kind of like a premonition." Emily's voice trembled.

"Em, why don't you take one of those anti-anxiety pills your mother keeps for you? You just have to go! This will be the best party of your life!"

"Okay, Natalie, I'll go. Maybe those pills will help. I hate being like this--it's so paralyzing." Emily's mind had its own monsters.

"Just stay by my side, and I'll keep you safe," Natalie tried to be reassuring.

"Here's the plan. After dinner start walking toward Miller's Convenience Store. I'll meet you there. You decide what munchies to get-- chips and salsa, that kind of stuff. I've told KT to have the guys pick up the beer. They're dropping her off here first and then we'll all meet over at the lake. The other girls plan to be at my house around 9 p.m. so I figure we need to meet up by 8:45 to be back here on time."

"Can we really pull this off, Nat?"

"Like a hot knife through butter."

Emily's mother called out for Em. Natalie could hear Mrs. Martin's voice resound through the receiver.

"Emily, are you still on the phone? Can you hear me up there? I'd like to talk with you in the kitchen."

"Yes, Mom. One second."

"I'll see you at Miller's at 8:45. Bye."

"Coming, Mom."

"Are you girls still planning to have a sleepover at Natalie's? I spoke to her mom half an hour ago and she said she had to work tonight."

"We're still on, Mom."

"Emily, is everything okay?"

"Sure, Mom."

"You sound nervous, honey." Amanda Martin detected something.

"I'm just excited about graduating." Emily kept a straight face.

"I see," her mom relented.

CHAPTER 6

THE DRIVE FROM SOUTH BEND

IT WAS MID-AFTERNOON when the guys started their interstate drive. Patrick's two friends are amped-up and ready to party. Dylan Maguire is a lady's man. His black wavy hair, green eyes and deep cleft turn heads. While Colin Sullivan, at 6'4", has a chiseled face, straight blond hair, blue eyes and the body of an Adonis.

It's supposed to be a wild, promising evening with six girls all anxious to let loose and party. Patrick has assured his buddies sex is a sure thing so it would make the long trip worth it. But now, tired and hungry, the frustration between the two became evident as the trip turned ugly. All it took was one nasty accident to bring out the worst in people.

"Damn, how much longer is this drive going to take, Dylan? I know it's got to be less than four hours from South Bend to Macon County," Colin griped.

"Calm your heels, bud. I didn't figure on wall-to-wall traffic the whole way. We should be there in less than two hours. Hey, what's that you're holding?"

"Neat, isn't it? It's a medallion my dad gave me when I turned 16." Colin beamed.

"I've never seen anything like it before. What does it mean?"

“It’s an old Gaelic symbol called a triskelion. See these small stones around the edge? They form a spiritual circle that protects the person who wears it,” Colin said sanctimoniously.

“You’re not into that pagan witchcraft stuff, are you?”

“Chill, Maguire. I figured I’d have time to see my father’s old friend, Daniel McCloud. I called him before we left and asked if I could meet him tomorrow. He lives in the area. Since no one outside our little group knows about the party tonight, I told him I’d call for directions in the morning. Who knows where we’ll be waking up?” Sullivan smirked, then continued. “I brought it along to show McCloud I’m still part of the brotherhood. It’s kind of an old Irish thing,” he toyed with it.

“Don’t tell me you believe in all that Wiccan mumbo jumbo?” Dylan blurted.

“Let’s leave this conversation for another time. I want to talk about the girls we’re going to meet tonight. I’ve seen pictures of Patrick’s sister KT and she’s one hot babe. You could spend forever groping her tits. Patrick talks about her like she’s just another piece of ass. Says she’s a sure thing. Can you believe that? I heard these girls are looking for a good time. Speaking of Patrick, where are the brothers O’Neill? Weren’t they behind us just a short time ago?”

“They’re back there in the crunch. No worry, Colin, I know where I’m going.”

“Good. Nothing’s going to stop us from having the time of our lives tonight. By the way, I put three bottles of Jameson in the trunk. I figured the girls might be up for something a wee bit stronger than a beer,” Colin grinned.

"Smart thinking. Man, oh, man, look at all this traffic. This has to be the result of that nasty farm truck pileup we heard about on the radio. We're in deep shit."

CHAPTER 7

MELANIE AND DEIDRA STUART

THE TWINS FINISHED their celebration dinner. It was difficult getting their talkative mom out the door. Deidra was worried about the time. They'd have to hightail it over to Natalie's.

"Is she out of sight yet, Deidra?" Melanie whined.

"Mom's car just disappeared around the corner. Let's take off and cut through the hedge." Deidra led.

"Oh, no! I'm completely snagged on this bush. Deidra, did you remember to bring the flashlights?" Melanie moaned in protest.

"Of course I brought them along, you idiot, but we don't want to bring attention to ourselves. Remember, we're supposed to be in the high school gym right now. Get yourself untangled. We can take a shortcut through the shopping center's parking lot and swing around the convenience store. We'll save ten minutes that way." Deidra was certain.

"Great, walking through a pitch dark parking lot when we've got flashlights in our duffel bags. What seems wrong with this picture? You lead the way, Smarty Pants." Melanie trudged behind.

"Hurry up, Mel, we've gotta walk faster. We're supposed to be at Natalie's by 9 'clock."

"Deidra, I could sure use a Band-Aid. Guess I cut myself on those shrubs. Blood's running down my arm."

"Can you wait 'til we get over to Natalie's?" Deidra's patience was waning.

"If I have to. I just don't want blood getting all over my blouse. How will I explain that to Mom?" Melodramatics spiked Melanie's words.

"Okay, just wait 'til we get deeper into the parking lot, and I'll fetch out a Band-Aid from my duffel bag. Those dumpsters over there will give us cover, and I'll fix your arm. Darn, the security guard is driving around the parking lot. He's got a flashlight and is checking around the cars. Make a run for it."

"Deidra, you *do* know Mr. Abbott knows Mom."

"Shush, just keep quiet and don't move. If he shines his light on these dumpsters, he'll see us! I've got an idea, Mel. This one isn't piled up and is probably empty. Let's shimmy into it fast. We can make a mad dash for Natalie's once he's passed."

"Okay, Deidra. How are we gonna get in there and what about our stuff?"

"Throw the duffel bags in first. I'll give you a hoist up and then you can pull me inside, but be quiet! Hurry, his car is heading this way. Brace yourself on my shoulders and step into my hands. I'll push you up and over."

"I'm in. It's a miracle I didn't land on my head. What a drop. Your turn now."

However, Deidra had calculated wrong. Things quickly shifted to damage control.

"Melanie, can you reach the top of the dumpster with your hands? I can't get myself over without help."

"My fingers can, but not my entire hand." Melanie was too short.

"Can you stand on both of the duffel bags and try again?" Deidra pleaded.

"I would if I could. It's so dark in here. Gosh, I wonder where our flashlights are."

"Shut up, Mel."

"I can't see squat. I'm walking on some slimy, sticky stuff. I can't believe I didn't slip and break my neck landing on this goo. It stinks, too. Run, take a flying leap, do something, Deidra! You're smart, figure a way to get in. This was your brainy idea and I don't want to be in here alone." Melanie's apprehension grew like wild fire.

CHAPTER 8
MALL SECURITY

MALL SECURITY at Decatur Shopping Center was buzzing. Tips came in from unidentified callers throughout the afternoon that Decatur's least favorite resident had been released from jail and was seen back home in the neighborhood. Billy Smith earned his reputation seven years back as a pedophile. Everyone thought that he should rot in jail forever. But somehow Billy got himself out early on good behavior.

Concerned parents knowing their daughters would be shopping tonight wanted security to be on top of things. Several calls came into Decatur Police Department as well. Everyone knew Billy was back.

"Bob, Captain Green's on the horn, pick up." Head of Security was calling.

"I've got it, Max. Hi, Captain. Yeah, we've received several reports of possible problems in the area. I've got Abbott checking out the entire parking lot.

"His last clear communication was ten minutes ago when he told me he hadn't seen anything suspicious around the front. I've tried three times unsuccessfully to get him on the two-way radio. I told him to call for backup if he got in trouble," Officer Bob Banks reported.

"I'm using the darn telephone booth to call in. These two-ways are worthless crap. How good can security be when we can't even communicate with our security guard on patrol? Bob, where the heck is he?" A.J. Green was frustrated as hell.

"He's likely just taking a piss out by the dumpsters. He wouldn't recognize a criminal if one was staring him in the face." Officer Banks chuckled.

"You're probably right. Page me if you hear anything, and I'll call you right back. We don't need any more problems on grad night. We'll have enough rowdy kids to keep us busy. Talk with you later," Green clicked off.

"Bob, Abbott's trying to call in again. Can't make out what he's saying. Talk up, Abbott, are you there?"

Static…Static…

"This is Abbott, can anyone hear me? I hate this damn radio!"

At 59, James Abbott is a worn out man, with nothing to face but the people he saw daily at the mall. At this stage, he was stranded in Suburbia.

"There goes that radio again."

Static…Static…

"How the hell do they expect me to get anything with all the noise?"

Static…Static…

Abbott refocused his attention. *Oh, great, someone's walking in the parking lot. I'll shine my flashlight on them and drive up nice and slow. Don't want to scare somebody unnecessarily.*

"Who's there? Hey, I know…"

STATIC...STATIC...

"You!" He turns his light away. "What are you doing here?"

STATIC...STATIC...

"What did you say you were looking for? Let me get out of my car and I'll see if I can help. Hey, get that light out of my eyes! Turn that thing away..."

STATIC...STATIC...

"What the hell!"

CHAPTER 9

TRAFFIC JAM-ALERT
I-72 BOTH DIRECTIONS

BACK IN THE THICK OF THINGS, the road trip wasn't going as planned. Little did Dylan or Colin know the magnitude of the traffic snare.

"No, this really isn't happening."

"Shush!! Be quiet!"

"Update. Expect long delays on the I-72 expressway due to an earlier multiple car accident with one fatality." The reporter continued,

"At 5:20 p.m. today a farm truck going westbound on the I-72 lost control, swerved into the left lane hitting a ford Mustang. It then hit a van before flipping over unleashing several wooden crates blocking all lanes. Oncoming cars crashed into the crates creating a domino effect. As a result, there was an eight-car pileup. Nine people were being treated for minor injuries.

"The driver of the farm truck was pronounced dead at the scene. His name was not released pending notification of kin. The highway is temporarily closed during clean up and investigation. Highway Patrol is on-scene redirecting traffic Ambulances, fire engines and tow trucks are still trying to make their way through the sea of chaos that extends for miles in both directions."

"Turn that radio off! What a nightmare. Dylan, people are getting out of their cars. I guess the only party we're going to tonight is right here on this lousy expressway. A bottle of Jameson might get opened sooner than I planned. Maybe, I'll get out and walk down the line a ways and try to find the O'Neills. Unless they pulled off the expressway and knew of some other way around this gridlock they're stuck in this stinking mess, too. Or, I can stand on the hood and take a look instead of walking back there." Colin was wound up.

"No way, Colin. This is my father's car and you're not standing on the hood, trunk, or anything else. Why don't you just take that medallion of yours and make it do its magic and get us the hell out of here. Then, I'll become a believer."

"You just don't get it man. My medallion probably saved us from being caught up in that accident. We left 30 minutes later than we had planned, remember. I'm off now to go find the O'Neills. If the traffic starts up again, and I'm not back, take the next exit and I'll meet you there." Colin was gone.

Dylan sat in his dad's car, tired and frustrated. He couldn't understand the relationship between Patrick and Colin. Other than both of them being Irish, what was the connection? He wondered what he was getting himself into. The last thing he needed was to get involved in some kind of cult.

HAPPY TO BE OUT of the car and away from Dylan, Colin wandered back through the maze of cars looking for the O'Neills. Alone, he now faced the reality that he might have to quit college. Worried, guilt-ridden, and left with a sense of uncertainty about his future, he reflected on the web of lies he'd told his buddies back at school.

Where are they? They've got to be in this sea of cars somewhere. They couldn't have passed us. Not a chance. Patrick promised I'd forget all about my problems if I came down here to celebrate with his kid sister and her friends. Last night's phone call from Dad sure changed things…

"Money's tight, Son. We're in a severe drought, and if things don't turn around fast, I can't make your next tuition."

Gee, Dad, thanks for the ample warning. What if I really do have to quit college? First thing tomorrow I've got to go meet with Daniel McCloud. He'll tell me what's really going on. I wonder if that farm truck that caused the accident is from one of the farms Dad's associated with.

Talk about a moral divide. No one at school knows I'm the son of a farmer. Hey everyone, it's confession time! Dad's a poor Irish farmer who believes in unorthodox pagan practices, and Mom's a proper Catholic who split with me to Chicago when I was young. The perfect Irish family. Yeah, what a joke!

I don't even remember the farm it's been so long. I've heard about Whispering Lake, but I can't tell that to Dylan. Not a prayer. I do owe Patrick. He knew I lied, but never called me out. For crying out loud, our fathers are friends. How could I have known?

CHAPTER 10

BLINDING LIGHT

NATALIE COULD NEVER have imagined what happened to Deidra and Melanie next. Fortunately, the twins' visits to the hospital gave her a detailed account of their frightening experience. She now visualized their terror.

"MEL, OH, MY GOD!" Deidra shrieked.

"What's wrong?" Melanie yelled back.

"It's Mr. Abbott. He's lying on the pavement by his car. His flashlight's shining right on his face. He's not moving and his body is in a weird position. Oh, Melanie, he looks dead!"

"Deidra, you're frightening me! Please tell me you're kidding!"

"It's the truth, Mel. I wouldn't tease about this."

"Help me get out of here! I can't see anything and my shoes keep slipping on this slime. There's got to be something for me to stand on. Maybe, I can find our bags." Melanie barely touched the dumpster as she edged herself along.

"This dumpster didn't seem this big from the outside. I think I've found something, but...it's not the duffel bags." Melanie shrieks. "HELP ME! Deidra, get me out of here! NOW, Deidra, NOW!" Her screams reverberated inside the large metal vault.

"You're scaring me! What is it?" Deidra demanded.

"RATS, big ones, the size of cats. Do you hear me, Deidra? GET ME OUT OF HERE!"

"Stop shrieking, Melanie, I'll get you out. Just let me think a second."

I have to stay calm. That other dumpster has some crates that might work. I need something to knock them down.

She saw a rough metal rod on the ground. Deidra picked it up with her jacket to not get cut, then she snagged the crates.

"Mel, I've got a solution. I'm sending some crates over for you to stand on. Here they come. I'll stand on a couple out here so I can grab you. Once I have a good grip, I'll pull you out."

"I can see the duffel bags. One plopped on top of the other. My eyes are adjusting. I'm sending the bags out now." They landed outside next to Deidra.

"Stand on those crates, Mel, and let's get you out of there. Reach your arms up. You'll need to push off and climb up the inside of the dumpster. You know how to do this. Remember our wall climbing lessons." Deidra prayed she did.

"You better not let go of me, Deidra."

"The crates aren't going to hold long. We've got one chance to get you out. I promise I won't let you go."

Melanie made it over landing on her feet.

"Yuck, what's that all over your shoes? What did you step in?" Neither girl could tell in the dark.

"Some gooey stuff, I don't know."

"Hurry, take 'em off and shove them into the side pouch of your duffel bag. They won't dirty anything in there. I put a towel in with your other things. I packed an extra pair of shoes in mine. Here they are. Use me to lean on." Deidra braced herself.

Melanie muffled a scream. "He really *is* dead! What should we do? We have to do something, Dee." Melanie froze.

"I've been thinking about that." Deidra went into survival mode.

DEIDRA AND MELANIE'S shortcut walk through the darkened parking lot now had frightening ramifications. Were they seen? Neither girl could be completely sure. Clearly they were privy to a murder scene. What should they do? Call for help or shift into survival mode perceiving flight and distance their safest option? What if the murderer was still somewhere out there, possibly aware of their presence? Like two animals sensing danger they respond with their primordial instincts. They moved on impulse.

"Melanie, the way I see it we're in big trouble. If we go to the police they might think we had something to do with Mr. Abbott's death. What would we be doing out here in a dark parking lot with you in a dumpster? That looks pretty suspicious.

"Maybe, whoever killed Mr. Abbott didn't see us. You were in the dumpster and I was hidden behind it. I never saw anything happen, anyhow. If we stay here and get help, maybe the killer might think we saw him and come after us. Or, we can ditch this place and keep out of this entire mess. That might be the smartest thing to do.

"It's good we have extra clothes. We need to get out of these dirty things ASAP. Let's split up and find somewhere safe to change. We won't draw attention walking alone, but we would be more recognizable if we were together. Then we can meet at Natalie's. We could just say we got into an argument and walked over separately. No one will have any reason to suspect anything is wrong." Their agreement was unspoken.

"We better throw the crates and the rod back into the dumpsters fast. Don't want that murderer seeing them. Get your duffel bag, stay in the dark, and be careful. Melanie, look at me. We can do this."

"Deidra, I'm sorry for all the things I said to you while I was in that awful dumpster."

"It's okay, Mel. I'm heading out. Stay alert and be safe."

"You, too."

CHAPTER 11

MILLER'S CONVENIENCE STORE

LIKE A HORSE RACING down the track, Natalie's mind switched lanes to move ahead. She knew Emily would be at Miller's getting the snacks while the twins were dealing with their nightmare. As part of her interview with the cops, they viewed Miller's video tapes of that night in an effort to rekindle her vacant memory. She was at a loss then, not now.

With graduation parties, summer barbeques and weekend rallies, a larger than normal crowd of teenagers and bikers had descended on Miller's. The crunch of people grabbing food and supplies created a stampede of confusion. In the middle of this human tornado, Emily moved around slowly, preoccupied within her own anxious world.

Emily debated how many bags of chips she needed to buy for the group, but she didn't see any salsa. *Do they even have salsa at a convenience store*, she wondered? She'd have to ask. Suddenly, a feeling of fear started to overwhelm her. *Why isn't that pill working yet? I need some water. Boy, what a long line to get into that lousy restroom.*

Then she noticed the store clock. *Darn, my watch stopped almost an hour ago.* She gasped, *it's late. I'll find out about the salsa when I go to check out.*

A preoccupied Natalie walked through the human blockade hanging outside of Miller's. She saw Emily receiving change from the cashier.

"Emily, there you are. I've been waiting in the car, but I figured you might need a hand carrying things out."

"I'm sorry, Nat, time got away from me. The salsa was completely sold out. I was lucky enough to get two containers of cheese spread and chips. What's all the commotion about? I saw two police cars go flying past heading toward the back parking lot."

"Give me one of the bags, Em. Let's get out of here and avoid the scene. I saw them, too. I was just getting out of my car when they passed me. It's probably some drunk exposing himself back there. After all, it's graduation night and I'm sure everyone's drinking themselves silly.

"No time to be spectators. We need to get gas and check things out with the car. There is dark smoke coming out of the tailpipe. It'll only take us a minute. I'm parked off to the side over here."

The two girls tumbled through the frenzied rush of people racing over to see what was going on. Natalie and Emily climbed into their car unnoticed.

Natalie spoke first. "I know the mechanic over at the gas station. He offered me free gas if I promised to go out with him. This guy's not my type, but I'll worry about that later. I'll ask him to check under the hood as well. It's been five years since this car's been driven. Let's run it through the auto wash. I never did take a hose to it and it's really dirty."

"I think we're a little late, Natalie. My parents just gave me this watch for my graduation gift, but it's not running right."

"Maybe it just needs a wind up, Em."

"You're probably right. Now I understand why it was getting dark. I got here early so I took a walk around the shops in the center. Could you reset it for me?"

"Sure, let's wait 'til we get to the gas station. I need better lighting and we'll be there in no time." Natalie started the car, put it into gear and sped away. Moments later they arrived.

"Natalie, you're such a lead foot. Here's my watch."

"Okay, it's wound and reset." Natalie handed it back.

"Thanks. It's 9:18; we really are late!"

"Well, I wouldn't worry about the time. Did you hear about that accident on the expressway? I'm sure KT's dinner was delayed. Her brothers and their friends probably got caught up in that traffic mess. No big deal. Anyway, I put a note on the front door saying we'd be back in a flash, that we've gone to get snacks and gas." Natalie tried to minimize Emily's angst.

"Natalie, I'm glad you talked me into coming. I need to get over my fears."

"We all have fears, Em. That's what friends are for, helping each other. If we stick together no matter what, we're invincible."

The acne scared, overweight mechanic walked up to the car.

"Hi, girls." He smiled at Natalie.

"Tony, I'm here to collect on that graduation gift you promised me. I need some gas and maybe a quick wash. Any chance for both?" she teased biting her lower lip.

"It's your night, Ms. Graduate. The car gets the full treatment on the house. I'll be calling you for that date." Tony winked back.

"A deal's a deal, Tony. About the car…"

CHAPTER 12
THE TWINS TAKE OFF

MELANIE WAS CONSUMED by anguish on her walk. The teenager's mind was racing. *I can't believe Mr. Abbott was murdered. There's no way he was alive with his neck twisted like that. What has Deidra gotten us into walking through that parking lot? And those nasty rats will haunt me the rest of my life. Fortunately, they were more interested in whatever it was they were eating.*

Natalie could feel Melanie's profound horror.

Melanie continued to agonize. *Where can I change in private? I smell really gross. I've got to see myself under the street light.* Melanie walked out of the shadows.

Wow, did those rats bite me? The cut on my arm wasn't this bad, so why do I have blood on my pants? Yuck, there's blood on my hands and under my fingernails! It's even on my duffel bag. Where did all this blood come from? This is scaring me--I've got to get this stuff off now!

She searched her surroundings, then noticed a hose by the side of a house with a For Sale sign out front.

Looks like the people moved out. I sure don't need any company now. When I get to Natalie's, I'll wash my clothes in their washing machine. I'm lucky Deidra packed a towel. I'll just tell Nat it was that time of month. She'll understand.

Ugh, the water's still running red. At least the blood's coming out of my clothes, but these sneakers will never come clean. I'll have to ditch them somewhere. A storm sewer would be perfect.

Then she gasped aloud. "Why was there blood in the dumpster?"

DEIDRA DELIBERATED as she hurried down the street. *I sure hope we made the right decision. What if Mr. Abbott was still alive? Maybe, he was just knocked out. No, he was dead all right.*

Oh, no! Natalie and Emily are at the gas station. There goes my plan to change in that restroom. At least now I have a chance to get over to Natalie's before they get back...

She stepped back into the shadows and raced over to Natalie's house.

"Deidra, Deidra, I'm over here."

"Why are you hiding in the bushes? There's nothing to worry about. Are you the first one here?"

"Yeah." Melanie was shaky.

"It's past 9:30. Where is everyone? We're a half an hour late."

"Natalie left a note on the front door. She and Emily went to buy snacks and gas up. They won't be long."

"That figures. I was going to change in the station's restroom but had to switch plans once I saw them there. Fortunately, they didn't see me. Melanie, you've really got to get a grip on yourself. Everything is okay."

"Are you sure, Deidra?" Melanie stared hard at her sister.

"I don't have time to debate this now. We'll discuss it after I change."

"But, Deidra, wait. I have to tell you something. I caught a glimpse of myself under a street light. There was blood on my hands and clothes, and I don't think it was mine. I went to that empty house on Main Street with the For Sale sign and used their hose to wash off.

"When I took out the dirty sneakers, they had blood on them, too! I couldn't get them clean so I shoved them down a storm sewer. I figured I could tell Natalie I had an accident with my period and ask to use her mom's washer and drier for my clothes, but the sneakers were another story. I still have blood under my fingernails." Melanie stressed as she babbled on.

"I checked my body all over to see if any of the rats had bitten me, and I couldn't find any bite marks--just that cut. Did you bring our nail clipper?"

"Maybe the blood was from a dead animal. A dog or cat could have gotten hit by a car and someone threw it into the dumpster. We've both had a horrible experience tonight." Deidra became solemn.

"We have to make a decision right now to forget everything that's happened. Once we get to Whispering Lake, we'll shake this whole thing off."

"I sure hope so, Deidra. Right after I got out of the parking lot I heard sirens. I'm sure the police have found Mr. Abbott."

"I heard them, too. Please try and let this go. Here, I found the nail clippers."

"Deidra, there's blood on your blouse where I leaned on you. Right there, do you see it?"

"Yeah, I do. You better wash my blouse, too." They walked to the side of the house into the shadows. Deidra quickly changed, then they returned to the front.

"Deidra, here come Natalie and Emily. Put on a smile. Talk about timing."

"Hi, there. I hope you haven't been waiting too long. Did you see the note on the front door?" Natalie appeared distracted.

"Yeah, we did. Mel and I got here a short while ago. We're really excited about the party tonight." Deidra tried to be convincing.

Natalie asked, "Have either of you spoken with KT or Jennifer?"

Both girls shook their head no.

"That's odd. I was hoping KT would have been here by now. Her brothers were supposed to drop her off by nine o'clock. Looks like they might have gotten stuck in that nasty traffic mess. Let's go in the house and I'll check the phone messages.

"Em, just leave the bags of food in the car. We'll wait 15 minutes and if KT and Jennifer still aren't here we'll leave them a note and take off for the lake."

"Natalie," Emily interrupted, "it's not like Jennifer to not call or show up especially after making plans for a sleepover."

"Em, don't you remember Jen's mom offering to drive her over here after dinner? Come to think of it, I've been so preoccupied all day I never did get to tell Jen about our plans to go to Whispering Lake. She still thinks she's just coming over for a sleepover."

Then Natalie noticed something. "Melanie, your duffel bag is all wet."

"Yeah, I need to explain a little problem I have." Melanie acted sheepish.

"Okay, let's talk once we get into the house. Just leave your duffel on the porch or you'll drip water all over my mom's carpet. I don't want to have to answer any questions I don't have answers for."

"No problem." They all walked inside.

"What's up, Melanie?" Natalie asked as she closed the door behind them.

"Well, I'm kind of embarrassed. It's that time of month and well, I had an accident on the way over. I had to change my clothes in a public restroom, and I need to do a quick wash and dry if that's all right with you." She hoped her lies were believable.

"I don't see why not. We're going to be here 15 minutes unless KT and Jennifer arrive sooner. You can put your things into the dryer when we come back. Just don't forget. I'll go get you a towel. Here, you can wrap your duffel bag in this so it won't drip. The laundry room is the last room on the right. In the meantime, I'm going to check the answering machine to see if there are any messages from KT and Jennifer." Natalie was on her way when Deidra intercepted her.

"Natalie, are you wearing that leotard and tights tonight?"

"Don't be silly. KT's lending me some clothes. I did some ballet when I came home today; after all, we are going skinny dipping with guys later. I want to be limber. That's one thing my dad always taught me, be strong and fit, yet light on your feet." Natalie mused.

"You just look kind of funny with your hair all sprayed up with that outfit on."

"Just wanted to see how I'd look with my hair in a French twist. A sophisticated Natalie, a new me. Let me go check the phone messages. Jennifer probably flaked out on us. You'll see."

Beep, beep. 6:30 p.m.

"Hi, Natalie, it's Sally Lawson, Jennifer's mom. Jen hasn't come home yet. She was so busy talking with classmates and taking pictures she decided to stay a bit longer at school so her dad and I left without her. I was hoping you might know where she is? Dinner's at 7 o'clock and we've got a special surprise for Jen. I offered to drive her over to your house after dinner for your party so I thought she just might have gone over there sooner. Please send her home if you talk with her but don't mention the surprise."

Beep, beep. 6:45 p.m.

"Natalie, have you seen or heard from Jen? She still hasn't come home, and I'm starting to get worried. Please call me as soon as you get home. I've tried a couple of her other girlfriends and they haven't seen her either. The only place she could possibly be is with you girls."

Beep, beep. 7:13 p.m.

"Natalie, this is Chuck Lawson, Jennifer's dad. We're pretty upset here. Jennifer still hasn't come home. She hasn't called and no one has seen her. My wife is starting to panic. Just call us, please!"

Beep, beep. 8:35 p.m.

"Hi, it's KT. My brothers finally made it back to the farm and we're just now sitting down for my celebration dinner. What a miserable drive they had on the expressway. I'm sure you heard all about that accident on the news. Fortunately, they needed gas and got off early. Unfortunately, Dylan and Colin were already stuck in the mess. My brothers had no way of telling them they would be taking a different way home.

"Are the plans still on for Whispering Lake? Patrick is so tired from their marathon drive he would prefer driving us straight there. He already picked up plenty of beer. He's sure Dylan and Colin would head straight to the lake, too. Patrick gave them directions just in case they got separated. Call me as soon as you get this message so I know what to do. Where are you anyway?"

CHAPTER 13

I-72 EXPRESSWAY

COLIN HADN'T FOUND the O'Neills on his walkabout. All he saw was a mass of cars and agitated people milling around. Then, all at once, he saw people getting back into their cars.

He asked a nearby motorist, "Excuse me, sir, but have they cleared up the accident?"

"Yes, young man, finally! They said it was one of the worst traffic jams on the I-72."

"Thanks." *I better run for it,* Colin thought as he made his path. He spotted Dylan.

"Hurry up, jump in! I can't believe this nightmare is finally over," Dylan sighed.

"The O'Neills aren't back there. They must have gotten off the expressway."

"I bet they needed gas and took an alternate road. We're running low ourselves. I'll take the next exit and gas up. Patrick gave me a map in case we got separated. Let's just go straight to the lake."

"What a disaster this day has turned into. So much for a good home-cooked Irish meal." Disappointment painted Colin's face.

"Don't worry, I'm sure Patrick will grab some food for us. Is your stomach the only thing you ever think about?"

"No, it isn't the only thing on my mind. I'm also thinking about those girls and having a blast tonight. It sure has been a lousy start, but we can turn things around." Colin snapped out of his funk.

"Of course we can, Colin. We are the fighting Irish, after all." They both laughed.

CHAPTER 14

THE GIRLS MAKE A CHOICE

UNABLE TO CONTROL herself, Deidra slipped up behind Natalie and listened to the Lawsons' alarming messages.

"You scared me. Don't sneak up on me like that." Natalie blurted.

"What's this about Jennifer. Is she missing?" Alarm swept over Deidra's face.

"I doubt it. She's probably with that guy, Scott Ryan, she met a few weeks ago."

"She's never mentioned anything about him to me." Deidra contested.

"I heard about Scott from KT. She's pretty ticked off. Apparently KT and Jennifer both like him and there's some rivalry. KT met him first and then introduced him to Jen. Anyhow, I'm staying out of it. Plus, her brother let it slip to me that she was getting a new car this evening for a graduation present. Need I say any more?"

"Mrs. Lawson's message didn't sound like Jennifer got her car yet. That sounds really cold. Jennifer's been a great friend to all of us." Deidra was incensed.

"What do you want me to do? Run around and look for her? I'm trying to plan a wonderful party for all of us!" Natalie's face reddened.

"Hey girls, STOP! We've all had a tough day. My sister and I have for sure." Melanie intervened.

Deidra gave Melanie a look to kill.

"I don't think the girls want to hear about our petty little problems when a friend of ours is missing. Natalie, why don't we just try to figure out where she is and not get into quarrels between ourselves."

"That's fine, Deidra."

"What's up? What's all the chatter about?" Emily walked into the snake pit.

"We just have a dilemma that needs fixing," Natalie said calmly.

"That's a nice way of shutting me out. What messages came in from KT and Jennifer that's got all of you in a tizzy? Stop looking at one another and spill the beans."

"I think we should call KT and have all of us decide together what to do about Jennifer." Natalie started dialing.

KT picked up on the first ring.

"Finally! Where have you been? I left you a message over an hour ago."

"Sorry, I've been so preoccupied with doing things for tonight I never heard the phone ring. I had the radio on pretty loud while I was blow drying my hair. Emily and I just got back from picking up snacks for the party.

"KT, a problem's come up that we need to discuss. I'm putting you on speaker. Emily, Melanie and Deidra are standing here with me."

"Hi, everyone."

"Hi, KT."

"What's up? Why all the intrigue?"

Natalie spoke for the group.

"When Em and I got back home, Deidra and Melanie were waiting here. Since you and Jennifer weren't, I decided to check the phone messages. I had four: three from Jennifer's parents and one from you. It seems that Jen hasn't been home since we left commencement this afternoon and her parents are really concerned."

"I think I'm going to need another pill." Emily blurted.

"Hush, Em! Don't interrupt. Anyhow, her mom said she was talking with friends, taking pictures and wanted to stay a bit longer so they left without her. She knew she had a 7 p.m. celebration dinner."

Emily interrupted again. "Are they sure she's just not out with other friends, maybe having a soda and just forgot about the time?"

Natalie ignored Emily and continued giving KT the worrisome news.

"Her parents already contacted the two girls they saw her talking with at school. What disturbs me is that Mr. Lawson called also. We're worried maybe Jennifer has gotten herself into some kind of trouble." Natalie stopped talking.

KT took it all in, then spoke. "I doubt anything bad happened to Jennifer, so if we disappear for a couple of hours and have a small party what will it hurt? What could we do, anyhow?

"I've got my own situation here. Patrick had to take Mom and Darcy down the road to a neighbor to meet up with my dad. Some kind of emergency farmer's meeting. He should be back soon.

"We haven't heard from Dylan or Colin so we figured they just headed straight to the lake. My brothers are all tired from the drama on the road and can't wait to have some fun and let loose."

"I want to say something, KT." Melanie went into attack mode.

"How would you feel if it was you out there, God knows where, and your friends abandoned you?"

"We're not abandoning anyone and Jen wouldn't do anything stupid. Come on, girls! Melanie, you don't have five people that drove from one state to another just to make your graduation night a party you'd never forget. Well, I do. I'm feeling responsible for a lot here. Don't make me out to be some kind of monster.

"We don't even know where she is. We can't call her parents and tell them what we had arranged tonight, unless you girls are up for confessing you lied to your parents?" KT got quiet.

"KT's got a point, Mel." Then, Deidra gestured softly, "Can I speak with you in private, sister to sister? We'll be right back." They darted out to the front porch.

Out of earshot, Melanie stated, "This is really getting complicated, Deidra. Too many bad things are going on tonight. I've been trying to forget what happened earlier, but this isn't making it any easier." Melanie's voice quaked.

"Mel, we *need* to go to Whispering Lake. We *have* to stay together. If Mom and Dad find out, we'll have a lot of explaining to do. If we go to the lake, the girls will cover for each other so we'll all be protected." Deidra prayed she was right.

"I understand." Melanie grasped the gravity of the situation.

Natalie's voice rang out. "Would you two come back in here, please!"

The twins returned immediately.

Natalie continued. "I think the best thing for all of us to do is to stick to one story. The five of us were together this evening and saw and heard nothing. We're just a bunch of high school graduates looking to go out on the town and party. In fact, I told my mom everyone was going to surprise me so I think it's a smart idea we get over to Whispering Lake. If there's any fallout because of this, we better be far away when it happens."

CHAPTER 15

THE POLICE ARRIVE

NATALIE HAD TRIED years ago to reconstruct things, but with so many missing pieces it was impossible. She had learned crime scene records weren't that hard to come by as a journalist. The internet was her sleuth. With more memories now streaming in, the murderous puzzle was materializing.

"You better radio dispatch, this isn't good."

"Brenda, units 45 and 42 on scene, responding patrolmen Mitch Emerson and Jim Doyle. Looks like we've got a homicide. Who's on duty tonight?" Officer Emerson asked.

"Mike Duffy and Rick Lombardi," the efficient operator replied.

"Get them down here right away. And we need backup, too. Officer Doyle and I both responded to the 2110 hours dispatch of a possible homicide in the southeast parking lot at Decatur's Shopping Center. There's a man down." Officer Emerson waited.

"Mitch, go to channel 2 and we'll take all your information."

"Officer Doyle is cordoning off the entire area. The victim's name is James Abbott. His name and Decatur Shopping Center Security were on his identification badge. His keys are still in the ignition of the security car and the motor's running. The driver's door is open. We found him lying only feet away on his back with his head twisted, neck looks slashed." Officer Emerson stopped.

"That's awful. I'll notify Duffy and Lombardi right away."

"Thanks, Brenda. Bye."

"The front's cordoned off, Mitch, but we need backup immediately! Everyone's running for their cars. I couldn't stop them all." Doyle was sweating.

"You better cordon off the back exits by that Mexican restaurant and the ones around those dumpsters. I'm holding ground here. We don't need any evidence being compromised on our watch." Emerson took charge.

"And Jim, if you run into any problems, scream your ass off."

"Don't worry. I don't want to be a dead hero. I'll be fast." With that he was gone.

"Impressive!" Emerson exclaimed as Doyle quickly reappeared.

"Cruisers should be here any moment. They'll barricade the streets around the center. No one will be able to get in or out of this place." Doyle was confident.

"I wonder what made Abbott stop in the middle of an empty parking lot and get out of his car."

"Obviously, someone either drove up or walked up to him."

"But why would he get out of his car? He's safe inside, right?" Doyle commented.

"Beats me. He made himself vulnerable and got slashed to death."

"Do you think it could have been that guy who was harassing girls over at the schoolyard earlier today?" Doyle wondered.

"I doubt it. Why would he bother with a security guard out here? I heard he's just another drunk who has a reputation for mouthing off. This guy keeps a bottle of booze in his hands, not a knife. News is some concerned citizen called the Department a few hours ago and said Billy Smith, Decatur's famous child molester is back in town.

"The caller claimed to be his neighbor. Just saw him sitting on the porch of his mama's house staring out at the street and figured that was enough to alert the cops. Reckon his local fan club is keeping tabs on him. Guess 'cause he's been such a good model citizen they let him out on good behavior, hah!" Emerson didn't buy it.

"They should keep those perverts locked up forever." Doyle passed final judgment.

"Some of the calls could have been from punks wanting to stir up trouble." Emerson opened up a small pouch and grabbed some chewing tobacco.

"Yeah, the 6 o'clock news was filled with all the local drama. People's doors will surely be locked tonight when Decatur's upstanding citizens hear about this." Doyle was convinced.

Backup blew into the parking lot. Both officers straightened up.

Mitch recognized the cops. "It's Fernando Vasquez and Brad Patterson. They're both five year veterans. They'll help tighten the noose around this place real good."

"Hi, boys." It was Patterson. "All the streets around the center have been barricaded. Got a couple of black and whites re-directing traffic. What else do you need us to handle?"

Officer Emerson responded. "There's a growing group of disgruntled shoppers in the front parking lot waiting to get out of here. We need to get names and contact information. Find the mall security's head honcho and get him over here ASAP!"

"Will do." Backup took off.

"Once the crime boys get here things will move right along. Duffy's a pretty good detective, but Lombardi is wet behind the ears. Don't think he's ever shaved." Doyle chuckled.

"Duffy's going to have his hands full with his new young Pisano partner. Lombardi was only on the job a short time when he got promoted to detective. Bet this is his first homicide." Doyle watched the growing crime scene.

"Rick Lombardi may be young, but I have a gut feeling about him, Jim. He plays a good game of chess. I'm banking the kid figures it out." Emerson spit the wad of tobacco into a baggie.

"Well, someone's got to 'cause it just doesn't make any sense to me," Doyle admitted.

"That's why we do patrol and stay clear of homicide." Emerson smiled.

"You're right about that." Both officers nodded.

CHAPTER 16
WHISPERING LAKE

UNDER THE UMBRELLA of night the four girls slipped into the waiting car and Natalie drove them away unseen. Her dad's car was running fine. She'd have to thank Tony properly at another time. The night was finally looking up for the girls. Natalie knew the route by heart, the turn off to Whispering Lake was just a little further and party time was close at hand. Only time would tell if they made the right decision.

"Wow, it's creepy out here. The water is so dark. How do I know what's under the surface?" Em's eyes were wide with fright.

"Em, why don't you come over here and help us out." Natalie was exasperated.

"Natalie, did you remember to bring towels?" Melanie asked.

"There's a whole bunch of towels in the back seat. Here are the keys. Don't lose them and don't forget to relock the car." Natalie was tired of thinking for everyone.

"Where are we going to set everything up?" Emily seemed unsettled.

"Go over toward the restrooms, there're several picnic tables and a barbeque and fire pit. Here, take this flashlight."

"Natalie, would you mind going with me? I'm feeling kind of nervous about walking in the dark alone and you promised you'd stay with me. My mouth is really dry and it's hard swallowing." Emily was childlike.

"Of course I'll walk with you, silly goose. Deidra, you keep a lookout for KT and her brothers. Em, take this bag. I'll take the heavier one. We'll come back for our duffel bags." They headed off.

"Thanks, Nat, for coming with me. You always make me feel safe. What do you think happened to Jennifer? I can't seem to get her off my mind."

"I don't know. We hugged, took pictures, and threw our caps up into the air. After that, so many people came over to congratulate us, I didn't pay attention to where Jen went. We had a quick moment just before I left school when she was standing by her mom. You were there. Remember? I told her about the sleepover tonight, got a nod from her mom and a promise she'd drive Jen over after dinner. That was it." A distant look came over Natalie's face.

"Do you think she's pretty, Nat?"

"Sure, I do. She's probably back at her parent's house right now." Natalie thought for a moment. "I bet Jen's already left a message explaining the whole screw up."

"I guess you're right," Emily sighed.

"There're the picnic tables. We'll put this table cloth on that table. After all, this is our graduation night and I want everything perfect. I even brought balloons. How are you for blowing some up?" Natalie pulled one out.

"Oh, Nat, this really is wonderful. You are the best party planner. Sure, I've already got red hair, might as well have a red face to match." She grabbed the balloons.

"You can always make me laugh, Em. Here are a couple of candles and holders, too. The matches are in my bag. There are some hot, sexy guys coming. KT assured me. Maybe, now's a good time for you to take another pill. It'll start working just about the time they show up. We don't want you being nervous now, do we? Are you okay to stay here alone while I go back and get our duffel bags? I'll see if Melanie and Deidra need any help." Natalie waited for a response.

"Yeah, I'm fine now." Emily started blowing up the balloons.

"Good, I'll be back in a flash." Natalie was gone.

CHAPTER 17
LOST IN THE WOODS

BY NOW THE JUNE SKY had lapsed from a boiling caldron of red, orange and gold into deep purple. Two young men made their way into Macon County at the mercy of a handmade map.

"Some map this is! Now I know why Patrick gave you instructions to go along with it. We'd have problems finding this place even if he was driving right in front of us." Colin was seething. They were good and lost.

"Darn it, I have to pull over. My allergies are kicking up, and my meds are in the trunk. Hey, Colin, look out your window. There is a gate and an old sign that says Whispering Lake. How do ya like that? Lucky we stopped. The brushes and tree branches have it hidden." Dylan started sneezing.

"Guess that's what the "X" on the map means, you idiot! "X" stands for gate, fence, or pass through!" Colin was exasperated.

"I didn't sign up to drive through two states to find this party. Do you want to drive, shithead?" Dylan couldn't stop sneezing.

"You're doing a great job, Dylan. Take your meds," Colin smirked.

Dylan got back in the car.

"Patrick never said the lake was on private land. I should have figured out something was off when he handed me a handwritten piece of artwork with squiggles, signs and arrows. A first grader could have done better. Can you make it out?" Dylan asked.

"That map was just supposed to be a backup. Remember, we were going to meet up once we arrived and finalize things." Both guys were tired and fed up.

"Okay, we've come this far, I'm driving in." Dylan pulled through the gate onto a rough gravel road.

"Great, more surprises. Be my lookout for potholes. All we need now is to get a flat tire." Dylan drove slowly.

"All I see is the road, the trees and the sky and it all looks alike--dark. Did we miss a turnoff somewhere? I feel like we've been driving around in circles. Is it possible we are?" Colin had his head out the window.

"Anything's possible. Tell me again what the directions say." Dylan was frustrated.

"We've followed Patrick's instructions to a 'T'. So where the heck is this lousy lake and the hot babes? My stomach hasn't stopped growling for the past hour. I'm starving!" Colin's patience was tapped.

"Let's pull over and get out. Maybe we can work our way to a rise and get a better prospective. I've got a couple flashlights in the back." Dylan turned off the engine.

"Now that's the best idea I've heard since we started this crazy journey."

Dylan had come prepared. "I have a switchblade and compass in the glove box and kite string in the trunk. We'll leave a trail. The last thing I need to do is get lost in this wilderness."

"I'm getting a bottle of Jameson out. Tonight I'm going to have fun no matter what. Would you care to join me in a little libation?" Colin grinned.

Finally, they agreed on something.

CHAPTER 18

THE O'NEILLS ARRIVE

BETWEEN MISSING AND LOST friends, a nightmare interstate drive, and unknown consequences from a major drought, each individual had his or her reason for wanting to forget the havoc of the day. The lake party hopefully would be the ultimate elixir to celebrate with complete abandon: sex, booze and total privacy—what could be better?

The O'Neills arrived at Whispering Lake.

"KT, is that Natalie Grant's car in the parking lot over there?"

"It sure is, Aidan. She's got her father's car. Remember the boating accident a few years ago?"

Aidan resembled his mother's pointed features, dark eyes and hair.

"I recall hearing about a boat exploding out on the lake. That was Natalie's father?"

"Yeah, it was pretty bad. I heard he never knew what hit him."

"What a gruesome way to die." Aidan grimaced.

"I think the two of you will really hit it off. I can hardly wait to introduce you. Where do you think Dylan and Colin are now?" KT appeared concerned.

"It may take a miracle of faith to find this lake following Patrick's directions." Aidan chuckled.

Patrick walked up and said, "Gee, thanks, Aidan. My directions were just fine."

The oldest O'Neill son had blue eyes, black hair and pretty boy looks.

"Then where are they, Brother Patrick?"

Patrick turned to his other brother, "What do you think, Liam? Should we send Aidan off to find my friends?"

Liam was the only O'Neill with hazel eyes and curly brown hair. He was the most sensitive of the lot.

"We came out here to celebrate with KT and her friends, not to have family squabbles. If my eyes don't deceive me, here come two of your girlfriends now. These must be the twins you told me about." Liam pointed to the two girls approaching.

"That's Deidra and Melanie Stuart. Hey girls, over here."

"Hi, KT," they replied in unison.

"Deidra, Melanie, I'd like to introduce you to my brothers: Patrick, Aidan and Liam."

"Nice to meet you," the twins giggled.

"Deidra, where are Natalie and Em?" KT asked.

"They're down by the picnic area setting up things."

"We brought plenty of beer," KT added.

"Sounds good," the twins agreed.

"Where are your two friends from Notre Dame?" Deidra asked.

"Yeah, where are they, Patrick?" Aidan prodded.

"Aidan was just going out on a search and rescue mission to find them," Patrick replied.

"Are they lost?" Melanie tensed up.

"No, girls, they're just following Patrick's directions so they could be anywhere from Wisconsin to Iowa," Aidan laughed.

"You guys really are funny." Melanie relaxed.

"Okay, girls, get ready 'cause the O'Neills are here and we're gonna show you how to party the good old Irish way. Let's go find your other friends and get this party rollin'!"

"But what about your buddies?" Deidra asked.

"I'm not sure if I want to find them. I kind of like the odds the O'Neills have right now." Patrick was grinning from ear to ear.

"KT also told us you were shameless flirts." Deidra blushed.

"You're only seeing the tip of the iceberg darlin'."

"Patrick, why don't you and KT go with the girls to the picnic tables; we'll get the beer and meet you there." Aidan had had enough.

"That's what I like, brotherly spirit. Don't be long bringing the beer." Aidan and Liam split.

"Aidan, something's going on in our family and we're not being told what it is." Liam was apprehensive.

"Whatever it is, Patrick seems to know about it."

It was clear Aidan and Liam were out of the loop. The O'Neills had plenty of secrets between themselves. They grabbed the beer and returned.

CHAPTER 19

SEARCHING ON FOOT

AS IF FINISHING the last leg of a marathon, Dylan and Colin headed out on foot into the dense forest that shrouded Whispering Lake. Working off of stretched nerves, empty stomachs, and waning optimism, they were still determined to find the lake.

"Colin, there's a clearing through these trees, let's get over there. I need to get my compass out."

"I bet you never leave home without it," Colin clowned.

"Enough already! Maybe we can look at that map again and recognize the terrain. Follow the squiggles." Dylan honestly doubted it.

"Not likely." Colin wasn't buying it either.

"Okay, wonder boy, you lead!" Dylan demanded.

"Not me, I'm too tired and hungry. How 'bout we sit down and have a swig of this whiskey?"

"Give it another five or ten minutes and if we can't find the lake we'll call it a night and stay out here under the stars."

"We're not going back to the car? You threaded string all over trees marking a path back there." Colin was confused.

"We could, but I'm actually hoping we'll be able to hear voices through the woods. The lake can't be far off and sound carries. If we're in the car it'll be harder for us to hear anything."

"You've got a point there, guess you're the smartass." Colin grinned.

"Since we're just walking, it seems like a good time for you to tell me about that medallion of yours. Maybe we can use it to show us the way." Dylan's sarcasm hit home.

"Dylan, sometimes you really tick me off."

"Why? I just want to know why you think it's so special. Let's sit down and crack that bottle open. I'm tired as hell." Dylan flopped down next to a tree, Colin followed.

"Okay, Dylan, you asked for it. What do you know about the Great Hunger?"

"Other than what I'm feeling now, I guess what most Irish know. Lots of people died of hunger, and I don't want to be one of them." Dylan took a swig.

"Do you want to hear this story or not?" Colin raised his voice.

"Yeah, go ahead." Dylan was resigned to the impending history lesson.

Colin recounted in detail how the Irish peasants suffered at the hands of the land owners. He told how his ancestors and friends escaped sure death by pooling their assets so they could board a "Coffin Ship" for the perilous journey to America. Telling the story made him thirsty.

"How about some of that Jameson?" Colin grabbed the bottle.

"Hey, Colin, do I need to hear all this? All I asked about was that medallion and I'm starting to have regrets." He closed his eyes.

"I'm getting to that. It has to do with my ancestors' pledge."

Colin then shared what happened when they arrived at New York Harbor. The docks were filled with thugs and scam artists promising them pie in the sky. Lost and discouraged, his ancestors heard about a soup line and headed over. Their luck was about to change.

Dylan screamed at Colin, "I've had enough of your long-winded story. Keep your tale to yourself. All I want now is for you to shut up. Can you do that, Colin?"

Colin shouted back, "I'm almost done. This is my story, Dylan, my roots! You wanted to know, now listen up," Colin continued.

"A wealthy businessman, Richard Barrett, had just arrived from Chicago looking for Irish workers to farm the land he acquired in Macon County, Illinois. Being Irish himself, he understood the Irish were grateful to be out from under the tyranny in their homeland and wanted a chance at happiness in America.

"Barrett saw my ancestors huddled up trying to keep warm in the center of that soup line. He walked over to them, made his offer, and gave them their future. Two days later, after hiring wagons for the trip to Illinois, Barrett and the nine clans made a 12 day journey to Decatur."

"Get to the medallion already or I'll have to kill you!"

"Dylan, you're such a pain in the butt. We're sitting on land Barrett originally owned. There's a lot of history here.

He knew that planting corn and soybean would pay off. In 1854, the Illinois Central Railroad was completed through Decatur. That meant the population would skyrocket and Barrett's crops could be shipped out by rail. He smelled money right from the get go."

"I thought you said your father was a successful businessman from Chicago?" Dylan was puzzled.

"I know I did. Let me finish, then I'll explain." Colin would figure that out later.

"You better hurry up." Dylan was fading.

Colin couldn't be stopped. His story was more for himself than for Dylan anyhow. He was trying to keep his moral compass balanced.

"When the clans saw the land they knew they had found their new home and life. It was ideal for farming. Besides that, Barrett had promised each clan land of their own. It would be worth their labor.

"They even had their own small, unmarked lake that had been omitted from the property map by the land surveyor. They figured Barrett paid an arm and a leg for that oversight. The clans decided to make a pact to stick together and not lose the old traditions. But they never stopped being Catholic; in fact, they built that church on the hill past Heaven's Door."

With one eye open, Dylan commented, "That's why Whispering Lake isn't on a real map! How do you know so much, Sullivan?"

"My ancestors didn't want their story to be forgotten. In fact, each clan wrote their trials down in their own private leather bound journal. My dad has the Sullivan book and it will get passed down to me some day. The elders wanted their children's children to understand what they had endured."

"Where does the medallion figure into it?" Now things were making sense to Dylan. He straightened up a bit.

"There was another journal that was left as well. It's a pretty interesting accounting of how they planned to practice the old ways. It was kind of a combination of their Celtic roots and Catholicism, a melding of what they took from their heritage going back to the times of the Druids. Have you ever heard of the Brehon Laws?" Colin was posturing.

"No, can't say that I have." Dylan was drifting again.

"Well, the Brehon Laws were the oldest form of European laws, at least according to old Irish records. That's how generations kept alive the old ways: the lore, kinship, and traditions. One of the clans that came across the Atlantic with them was part of the O'Flaherty Clan, one of the oldest Irish families of that region. They were well-versed on Brehon Law and shared their knowledge with the rest of their friends. But the clans in America had to assimilate their Irish culture with the new laws of the land. The Catholic churches were built, but many Irish secretly practiced their pagan beliefs. They didn't want to lose their roots. As a tribute to the old ways, my ancestors designed a gold medallion with a triskelion symbol in the center to …"

Dylan interrupted. "Colin, as much as I would like to hear the rest of your story, the whiskey is kicking my ass." He passed out.

"Are you sure you're Irish? I could drink half that bottle and not flinch." Dylan was already snoring. Colin thought, *I'm going to see if I can find that fantasy lake by myself. I'll take the compass, flashlight and knife; sleeping beauty here won't need them. Besides, I'll be back before the booze wears off. Whispering Lake can't be that far away.*

CHAPTER 20
LOOK TO THE STARS

UNOBSERVED, NATALIE GRABBED the pants and tank top KT had left on the picnic table and quietly disappeared into the woods to change. Colin had just ventured off as well.

Once in the clearing, Colin strategized, *I'll align the compass with the North Star. I should be able to get my bearings straight from now on. There's enough clearing out here to stay on course. We must have passed the turnoff somewhere along that road.*

Suddenly, he heard a noise. It sounded like a moan. He flashed his light and yelled out,

"Hello. Who's there? I'm Colin Sullivan, a friend of Patrick O'Neill's." He moved toward the rustle.

"Over here, Colin, I'm Natalie Grant, KT's friend. Can you see me?"

"Stay right where you are and keep talking. I'll find you. Good evening, Ms. Grant, Colin Sullivan at your service."

"Hi, Colin, are you here to rescue me? Did you hear me fall on my butt?" Natalie giggled.

"I was actually hoping someone was coming to rescue us. My buddy and I got lost after we turned onto Eagles Pass Road. It's so dark and confusing out here we couldn't figure out where we went wrong. So we started hiking thinking we would spot the lake. Dylan is passed out under a tree across the clearing over there thanks to some Jameson. I decided to find the mysterious Whispering Lake by myself. Enough about us, you're okay, right?"

"Yeah, I guess I'm not as graceful as I thought. KT lent me these clothes for tonight. I slipped away from the group to change and fell when I tried to put my shoes back on. You startled me."

"Well, there you are my damsel in distress. You should have waited for me to come put your shoes on so you wouldn't have slipped." He thought this girl was hot.

"Prince Charming only exists in fairy tales. No one has ever come to my rescue before. Not ever." Natalie stared at the man of her dreams.

"Maybe we both need some rescuing tonight."

"You know, Colin, you sure look better in person than your photo." Natalie beamed.

"You've seen my picture?" He was surprised.

"KT showed me a picture of you, Dylan and Patrick. She told me she had dibs on you, to stay away. KT always gets what she wants." Natalie played coy.

"What about you, Natalie. What do you want?" Colin flirted back.

"Just once not to be disappointed." She seduced him with her eyes.

"I won't disappoint you." The seduction went both ways.

"Isn't it beautiful out here under the stars?" Natalie looked up at the night sky.

"It sure is and it just got a whole lot more beautiful since you showed up. So tell me about this illusive lake." Colin was captivated.

"I used to fish out here a lot with my dad. Whispering Lake was his favorite fishing spot." Natalie looked away but continued. "My father was killed in a boating accident here five years ago. There was a terrible fire and an explosion."

"That's horrible!" Colin was shocked.

"My girlfriend and I heard the explosion from the shore. It was too late. We couldn't do anything."

"I'm so sorry, Natalie. Is it difficult for you being out here?"

"I actually feel like he's spending my graduation party with me," she said with a smile.

"Have you ever been out here at night before?" he asked.

"No. The night sky is amazing." The vastness thrilled her.

"I've been enjoying the stars for the past half an hour. Do you know where any of the constellations are?"

"No, I never took astronomy in school. Do you know where they are?" Natalie fed right into him.

"Yes, I've studied astronomy for years. Let me point some out to you." Colin slipped his hand around hers.

"This sounds like fun." She loved his touch.

"Let me guide your hand. Look straight over where my index finger points. That's Hydra, the largest of the 88 constellations. It's known as the water-snake. It was believed that Hydra had nine heads, the middle head being immortal. We only see one head in the sky. Maybe that's the immortal one." His heart started racing.

"Wow, I can see it. This is so neat."

"I know you've heard of the Big Dipper. Now, you'll have to use your imagination here, it's an outline of a bear. Some say the chain of stars leading away from it represents its tail, but everyone knows bears don't have tails. In Ireland they call it the Plough, the pointer toward north." He could smell her scented skin as he held her close.

"Have you ever been to Ireland?" Natalie asked.

"No, I haven't been that fortunate, but I feel very connected to my Irish roots." He was becoming aroused.

"I'd like to hear about your family." In their closeness, she felt his growing erection. He pulled away slightly.

"Natalie, do you know the name of the star that travelers use to find their way back home?" He wanted her badly.

"The North Star," she said proudly.

"You're right. Its real name is Polaris and it is actually True North. Sailors have been using Polaris for hundreds of years for navigation. Are you familiar with compasses?"

"Not really," she lied.

He shined his flashlight on the compass. "It's a life saver when there are clouds at night and you can't see Polaris. (N) is magnetic—just move the arrow to (N) and the rest is aligned. You can never get lost if you have a compass. When is your birthday?"

"September 2nd."

"You're a Virgo. That sign actually originates from the constellation Virgo."

"You know *that*, too? I'm impressed. Go on." The seduction continued.

"It's considered the feminine sign and also an earth sign. By nature, you're a perfectionist, very detail oriented. Am I right or are the stars playing tricks?" He could see her naked breasts in his mind.

"I guess the stars have me pegged. I definitely obsess about details." He was so tall and handsome. She wondered if he was a good lover.

"Well, the good news is according to the stars you and I are definitely compatible. Can you feel the gravitational pull drawing us together?" The sexual tension was building between them.

"Yes, I do." Natalie inched closer.

"Is the chemistry between us obvious to you, too?" He rubbed up and down against her now.

"I made a vow to let my hair down tonight. Why don't we just stay lost for a while? We can go around to the far side of the lake and skinny dip. With your compass and me guiding you, I'm sure we can find our way back. I know a few secluded hiding places." Natalie threw caution to the wind.

"What about your friends? Won't they be worried?" Colin hesitated.

"They know I've got my flashlight and can take care of myself. It's your decision, Colin. We've got maybe half an hour to have our own little party. Consider it an appetizer." Natalie felt him.

"What's to decide? There isn't anything else I'd rather be doing. First, all I could think about was food, now all I crave is you." He wanted to take her right there.

"Well, in that case, I'll give you a six-course meal. We need to be very quiet. Take my hand." Natalie and Colin disappeared into the night.

CHAPTER 21

DECATUR POLICE DEPARTMENT

IT WAS ANYTHING but a typical Friday night. Graduation parties were in full swing, bikers gathered for motorcycle rallies, and petty crimes generated tons of phone calls and visits from irate residents. The skeleton force on hand could not accommodate the swell of humanity that overtook the station so the entire Decatur Police Department was mobilized. The tank was full. The smell of booze, vomit and urine choked its stagnant vents. In the thick of things were Jennifer Lawson's parents who stood like two lost sheep waiting to be slaughtered.

"Mr. & Mrs. Lawson, hello, my name is Sergeant James McDougal." A potbellied, middle-aged officer greeted the anxious parents and ushered then into an office.

"Would you please take a seat. The Police Department understands your concern about your daughter, but we have to follow procedure. We'll need to have you fill out a Missing Person Reporting Form—is this the correct name?"

"We can't sit down. Our daughter's been missing for hours. Something must have happened to her. She would have called if something came up. Please, you've got to help us!"

"Mr. & Mrs. Lawson, we still don't know if Jennifer is officially missing, or if she just took off. Your assistance is vital here. Is it possible she is with some friends and has lost track of time?"

"Not a chance. Jennifer wouldn't do anything like that. She just graduated high school today and was looking forward to her graduation dinner. She would never miss her own party. She'd call." Chuck and Sally Lawson were inconsolable.

"I understand your concern, but we must take the proper steps. We'll do it as quickly and easily as possible. Once we have all your information it'll give us something to go on. I can start one man on it right now. We'll send out an APB and at least make our officers aware."

"Mrs. Lawson, why don't you take a seat and start filling out this report."

"Sergeant McDougal, this report is so detailed!" She was traumatized.

"Why don't you just fill out what you can and leave the rest blank. We'll go over it together once you're done." He tried to be sympathetic.

"Do you have a picture of your daughter with you?"

"Yes, I have pictures of all of us. I also brought the camera we used today at school for graduation." Chuck Lawson responded quickly.

"Good, we'll need that camera film when we're done. Please sit. I don't mean to upset you with these questions, but we have to be thorough. Let's start with this morning. Tell me everything that happened today to you and your family. Try not to leave out any details no matter how small." Lawson complied.

"I work for Alumni Insurance Company in Decatur as an agent. I took the day off so I could attend Jennifer's graduation ceremony from Eisenhower High School. We have one other child, Jeffrey, he's 15. He was with us. Sally and I had gone out last weekend and bought a Mustang convertible for a surprise graduation gift. Jen was accepted into Wheaton College so we wanted to give her something special. It's sitting in our garage with a big ribbon wrapped around it."

"Please just stick with today, Mr. Lawson."

"Fine. Jennifer woke up this morning and got herself ready for graduation. Commencement started at 3 p.m. at Eisenhower by the track field bleachers. They weren't a large graduating class so we figured two hours for the program and scheduled dinner for 7 p.m.

"Just before we left, Jennifer's friend Natalie Grant mentioned a sleepover party for the girls at her home tonight. Sally offered to drive Jen over after dinner. The girls hugged. Natalie said goodbye and left. Jen told us she'd be home shortly. She wanted to say last minute goodbyes and take some more pictures with friends.

"We left at 5 p.m. along with most of the other families. We didn't give her decision a second thought." Chuck Lawson swallowed hard.

"Mr. Lawson, what would you say was the demeanor of your daughter before the ceremony?"

"Thrilled, she was looking forward to going away to college."

"How would you describe her demeanor when you said goodbye at the school?"

"She was happy, running around chatting with friends. It was chaotic."

"Mrs. Lawson, how are you doing over there?" The sergeant shot her a glance.

“I’m doing fine I guess.” She choked inside.

“Mr. Lawson, when Jennifer walked off, which way did she go?”

“I don’t know.” Lawson looked to his wife.

“Chuck, I saw Jennifer heading toward the girl’s restroom when we were leaving.”

“Was she alone?”

“Yes.”

“Thank you, Mrs. Lawson. Okay, your family drove home, what happened then? When did your family first think something was wrong?”

“We expected Jen to come straight home after her goodbyes. Sally had invited her sister Elizabeth over for the celebration. Elizabeth couldn’t stay for dinner but was waiting for Jen to come home to give her a graduation gift in person. She had been there for about half an hour and was getting impatient. That’s when Sally put on the 6 o’clock news and learned about Billy Smith, that sex pervert that was released. She freaked out and started calling all of Jennifer’s friends. We left several messages at Natalie Grant’s but no one ever answered.”

Then Sally Lawson spoke up.

“Sergeant, I’m finished. I couldn’t answer several questions.” She was overwhelmed.

“We’ll deal with the report shortly. Is there anyone that may have a grudge against your daughter? Has she received any threats or told you of any problems with anyone: teachers, students, friends or family? Any disgruntled ex-boyfriends?”

"Our daughter doesn't have a mean bone in her body. No one would have a grudge against Jen--why would they? Sally, please don't cry." Chuck Lawson fought back his own tears.

"Before you came here tonight did you check her closet, notice a suitcase or small overnight bag missing? Was her bike still there?"

"No, we never checked. It didn't occur to us," they responded together.

"Any money withdrawn from your accounts? Does she have access to your credit cards?"

"Chuck, Jennifer has one of my credit cards! I gave her my visa this morning."

"That's good, Mrs. Lawson. I'll need the card information. That might be a lead." The sergeant wrote something down.

"Jen was robbed a while ago and doesn't carry a purse. She only takes a small wallet or a credit card depending on where she's going. I'll call my son and have him check the garage and her bedroom. He can also bring a credit card statement to the station for you."

"Let's wait on that for the time being." He tried to keep them focused.

"I'll need telephone numbers, addresses and anything else you can help us with in regards to your daughter's friends and acquaintances. Let's go over the report now."

"I've answered all the questions that I can. I don't know Jen's social security number. This other form, why do I need an Authorization to Release? I'll also need to get my address book from home. Our son can bring that, too." She was scattered.

"Mrs. Lawson, right now we're not sure where your daughter is. Based on your answers, unless your daughter shows up tonight with an unbelievable story, we'll consider this case as a Missing Persons. We get calls every so often that someone's missing. Usually they show up. Let's not get too worked up yet. I'm going to assign your case to someone now." His gut told him this wasn't good.

"Mrs. Lawson, why don't you go get that camera now and make your phone call to your son. Mr. Lawson, please stay."

"Chuck, I need the keys to the car. I'm so scared. Where's our baby girl? No one would hurt her, would they? She's never hurt anyone in her life."

"We don't know anything yet. Let's not panic. Jennifer means the world to me, too. Here are the keys. I love you, Sally."

The Lawsons held onto each other. Their world was about to collapse.

CHAPTER 22
THE CRIME SCENE

THE SHOPPING CENTER'S parking lot was humming. Uniforms and detectives began an intensive investigation. The surrounding streets had been blocked off and the entire lot was sealed tight. Spectators were pressed up against the crime scene tape. The quiet community of Decatur was rocked by murder.

"It's about time you guys showed up," blurted Officer Emerson.

"Good evening, officers." They shook hands.

"Jim, I think you know Mike Duffy and Rick Lombardi," Mitch Emerson stated.

Duffy, 45, a veteran homicide detective with 15 years, had the ultimate poker face. Yet, his penetrating blue eyes were an effective tool in interrogations.

Lombardi, 22, joined law enforcement straight out of college. Of Italian descent, his dark, wide-set eyes and cropped black hair made him look convincing.

"Mitch, I'm sorry it took us so long. You got anything yet?" Duffy's voice turned to steel.

"This is what we know." Officer Emerson took the lead. "According to mall security, their guard, James Abbott, was responding to a call he received from his supervisor while he was on his regular hourly patrol. Abbott was told to check out the parking lots front and back for any suspicious looking characters and to notify them immediately and, if necessary, get back-up.

"He was only supposed to observe, not engage, if there was a problem. Apparently, they'd received tips about some unsavory chaps in the neighborhood. Security had problems with their two-ways. Static kept hampering their communication. Last time they actually spoke with Abbott, he was just heading toward the back parking lot. He reported he hadn't seen anything unusual in front of Miller's Convenience Store. That was about 2056 hours. All they heard were garbled words and static from that point on."

Officer Doyle added, "As we cordoned off the parking lot it looked like a speedway with motorists zigzagging everywhere trying to get out. Plus, we couldn't stop everyone on foot. Fortunately, none were motivated to come this way, so hopefully the crime scene hasn't been compromised."

Officer Emerson continued, "Officers Vasquez and Patterson are dealing with the line-up of traffic waiting to get out of the front exits. We're taking statements from everyone. The owner of Miller's Convenience Store came over to talk with us. Stan Miller is his name.

"We've also heard from A.J. Green, Security Supervisor for the Decatur Shopping Center. His security people have their hands full. I told him to report to us as soon as he can. I think that's about it. Everyone's been notified. We're here if you want our assistance." Officer Emerson finished up.

"Thanks, Mitch." The officer nodded and walked off.

"We need the crime scene technicians ASAP. Take as many notes as possible, Rick. Their validity could mean the difference between a conviction or an acquittal in court later on."

"They'll be good enough to convict," Lombardi assured.

"That's what I want to hear. I haven't slept in two nights doing the Brady homicide. My notes would be worthless crap now. And I'm staring at a new murder case. It never ends."

Peering down at the corpse, Duffy noted, "The victim's throat was slashed straight across his left jugular. Got your camera? Photograph his face from all angles first. Then photograph his body, capturing everything you can. Make sure you use your compass so we have proper alignment." Duffy straightened up.

Lombardi observed, "He looks bizarre with his head in that position. It appears he was also slammed pretty hard across the left temple. Look at all that blood on the ground. Bet he knew his assailant; otherwise, I don't think he would let him get that close." The young detective was astute.

"Good eye, detective." Duffy looked at the setting. "Come on Abbott give us some help here, buddy. You got out of your car in the middle of this empty parking lot, why?

"Rick, I need to call dispatch for a few more men. This center has a huge lot to cover. Hopefully, there's some evidence waiting for us out there and it hasn't been compromised."

Duffy pulled a thermometer out of his pocket. "The temperature is 73°. Log that in when you're done. We'll also need the lighting truck ASAP. It's going to be a long night. I'll be right back."

Lombardi was observant while taking pictures of the corpse. *This obviously wasn't a robbery,* he thought. *You're wearing your watch and your wallet's bulging out of your pocket. Why would anyone want to kill a security guard unless he's on the run?*

Duffy returned.

"We've got the cavalry on the way. The coroner should be here shortly. We might as well go pay a visit to that convenience store before everyone arrives."

Duffy motioned to the officers, "We'll be back soon. We're going over to Miller's."

Lombardi put his camera away and made some notes. He would be sure to discuss them with Duffy later. They walked off. The two officers resumed command.

The convenience store was closed, but the lights were on and a young, attractive Latina was standing at the front register. Lombardi knocked, she opened the door.

"Hello, we're Detectives Mike Duffy and Rick Lombardi from the Decatur Police Department. Are you Norma Trevizo?"

"Yes, I'm Norma. I made the call to the cops." She fidgeted.

"We need to interview you, but first we'd like to speak with the owner, Stan Miller."

"He's in the back. I'll go get him." Norma turned into Stan Miller's path.

"Thank you, Norma. That won't be necessary; I can take this from here." Miller, 50ish, was a short man with beady brown eyes.

"Gentlemen, let's go into my office. I've been watching the front door ever since I first heard the sirens and saw two cop cars go whizzing by. I heard James Abbott was killed. Who would fathom such a thing could happen in a quiet, safe neighborhood like ours?"

"We agree, Mr. Miller," Duffy said as they followed him.

"Please call me, Stan."

"Stan, this is my partner, Detective Rick Lombardi, and I'm Detective Mike Duffy."

"Nice to meet you both. Please sit down." Miller sat at his desk.

"We'll stand," Duffy replied.

"We will interview Norma as she's the person that called in the report, but we'd like to begin with you." Duffy spoke dispassionately.

"Can you tell us if anything out of the ordinary happened tonight? Did you or any of your employees notice anything suspicious or anyone strange hanging around inside or outside your establishment?"

"No sir, nothing at all," Miller answered deliberately.

"Did you hear any unusual sounds?" Duffy continued.

"No."

"See any cars that drew your attention?"

"No." Miller was getting anxious.

"Thank you. We'll need your contact information and the names and phone numbers of all your employees."

Miller replied. "Norma is my only daily employee. She works after school, 4 p.m. 'til 10 p.m., Monday through Friday. I have one part-time employee that does weekends and can come in if I'm in a pinch. Andy Murray graduated today so he wasn't available; therefore, I was short staffed. Because of graduation day we've been busier than normal. But business stopped the minute you guys cordoned off the parking lot."

"I wouldn't worry about that, Stan. I think your business will survive," Duffy quipped.

"I hope so. I've put my life into this place." Miller was sweating profusely.

"Stan, do you have surveillance cameras?"

"Yes, two."

"Will you show us?" Miller scrambled up.

"This one watches the entire inside and that one over there covers the outside directly in front. I get a few bums coming in for a free handout now and then. The inside camera is to discourage petty theft, but a stolen candy bar here and there always happens regardless of surveillance." Miller checked his watch.

"Can we have the tapes from today?"

"Yeah, sure. I'll go get them." He returned with two cassettes in hand.

"Thank you for all your help, Stan. We'll review the tapes and contact you when we're done. We may need you and your clerk to try and help identify faces for us."

"Hope the tapes help." Miller took their cards.

"So do we. Now we need to talk to Norma."

"I'll send her back." Miller scurried away.

The anxious employee appeared. "Have a seat Norma." The two detectives hovered.

"We'd like to talk to you about what happened here this evening. Why did you call the police tonight?" They waited.

"I saw the security guard on the ground when I looked out the window."

"Tell us about that," Duffy pressed.

"I was working with several customers at the same time. One was checking out and asked if we had any salsa. I said we were out. The front window next to the cash register has a pretty good view of the entire parking lot so I looked out left to see if Cisco's, the Mexican restaurant at the far end of the back parking lot, had their lights on. They're a family run business and don't always keep regular hours.

"I figured I could send the girl over there to get fresh salsa. That's when I saw the security car stopped with its lights on, and the door open, and the security guard lying on the ground. We were really packed at the time and I didn't want to create a panic. I checked around for Mr. Miller, but he was back here so I pretended I was looking for something, faced away and called the cops."

"Then what happened?"

"Two squad cars showed up right away and went into the back parking lot. I wanted to run back here and get Mr. Miller, but he told me never to leave the register area unattended."

"Did anything else look unusual to you, customers being inappropriate? Were there any odd sounds you heard?" Duffy continued.

"No, Sir. It was pretty noisy in here, but customers were being very patient. Nothing was wrong until I looked out the window. After I made the call everything happened so fast. I heard the sirens, then Mr. Miller and customers ran out the door to see what all the commotion was about. I just stayed at the register."

"Norma, you acted very responsibly tonight. If we need to speak with you further we'll let you know. Please take our cards." They turned to leave.

Reaching the front they said goodbye to Stan Miller who was watching out the window at the developing crime scene.

Outside, the detectives walked at a fast clip.

"Hopefully, the crime boys have arrived. Things here don't fit a pattern. Instinct tells me there's a much bigger picture than the one we're facing right now in this parking lot. I think Abbott was simply in the wrong place at the wrong time. What did he stumble onto that caused somebody to murder him in cold blood?" Duffy's finger tapped at the air.

"If you've done something illegal and you see a security car approaching why not just run for it and get the hell away? Why risk a confrontation that could expose you and a crime? If it was a robbery, the guy wouldn't be hanging around leaving himself open like this. He would have left the parking lot and hit the street running." Duffy's gut nudged him.

They stopped just short of the mounting crime scene. Lombardi offered his analysis.

"The assailant manages to coax Abbott out of his car, then simply kills him. Why? Abbott apparently wasn't concerned about his safety, maybe he recognized the person. We agree on that.

"Makes me think the attacker approached him on foot. If he drove in, Abbott would have been suspicious and had his club out and ready. Abbott only had his flashlight, almost like he was planning to look for someone or something. The driver's window was half down. Maybe the thug told him he lost something and asked Abbott for help.

"What was the killer doing out here? Mike, why would Abbott leave his motor running?" Lombardi saw the inconsistencies.

"He must have thought he'd only be out of his car for a short time. It looks like he voluntarily got out--ended up dead," Duffy concluded.

They moved forward.

"Good job, Mitch, I see you've got the whole force working." Duffy appreciated good police work.

"I gave all your instructions to the tech guys when they arrived and they've been busy. Hank Robbins, Carl Brewster, and Joel Cohen are your crime scene boys here tonight. The coroner's finishing up. The morgue's on its way over to pick up the body." Officer Emerson waited for further directives.

Duffy didn't miss a beat.

"When you spoke with the mall security did you find out if there were any security cameras around the outside perimeter?"

"Just scattered ones inside the mall and stores. Nothing along the perimeter of the lot. The owners hired security guards for that."

Lombardi interjected, "Mike, even though the lights are out over at the Mexican restaurant do you still want me to go pay them a visit?"

"Yeah, we need to see if they have a security camera and if someone is around that noticed something, but first let's see what the boys are coming up with."

They walked over to the corpse.

"Has anyone seen the top security honcho, A.J. Green here yet?"

Hank Robbins, the youngest criminologist onboard was their spokesman. At 26, Robbins proved his capabilities shouldn't be underrated. In a previous case he had discovered obscure evidence that ended up solving a double homicide.

"While you were at Miller's, he sent one of his underlings, Bob Banks. Banks was covering ass for Green. Said all hell broke out in mall security when the owners found out what happened. Green was on the mat about potential liability, he'll be over here as soon as he can."

"Great, blame's being shifted and we don't even have a suspect yet," Duffy griped.

"Hank, what have you and your boys got so far?"

"We haven't figured out a whole lot, unfortunately."

Lombardi interrupted, "I'm heading over to the restaurant if you need me." He took off.

"Hank, have you determined where Abbott was killed?"

"Yep, probably right where he got his neck slashed and head slammed. There were no drag marks or blood trails, only the blood on the ground beneath his head. There's no evidence of a struggle.

"We didn't find any bloody fingerprints or shoeprints. The asphalt is pretty uneven in this area with lots of loose gravel. There's no obvious blood inside his vehicle but there is some blood splatter on the car door.

"The vehicle and flashlight were dusted. Photos and drawings have been taken of the body and the immediate crime scene so we're wrapping it up. The vehicle will be towed to the evidence holding compound. The coroner's already done his analysis and estimates time of death at around 2100 hours." Not hearing any questions from Duffy, he resumed.

"We've scanned the bordering streets and alleys. Whoever did this had any of a number of ways to enter and exit the lot. They didn't even need to walk on the grass. They could have easily walked across the sidewalks and onto the asphalt parking lot. The perimeter lights are spaced far enough apart that the darkness could shield anyone not looking to be discovered, especially if they were camouflaged. The trees on the perimeter provide further concealment." Robbins continued with his own hypotheticals.

"It makes sense the assailant had his own flashlight. There would have been a struggle to get Abbott's away from him to then clout him over the head if that's what his assailant planned to do. It's hard to see where you're walking out here, especially in the dark on this uneven surface. Anyhow, that's what I'm thinking. Found no other evidence or potential weapons," Robbins concluded.

Mike looked out at the huge empty parking lot and shook his head. It was a lot of area to cover.

"Mike, I also noticed there are quite a few cars parked on the street," Robbins added.

"A car could have easily pulled in and out without suspicion. Anybody in those big old houses directly across the street may have seen what happened. The neighborhood needs to be canvassed."

"Thanks, Hank."

"Do you think it's worth bringing in the dogs?" Robbins asked.

"Not at this point. We need to start knocking on doors," Duffy groaned.

"It's kind of late. You won't be getting smiling faces answering those doors." Robbins shrugged.

"That's for sure. But many of them are probably staring at us right now through their curtains. They might love to get their name in the newspapers as star witnesses in a murder investigation. Someone has to have seen something."

Robbins responded. "Sure hope so, we're batting zero so far. This is a big lot. It's going to take some time."

"Have your guys gotten over to those dumpsters at the back of the lot yet?" Duffy inquired.

"Yeah, Carl and Joel are on their way over there right now."

"Okay, I need to speak with the coroner." On that, Duffy walked off.

"Wait up, Mike," Rick called out.

"Struck out. There's no surveillance camera there either. There was one cook still cleaning up. He said they closed early tonight. The owner's kids had parties and wanted to skip out. They saw the crowd over at Miller's and figured people might come over but gave up after 8:30 p.m.

"The cook didn't see anything. He was preoccupied doing his chores with the radio turned up. When he heard the sirens he came outside. His name is Manuel Cortez. I've got his contact information, but his English and my Spanish are about the same, no es bueno."

"I'll send Vasquez back if we need more information." Duffy turned to the medical examiner.

"Hi, Alfred, how's my favorite coroner doing these days?"

Alfred Sweet was a short, average looking man of about 60 who walked with a noticeable limp. His personality was his best asset though the dead never noticed.

"Hi, Mike. No complaints. I can't say the same about our victim."

"Rick, I want you to meet the best medical examiner in town, Alfred Sweet. Alfred, my new partner, Rick Lombardi."

"Hi, Rick. You've got yourself the best detective in Decatur to partner with."

"I believe you're right, Alfred. Nice to meet you."

They shook hands, then assessed the corpse.

"Whoever slashed his throat knew what they were doing. They went straight for the left jugular. I figure the blunt force knocked him out and the knife did him in. The hard bang on his forehead looks like it came from a flashlight or metal pipe. Something heavy. Don't see any defensive wounds. Once he's in the morgue we'll get the full picture."

Officer Emerson interrupted, "Alfred, the morgue's here."

"Good luck with your investigation. I'll talk to you guys later. I've got work to do." Alfred attended to the victim.

"Mike, I agree with you about the logistics of this case. Killing him here doesn't make any sense unless whoever did this needed to cover up another crime. Abbott made his rounds a little early before his scheduled 9 p.m. run. He surprised his assailant who was probably on foot. I also believe Abbott knew his assailant and that's why he left himself vulnerable. Turning your back on someone in a dark parking lot indicates trust."

"Lombardi, welcome to your first homicide." Duffy grinned.

"Your radio's going off, Mike." Lombardi heard it first.

"Mike Duffy, Carl Brewster here. This case just hit a whole new arena. You and Lombardi need to get over to the dumpsters right away!"

"Let's go, Rick."

"What's up?"

"Carl just called and it doesn't sound good. We need to get over there on the double." The detectives moved quickly.

Carl Brewster, 35, had been with the Decatur Police Department for a little over one year. He had great instincts and a nose for detail but was also known for being a wise ass. He and Duffy were two of a kind.

Brewster greeted them. "Hi, guys, it looks like we've got ourselves a much bigger crime scene. Don't walk any closer to the dumpsters. We're still checking for evidence.

"There are bloody shoeprints around one of the dumpsters and then they abruptly end. It looks like someone eliminated or changed their shoes right here. Clearly, at least two people were out here standing together at some point. There's also a lot of smeared blood on the ground. Take a look. Don't know if it's human yet." The detectives peered down with their flashlights.

Carl continued, "Obviously these dumpsters aren't run of the mill in size. They're the biggest mothers I've ever seen. I called out to see if we had an injured person in there but got no response. There is movement inside, but it sounds more like rodents.

"Maybe the blood is from a dead animal, but I'm banking we've got ourselves another victim or victims. We've called backup for a ladder to see inside and we've already started dusting all three dumpsters. The lighting truck will be here shortly."

Mike Duffy commented, "I had a gut feeling that the security guard wasn't at the center of this case. We need pictures."

"Jonas Spike just finished taking shots at the other crime scene and is on his way."

"How long to do your work, Carl?"

"We need at least a couple of hours. That should be enough time unless something else erupts." Carl exercised caution.

"You've got it." Duffy gave his approval.

"Mike Duffy? Hi, I'm A.J. Green, Security Supervisor for Decatur Shopping Center. It looks like our security really failed tonight. I feel awful about Abbott. I just heard we may have another problem here at the dumpsters."

Green, 52, appeared to have aged a decade in just an evening. Duffy nodded. They moved away from the dumpsters to have a talk.

"Yes, unfortunately there's another victim or victims in one of them. This is my partner, Detective Rick Lombardi."

"Hi. Not a good night, detectives."

"Our crime scene technicians will need a couple of hours to process these dumpsters. We've got a nasty situation growing by the minute and we can't let anyone compromise what's going on with my team. Understood? So if your guys could help us keep people on their side of the crime tapes it would be appreciated." Duffy was adamant.

"No problem. I apologize for not getting over to you sooner. Bob Banks explained the situation I'm sure. I brought a current list of everyone who does janitorial work for the store keepers. It doesn't account for people in the area that use our dumpsters every week as their own personal dumping site. We know we have several of those. My guys will comply with whatever you direct them to do."

"Mr. Green, what was the last clear communication you got from Abbott? Did he indicate he saw anything suspicious in the front or back parking lot? Anything at all?"

"Call me A.J. Abbott's last complete transmission was received while he was still in the front parking lot. He didn't seem concerned other than bitching about the two-ways having static. Abbott said he was off to check out the back lot.

"We had gotten calls earlier in the day regarding Billy Smith being back in Decatur. They were from nervous parents saying their daughters were shopping here this evening. Everyone knows he's a scumbag who had a liking for little girls. Detectives, this shopping center caters to the younger crowd so we were on high alert.

"Anyway, we never did talk with Abbott again. If he saw anyone that looked suspicious I can't see him just getting out of his car. We did hear just three words through the garbled communication. Not sure if he was trying to talk to us or not. It was, "Hey, I know…"

"Thanks, A.J., that could definitely be of some help. Call us with any new information you come across. I'll let you get back to your duties. We may need you to come down to the station at some point." Duffy was done.

"Sure, no problem." Green walked away.

The two detectives began to rehash the security honcho's comments.

"What did Abbott know? He knew something or someone. Maybe the killer? Maybe his assailant was there and Abbott was talking with them and security got a sliver of their conversation? There's a telling in those three words. Let's think on it." Lombardi listened.

Then Duffy said it was time to hit the pavement knocking on doors. He would go left and Lombardi would go right. They took off.

<u>ONE HOUR LATER</u>

Batting zero, they decided to walk one block over to Water Street. They hoped to find people who had been out for a stroll or walking their dog, or just sitting on their porch. It was a long shot, but they had to try. The following day Duffy knew he'd have to assign men to canvas a bigger area surrounding the center. Evidence would be harder to find.

After striking out on Water Street, they headed back to see what the boys had come up with at the dumpster. They discussed Smith. It sounded almost too fishy, like Smith was being set up, and this even without these people knowing anything about the dumpster situation. Duffy felt the weight of his job. They arrived.

"Hank, what did you find?"

"Not good. When we looked inside dumpster number one with the blood, we saw three bloodied garbage bags with exposed body parts and a lot of busy rats. There are three crates stacked inside with bloody shoeprints on top next to the wall. Two random crates appear to have bloody shoeprints on them, as well. Maybe they were thrown back in. We were lucky to snag a metal rod that could have been used as a weapon. It was standing on edge against the frame. We haven't gone in yet.

"Regarding dumpster two and three, no other evidence of blood, clothing, or anything else questionable was found. They were both filled with pretty much your normal gambit of garbage from a shopping center, lots of wooden crates, boxes and junk. Nothing suspicious was discovered. Both of these dumpsters have been processed.

"The only other thing of interest found was a small gold hoop earring on the ground right outside dumpster one. The earring and rod are over here if you want to have a look. I dusted both. The rod had some blood on the end that touched the floor. The hoop was coated with dirt and hairspray--no blood. The backing was missing. Probably why it fell out of someone's ear." Hank appeared beat.

"That metal rod would make getting to those crates a whole lot easier especially if you're a short person. He might have used the rod like a hook to pull the crates out of the dumpster to be used on dumpster one." Lombardi suggested.

"So they tossed a few crates inside so the guy in there could use them as a step-up to climb out. That makes sense." Duffy nodded.

"How did you do on your neighborhood canvas?" Hank asked.

"Freaked out a lot of people but got no leads. We were just killing time waiting for you guys to finish up. Well, I guess we got back here in the nick of time for the unveiling."

"It's all about the timing, Mike. Now to the nasty part, victim dumpster. Joel, get the ladder back here. Who's the lucky copper that gets to go in?" Hank wasn't amusing.

"It might as well be me. Hand me some new gloves and a mask." Joel took a deep breath.

Joel Cohen had been with the Department for four years. At 33, his perspective usually took in nonconformist thinking. He was an asset and the boys knew he could unearth the smallest of clues.

"You're a trooper, Joel. Move the lighting truck closer. Let's get the inside of this dungeon lit up like a candelabra." Duffy and the whole group looked on.

"It's not a pretty sight in here. I see three blood soaked black garbage bags with a bunch of rats crawling around. Looks like human body parts poking out. Some long blond hair, an open-toe shoe with toes from another.

"Where's the camera guy? We need to get exterminators out here on the double. Hopefully, they can eliminate the rats without compromising this situation any more than necessary. That would make getting the body bags out a whole lot safer."

"Anything else, Joel?" Duffy questioned.

"Like we saw initially with the flashlight, a bunch of wooden crates stacked up. It looks like someone stood on them to climb out. I see bloody shoeprints on them and also tracking up the inside wall of the dumpster. There are a couple more crates with bloody shoeprints and splatter on the walls a short distance away. From the looks of things probably heaved back in. Looks like a few smeared fingerprints are on the frame, too. They go maybe four feet in one direction, then stop short of the body bags and head back.

"Something landed in here, too. Not here now though. Whatever it was plopped in the blood and left a circular impression. Definitely not a crate. This was rounded, like a good sized purse or bag of some sort," Joel concluded.

Jonas appeared with camera in hand.

"Take shots of every inch of this metal tomb." He climbed out so Jonas could get in.

Once outside, Joel stood there perplexed. "What kind of person would want to go in there voluntarily with body bags and rats?" He said with disbelief.

"If someone couldn't get out readily, how the hell could they have gotten in? How and when did the body bags get in there? This case is getting complicated, boys." Duffy was noticeably troubled.

They concluded someone must have given him a hoist. Duffy moved away from the dumpsters.

"I've got to go make a call to the station again." He walked off.

"Hello, Brenda, Mike Duffy here. Our investigation just got a whole lot bigger."

"Go to Channel 2, Mike."

"We'll need all the manpower you can spare. Send out the coroner again. The crime scene now has more victims. We've got at least one more homicide."

"That's terrible. I'll get right on it. It's been a busy night here, too. We're jammed to the walls with malcontents."

"It looks like we all have a rough night facing us. Thanks, Brenda."

With that, Duffy moved back to the second crime scene. His mind was racing.

"Carl, how tall would a person have to be to get in and out of this thing?"

"Well, I'm 6 feet tall, so maybe 5'10"." Carl stood close to the side of the dumpster.

Duffy looked at the group.

"Someone used crates to get out. That we know. The other two crates with bloody shoe prints suggests someone tossed them back in. Joel says they were clearly thrown based on splatter. It's obvious the offender was trying to cover his tracts. Duffy was stumped.

"Maybe the bad guys pulled a car up to the dumpster, tossed the body bags over and something went wrong. One of them somehow managed to get in and the other asshole threw the crates in for him to get out." Joel surmised.

"Any other brainstorms, coppers?"

Lombardi interjected, "Only thing that makes any sense in this whole scenario is that there had to be at least two suspects."

"True, but things don't add up, Rick. Why would anyone want to get into a dumpster if you've just thrown a corpse in there? Wouldn't you just want to get the hell away?" Duffy argued.

"Maybe they forgot something on the corpse and went back in to retrieve it. Possibly some incriminating evidence. Maybe that missing bag that Joel referred to?"

"I hope you're right, Rick. Let's assume it and go with that scenario.

"So, even if they were both standing on crates it still doesn't explain the "why" except that they were short. Everyone listen up. Absolutely no comments with the newspaper boys or anyone else until we have something solid. I don't know where this is leading, but I sure hope we don't find any more corpses. Looks like we're doing an all-nighter."

Duffy refocused. "Hey, Rick, what does the bright young detective think about our budding crime scene? What are you doing over there anyhow?"

"I'm checking out these shoeprints. From the looks of them which, by the way, appear to be girls' tennis shoes, our suspects are rather on the small size. I see two sets close together. They both appear to be matching tennis shoes and the same size.

"Whoever made these prints was frantic. See here, both sets move around in circles. People just walking through a parking lot wouldn't do that unless they're nervous and panicking. Behind the dumpster we found the same tennis shoe impressions in the dirt. Carl believes someone might have been crouching down there. The imprints are deeper showing more weight bearing at the toe. Definitely the same kind of sneakers. Maybe one of our suspects was hiding or lying in wait for Abbott, just a guess."

"Any chance someone was just taking a leak back there?" Duffy questioned.

"Don't know yet." Lombardi knew he'd have to do better.

"Okay, so we have suspects running around creating two sets of identical shoeprints. I've never heard that one before." They walked back.

Joel wanted to add his two cents.

"Mike, the index and middle fingerprints in the dumpster were from a small hand, too. Probably female. Most of the prints were smudged, but we'll just have to wait and see if we can get one good lift that we can ID."

"What else?"

"Let's say they didn't have a flashlight, and it was dark in there. Isn't it logical that they would use their easiest fingers to guide them? Almost like an antenna."

"Let's say I accept that. So we have what amounts to a compromised person using the touch method to search for whatever they went in to get. As for the fingerprints, we'll get them examined more thoroughly.

"Another major question is how does all this figure in with Abbott? He may have stopped to investigate if he saw a car at the dumpster. Why get out of his car if he feared for his life? What did he see? He had his flashlight in his hand. If he was suspicious of something he would have turned around fast to get back-up because his radio was screwing up. We've got to come up with some logical explanations." Duffy was like a coach revving up his team.

"What about one of the perpetrators being at another location hidden behind one of those trees out on Main Street as a lookout? Abbott doesn't see the lookout guy but does see activity going on at the dumpster.

"What if the scout sees the security car heading toward the dumpsters? He intercepts him by running out in front of his car, surprises him and tells him some cock 'n bull story. Abbott steps out and gets wacked." Joel wasn't letting go.

"If that's the case, the murderer is throwing the body bags into the dumpster and the accomplice is out on the street. So the lookout guy did Abbott in? Is that what you think, Joel?"

"Yeah, why not? It would take two people to cut up the body or bodies. No shit, we probably have more than one psychopathic murderer running loose out there. What if there are more than two people responsible for these murders, Mike? Anyone else have any better ideas?" Joel threw his hands up.

"What about the crates? Could there be a woman, or two women? Remember, the small shoeprints Rick says are most likely female. Unfortunately, this parking lot gets a lot of foot traffic by girls. Maybe it's just a coincidence. We could run around for days investigating things that aren't even relevant. That's something we're going to have to look at long and hard.

"Females just don't cut up bodies, not that I've ever heard of. Sick, deranged males, yes. We need to check out the gangs in the neighborhood and see if that leads us anywhere.

We might be in the middle of a gang war when we get ID on the body." Duffy was determined.

"Mike, the coroner is waiting and the morgue has arrived, too," Officer Doyle reported.

"Thanks, Jim."

"The rats have been removed. I need a strong, able-bodied volunteer to go into that death trap and retrieve the body bags. The coroner's waiting." Duffy was waiting, too.

"Aw shucks, no rats?" Carl Brewster joked.

"Was that a volunteer I just heard, Carl? Didn't think so. Any other smug comments. No pied pipers in the group?"

"I think the boys have just volunteered you for the assignment, partner."

CHAPTER 23

CALLAGHAN FARM EMERGENCY MEETING

DESPITE AN UNFOLDING murder scene and a private party that was just revving up, another situation was also playing out. KT's father, Declan O'Neill, called to order an emergency meeting. It was 9:30 p.m.

"Hi, Declan."

"Hi, John." O'Neill and Callaghan exchanged handshakes.

"Before we go in I want to thank you again for letting us gather here tonight on such short notice." O'Neill was beholden.

"Not a problem, I'm glad I was able to accommodate. The barn will give us privacy. Will Patrick be coming tonight? I recall you saying your boys were coming in for the weekend for Caitlin's graduation."

"No, Patrick's covering for me at home. I missed Caitlin's graduation and celebration dinner because of this damn drought. I'm in the doghouse, but I'll have to make peace with my family later. I've been in my fields since sunup tending to my crops. I only surfaced when I got the news about Manas and decided we needed to meet. Finn was a basket case when he told me. I appreciate you spreading the word to the others. We need to deal with the emergencies at hand. This drought is serious business, too, and can destroy all our livelihoods." They walked into the barn.

"Let's call the meeting to order." O'Neill stood front and center.

John Callaghan, "aye"

Daniel McCloud, "aye"

Finn Sullivan, "aye"

Christopher Avery, "aye"

John Graham, "aye"

Ross Kelly, "aye"

Sean Murphy, "aye"

Kieran O'Flaherty, "aye"

Declan McNeill, "aye"

"All clans being present, The Sacred Order of Harvest will now come to order. Following tradition, Ross and Sean please perform the ceremony of lighting the candles bringing clarity and spiritual strength. Our sacred chalice symbolizes eternal wisdom. Let us drink its water gaining spiritual guidance and inspiration." The goblet was passed along.

O'Neill continued, "We, the descendants of the nine original clans who survived the Great Hunger and created a new beginning are ever mindful of the vows pledged so many years ago to continue in the practice of the old ways. As guardians of the sacred rituals of our forefathers, we honor our ancestors by giving homage to the elements of earth, air, fire and water. We respect the ancient Druids and Wizards of Old. We display the Celtic symbol of three conjoined spirals, our sacred triskelion across our lands showing respect for the continuation of life.

"I've called this emergency meeting to discuss the severe ramifications of the drought we're in and to acknowledge the loss of a longtime friend and worker, Manas. Finn Sullivan, you have the floor." O'Neill stepped aside.

Finn cleared his throat.

"As you know, we're in the midst of a nasty drought. With a dry spring behind us and now a record hot dry summer before us, our crops are facing devastation. The low groundwater levels are worsening at a rapid rate. Mandatory water conservation is being implemented all over the state. There's a good chance our crops may all be ruined by the time this season is over. Historically, the Sangamon River and the Mahomet Aquifer have always saved our farms. That can't happen this time.

"Our groundwater has reached a critically low level. Our wells in Heaven's Door were checked yesterday and they are more than two feet below the 1976 critical levels. We're in the mouth of a dragon, my friends, and will be devoured if we don't get additional water to our crops soon.

"We all know Barrett wanted to keep Whispering Lake a secret sanctuary for our clans. However, no other drought has been this severe. Our way of life is at stake here. I've looked into a few methods and am confident we can pump water from Whispering Lake to save our crops. Though its levels are considerably down I believe there is enough water there to last through this season. We will work on this and get back to you."

Finn paused. "Now with a heavy heart, I am sorry to tell you my headman, Manas was killed today on I-72. Two weeks ago Manas severely injured his hand in a pulley.

Regrettably, I allowed him to drive a large truck to pick up a load of crates. Due to the bandaged hand, being unfamiliar with the truck, and a poorly balanced load there has been an accident in which he perished."

"Finn, I'm sure I can speak for everyone here. You did nothing wrong. Fate just stepped in. Please give his wife our condolences and tell her we'll make all the funeral arrangements, if that's acceptable with her. We can bury him in the cemetery at Heaven's Door. I think Manas would want that." Declan was steadfast.

"Thank you, Finn." O'Neill moved back to the front.

"I wonder how difficult it was for our ancestors to deal with droughts and fires. I'll sleep on it and take action tomorrow. This meeting is now over. Ross, please extinguish the candles." The clans dispersed.

"Declan, wait. John, Daniel and I need to speak with you alone," Finn appeared concerned.

"Sure, let's go outside and walk out into the fields. The night air clears my mind. John, please thank Mary for her courtesy tonight."

"I will. We need to discuss some issues that weren't brought up this evening." Callaghan's tone reflected awkwardness.

"Finn, why don't you go first."

"Manas was still under doctor's care and I'm concerned about the liability. You're all percentage owners of my farm." Finn was worried.

"You need to check your insurance policy on that truck," Declan recommended.

"I'm insured with Farmer's. But before I call my agent, I'd like to speak with a lawyer. I'll feel more comfortable." Finn got quiet.

"Daniel, what about Ian? Isn't your nephew a Personal Injury lawyer in Chicago?" Declan inquired.

"Yeah, Ian McCloud would give you good advice. I'll get you the telephone number."

"Thanks. I'll call him first thing tomorrow morning. Maybe he can put my mind to rest." Finn appeared calmer.

"Okay, I think I'm done for the night. I need to get my wife and deal with the fallout. That's a conversation I don't look forward to having." Declan could hear it now.

"I thought you said Patrick would explain to Siobhan about the urgency of the situation and the need to have a meeting tonight?" John replied.

"He said he would, but I think Patrick was conflicted about his sister's graduation taking a back seat. My personal life isn't a whole lot better than the nightmare I'm facing out in my fields," Declan drew in a big breath and exhaled deeply.

"Finn, Colin called me before he left South Bend today and said he was planning to visit tomorrow. What's that about?" Daniel looked for clarification.

"Damn, I've been so preoccupied I forgot he was coming in this weekend. He didn't mention anything about calling on you, Daniel. I told him things were getting pretty bad around here. It's been difficult keeping up tuition and expenses for him at Notre Dame. I hinted he might need to quit college 'til things improved. With the worsening tide, I'm afraid my conversation with Colin is a foregone conclusion." Finn was resigned.

"I need to process things, Finn. We'll talk tomorrow." Declan was tired.

"Goodnight." Finn turned and left.

"Declan, I'm sorry, there's another situation I need to speak with you about. That's why I wanted to discuss this outside the house." John looked hesitant.

"Does Daniel need to stay and listen? It's very late."

"No, he doesn't."

"I'll call you tomorrow, Daniel." With that, Daniel McCloud walked off, as well.

"John, what is it?"

"There was a problem in my house. I had to call Maggie Grant here tonight to work on some emergency financials. When Siobhan and Darcy got here they saw Maggie. It seems Caitlin was going over to Natalie Grant's house tonight for a sleepover.

"I normally like to stay out of women's talk, but this conversation got real heated. My wife was concerned and brought me into it. It appears your daughter told your wife their friends would be at the Grant's tonight and her mother would be supervising. That was a lie because Caitlin knew that Natalie's mom was working here tonight. The two women got into an argument about Maggie being irresponsible leaving six girls unsupervised.

"On top of that there was a lot of discussion about the 6 o'clock news. There's some local child molester that's just been released from prison and he's back home in Decatur. Siobhan was so mad she picked up the telephone and called the Grant house but got no answer. Maggie told Siobhan the girls had a surprise for Natalie and that they probably went out for a short while. Well, that was some time ago and there is still no answer at the Grant's. Your wife is fit to be tied. I thought I'd warn you before you go in."

"This day just keeps getting worse by the minute. Well, I guess I have to go face the music. The wrath of a woman trumps the wrath of Mother Nature any day of the week."

"Aye to that."

CHAPTER 24
LOST TOGETHER

NATALIE INWARDLY SMILED picturing the heated argument that transpired between her mother and Siobhan O'Neill. They had no idea what was really going on. Natalie's heart raced as her rekindled memory sped back to Colin and a night filled with lust and secrecy.

"Be real quiet, Colin, voices carry. The lake is through those trees off to your left."

"Damn, we must have driven past it a dozen times, but it was so dark. I smell smoke coming from that direction," Colin noted.

"Patrick started up a fire so we could warm ourselves after skinny dipping," Natalie's insides yearned.

"I can hear the party, that's Patrick's voice for sure. It doesn't sound like the O'Neills are missing their buddies too much."

"The only girl that would be complaining would be KT. She's waiting for you."

"Well, she's going to have to wait for someone else. I'm spoken for; at least I hope I am." He tightened his hold on her hand.

"Colin, KT is sexy and you know it. I'm sure you've seen her picture. Her brothers brag about her."

"Are you having second thoughts? Do I get a choice here? Look at me." Colin stopped short.

"No, I'm not regretting this. You do have a choice. Honestly, KT had this evening mapped out before we got here," Natalie confessed.

"Well, right now I'm making a new map and you're in it. It's just the two of us. Is that okay with you?" His eyes implored hers.

"I'm leading you to a hiding place. Isn't that a clear enough message?" Natalie returned his gaze.

"Have I told you in the last five minutes that your body is amazing? Those pants and top really do your curves justice." Colin's groin throbbed.

"You're embarrassing me, but I love it. My hair will come down once we jump into the lake. It's naturally curly by the way." Natalie giggled.

"I can't wait to see you with your wet hair draped over your body with nothing else on you but me." Colin anticipated great sex.

She smiled coyly, "Over there, Colin, point your flashlight. Can you see that rock overhang by the big tree? Past it is a neat little hideaway that's totally private. We'll have to walk across these rocks and through some low hanging branches, but no one will find us. Be careful, the rocks are slippery." Natalie led slowly.

"Are you sure about this? Once we go over there, there's no turning back." Colin wanted confirmation.

"I know what I'm doing." She stopped and put her hand on his crotch.

"I want to be naked with you and feel you inside of me. Now come this way, duck your head and stay close."

"You weren't kidding. This truly is a hideaway," Colin declared.

"Close your eyes and don't peek." Natalie stripped down.

"No, I want to see you, touch you." Colin loved the game.

"You will in a minute. Now open your eyes." Natalie stood in front of him naked.

"You're perfect, fucking fantastic." He grabbed her.

"I love the way your body looks and feels and smells." Colin went wild.

"Let's get these clothes off of you. I'm hungry." Natalie kissed Colin passionately as she undressed him.

"Sit down and lean back against the rock and spread your legs." Natalie sat between his legs, at his feet.

"I don't know if I can wait that long, you're driving me crazy." Colin was beside himself.

"It won't take long, I promise. You look delicious. The first course is sucking your toes. The second will be my tongue up the inside of your thigh." She worked deliberately.

"Oh, Nat, you're blowing my mind."

"Actually, that's the third course, ready?"

"Stop teasing me. I can't take this anymore." Colin was in sheer bliss.

"Foreplay makes me hotter. How does my tongue feel? I can do this forever. You'll have to tell me to stop." Natalie kept going.

"You feel magnificent. How did you learn to *do* that? You're driving me insane." Natalie enjoyed being in control.

"Babe, I want to get inside you now. Get on top of me. I can make love to you as many times as you like. I'll stay hard for you all night." He penetrated her. Both moaned in ecstasy.

Colin and Natalie entered that domain where primal pleasure was all that mattered. They devoured each other. Then reality surfaced.

"Quiet! Did you hear that?" Colin listened.

"All I can hear are our hearts pounding. Don't move," Natalie pleaded.

"It sounds like a search and rescue team is calling your name."

"I don't hear anything. I love your sweaty body beneath me. Just stay where you are." Natalie was fixed in the moment.

"We'll get caught if we stay here together. Your call."

"Damn them!" Natalie slid off of Colin and stood up. She scooped up his clothes.

"What's this in your pants?" Natalie looked surprised.

"It's a family medallion. Another time."

"You're just full of interesting things. Do you always carry a switchblade?" Natalie stared at Colin.

"I just took it along for protection. It actually belongs to Dylan. I still hear them. They're getting closer." He raced to put his clothes on.

"Colin, I have an idea. You stay hidden. I'll slip into the lake and make it so they find me. I'll just tell them I wanted some time alone for a swim. They'll be so surprised when I get out of the water naked they won't question me. Then I'll figure a way to ditch them, get my clothes and go back to the party." Natalie was good at details.

"Great, you fuck me silly and then you disappear," Colin protested.

"Just for the time being. Wait 'til it's all clear, then hurry back to Dylan, get to your car and drive back down the road about ¼ of a mile. There's a dirt road on the right, you'll have to look carefully. It's the turnout for Whispering Lake. We'll meet back at the party and pretend we've never met before." Natalie turned to leave.

"By the way, you were amazing!"

CHAPTER 25

SEARCH AND RESCUE

THE WORLD SEEMED to stop as Natalie relived the events that occurred that fateful day. She had no idea that her friends would be so concerned about her whereabouts.

"Emily, stop it now. I'm sure Natalie's fine. She likes being alone doing her own thing. With all that's happened today I don't blame her. Jen is missing and the security guard was murdered. We don't know what's happened to Colin and Dylan. I'm really bummed out, too. My dad was too busy to go to commencement and my celebration dinner."

"I'm sorry, KT. I didn't know about your family."

"Em, I need to get something off my chest. I was so upset when I found out my dad couldn't make it to my party I just took off and went over to Decatur Shopping Center. While I was in Sander's Department Store, I was convinced I saw Jennifer but then she disappeared."

"Gee, I was there, too. I thought I had some extra time to waste. But I was wrong, my new watch had stopped. I never saw either one of you. When Natalie and I left the convenience store we heard sirens. Natalie said it was probably some drunk in the back parking lot taking a pee. We didn't give it another thought. How did you find out?"

"Patrick told me on the way over. He heard it on the news."

"I should have stuck to my first decision not to come, KT, but I didn't want to be a killjoy. Now I'm worried something's happened to your brother's friends. And Natalie's been gone at least half an hour. She could have changed in the restroom if she wanted privacy. My heart's really pounding."

"Do you have any more of those pills? Why don't you take one more?"

"Yeah, maybe I should. I'm starting to feel jittery again; I think I will take another pill. I'm sure it'll be okay."

"Well, remember her dad died here. Maybe she's out there kind of talking to him." KT hoped to pacify Emily.

"Oh, I forgot all about that. That would explain it." Emily calmed.

"KT, Emily, over here." Deidra waved.

"What's up, Dee?"

"Liam just got back. They found Natalie. She was on the other side of the lake. He said she just wanted some time alone and went skinny dipping by herself. Liam said she stepped out of the lake to greet them totally naked. Can you believe that?

"She went to get her clothes and said she'd rather walk back alone. Liam said Patrick's really pissed. He thought Natalie was coming on to him, but she was only teasing. Here comes Liam." Deidra hushed.

"I just saw your girlfriend Natalie in the nude. What a body. She isn't modest, that's for sure. Is Aidan back? He's going to flip!" Liam was bowled over.

"He should be back soon." KT replied.

"We went out there to rescue her. Boy did we get a surprise. Patrick's fuse is definitely lit," Liam warned everyone.

"Where's Patrick now?" KT asked.

"I don't know. We walked back separately. He needed some space."

"This was supposed to be a fun party with us all skinny dipping together. No chance your friends are still coming now, is there?" KT fretted.

"They're not my buddies, they're Patrick's. I'm going to get myself another beer and try to forget about this entire day." Liam took off.

Emily and Deidra were speechless.

"Where is Natalie? Damn her!" KT fumed.

Minutes later, Natalie walked out of the woods like everything was fine.

"KT, hi, I just love the way your pants and top fit."

"Well, the princess has returned! Has it occurred to you how worried you've had all of us? Just disappearing like that was really selfish of you. This entire evening has turned crappy and what about the security guard being found dead at the shopping center?

"What's going on with you, anyhow? My brothers went out searching all over the damn lake. We thought you had disappeared like Jen." KT was livid.

"I don't see what's wrong with me taking off for a little while to be by myself? You know this place has history for me. Are you so inconsiderate that all you can think about is yourself?

"The real reason you're pissed off is because your brother's friends aren't here. You got all of us out here just so you could seduce Colin. This isn't about Jennifer or any of us; it's about you and your selfish needs. I don't know what you're talking about with any security guard being found dead. What's that about?" Natalie was surprised.

"Would the two of you girls stop fighting and just shut up?" Aidan shouted over them as he arrived at the escalating scene.

"Aidan this is not the way I wanted this evening to turn out." KT turned and walked down to the lake. The rest of them stayed around the fire pit.

"Hi, Aidan. So sorry you had to see us like that." Natalie was apologetic.

"Girlfriends argue. It's O.K." Aidan tried to defuse the situation.

"Hey, look! Liam's walking back with your lost friends, Dylan and Colin. Good, they finally got here!" Natalie acted excited.

"It's about time those guys showed up," Aidan chimed in.

"Look who I just ran into when I was getting a brew." Liam was holding a Guinness.

"Sorry we took so long. We got lost. Where's Patrick? I want to thank him personally for the excellent map he made for us. Colin here, by the grace of God, found the dirt road entrance or we'd still be wandering out there." Dylan's lack of sobriety was obvious.

"Aidan, why don't you and Liam go get Patrick and the rest of the girls," Natalie suggested.

"And who might you be?" Dylan inquired.

"Natalie Grant, nice to meet you."

"I'm Dylan Maguire. Happy to make your acquaintance and this is my friend, Colin Sullivan." Dylan thought he had found his dream girl.

"Did you guys bring along anything stronger than that beer," knowing they had.

"We have just the right thing, don't we, Colin? How about a little Irish whiskey to warm you up." Dylan knew drunk girls gave it up easy.

"Excellent!" Natalie said enthusiastically.

"I'll go and get the Jameson. Hold down the fort, Colin, I'll be right back."

The second Dylan left, Natalie told Colin exactly what she wanted to do to him sexually. He was putty in her hands.

"I've had a hard-on thinking about you ever since you left."

Natalie suggested walking down to the lake. She knew everyone was excited to meet him, especially KT. She also wanted to get away before Dylan returned.

"Fine, but there's still some unfinished business that needs attending to." Colin grinned.

"You're just going to have to be patient. The girls are all coming back to my house for a sleepover. We'll work it out." She blew him a kiss.

At that point Melanie and Deidra walked up.

"Cool it. I want to introduce you to the twins. Deidra and Melanie, this is Colin Sullivan."

"Nice to meet you girls. Wow, you really are identical. How do people tell you apart?" Colin was stunned.

Natalie laughed, "That's easy. Just start talking girls, he'll figure it out."

"She's right. We're identical, but our voices and personalities are different. Where's your friend, Dylan?" Deidra purred.

"He went to the car to get us all a bit of Irish whiskey. Got any food? I'm starving."

"Oh, yes, over there by the tables. There are plenty of munchies." Melanie announced.

Dylan returned and handed the opened bottle of Jameson to Natalie.

"Thanks, Dylan. I think I'll just put it into my mouth and savor it."

"Easy going darlin'. We don't want you getting drunk on this so soon," he lied.

"Here, Colin, have a swig. It feels real good going down." Natalie was suggestive.

"I'm sure it does." Colin took a swig. "Girls, would you like some?"

"Sure, why not. Come on, Melanie," Deidra prodded, "after the day we've had, alcohol may do us good." Melanie took a swig.

"Okay, my turn." Deidra held the bottle high. "Here's to losing our fears and inhibitions!" Deidra gulped.

"Here they are. Time to party. Emily, KT, Patrick, come on over. Have a little libation," Dylan slurred.

"Well, if it isn't my very best friends Dylan and Colin. Why were you so late?" Patrick was still pissed.

"We'll discuss your map making ability later. Now it's time to let loose." Colin passed Patrick the bottle.

Dylan added, "We brought lots more to heat up the party and the girls. They're already drinking the fire. No one will be feeling cold after some good whiskey."

"Natalie, feel like another swim in the lake?" Patrick didn't take rejection well.

"Not now, Patrick, I think I just want to drink and sit by the fire," dismissing him.

"It's party time. To the Irish! Let's drink up. Keep the Jameson going round and it doesn't stop 'til the second bottle runs out. Then we'll see the worthy among you."

Emily approached Patrick. She told him she'd taken a lot of medication and wondered if the alcohol would be okay.

"Your decision, bright eyes, maybe one little drink won't hurt, but just one."

"Let me have that bottle then, I need to make the shadows go away." Emily let loose.

"Wow, look at Emily take down the whiskey. Emily knows how to party." Patrick didn't give it a second thought.

Everyone threw caution to the wind.

CHAPTER 26
THE MORGUE

NATALIE SORTED OUT the different scenes that played in her mind like a roadmap to murder. She remembered watching the news as the coroner was being interviewed. Alfred's tongue-in-cheek personality was a springboard for helping her visualize the morgue scene now.

"Mike, this is one of the most gruesome murders I've had to deal with in my 25 years of forensic examination. Let's start with the girl, Jennifer Lawson. I think her murder caused Abbott's. Not a pretty sight having to open up those body bags. ID by the father wasn't good either. The viewing was too much for him. He passed out. Rick Lombardi came in real handy to break his fall," Alfred reflected.

"Did you see the pictures of Jennifer at graduation?" Duffy asked.

"Yeah, I got to see them. Very different when the victim is alive and full of personality. This is my world, Mike. Corpses are strictly clinical and impersonal. They let me do my work without comment."

"I hear you, but I have to get into their lives to do my job right. What do you have for me to go on Alfred?" Duffy knew he had a tough one.

"Well, our victim died of multiple stab wounds to the chest, then her body was dismembered. I've calculated time of death somewhere between 6 and 8 p.m. based on her liver analysis, other breakdown calculations, and times you've given me. This is a much more difficult analysis. She was last seen at 5 p.m. and was discovered by 9:30.

"The body doesn't cool at the normal rate because of the disarticulations and plastic bags. The murderer definitely knew how to dissect a body. Other than the obvious there was no blunt force trauma to the head or bruises noted on her body. The nylon cord acted as both tourniquet and carrier for the body sections. Arranging the body parts back together has given us reliable information about the sequence." Alfred spoke matter-of-factly.

"Your murderer took her head off right between her cervical spine roots C5-C6, that's her lower neck. The assailant could have broken bones any of several different ways to get a complete dissection, but didn't. The body was actually disarticulated in a very professional way—very efficient.

The victim has multiple stab wounds to her thoracic cavity just to the right of center. See here? They bagged her pulmonary artery and ascending aorta. She bled out fast. The major bleed is on the inside. Probably used a switchblade or a hunting or fishing knife. The stab wounds are consistent with a right-handed person," Alfred continued.

"The killer wasn't much taller than the victim who measures approximately 5' 7". They were probably standing face-to-face at the time of the attack. The lab's doing toxicology on her blood right now. There's no indication of recreational drugs, but it's still too early to make the final call. Her skin doesn't show signs of needle marks, tracking, previous bruising or scars. She was killed with a knife but dismembered with a meat cleaver.

"I think someone planned out this murder very carefully. They had everything they needed waiting in advance. Even chose a strong nylon rope to tie off the body parts." Alfred drew Duffy closer.

"Take a look at this, Mike." Alfred held out his hand.

"Looks like a regular condom to me," Duffy said.

"The pervert stretched it over her tongue. It was shoved all the way down to the base. There was no semen or fingerprints. Very bizarre. We also found a few unused condoms tossed into the bags. Not sure what that means." Alfred shook his head.

"Maybe the murderer is sexually dysfunctional and this is how he gets his rocks off," Duffy suggested.

"Looks like he didn't want to leave any incriminating evidence, just meaningless clues. He clearly wanted the police to find his handy work. Serial killers love to be one step in front of the cops. Gives them an adrenalin rush and sense of power. Could be advertising more to come," Alfred assessed.

"I hope not. What else can you tell me?"

"There was booze poured on her torso but none found in her system. Perhaps another message from the killer? This rope could mean something. It's a four-strand twisted type typically used in the marine industry for mooring, anchoring and towing. What kind of mind thinks to place rope as both tourniquet and handles to facilitate this kind of murder?" Both men stood puzzled.

"Maybe your killer is a sailor. Definitely knows a lot about knots or possibly that's what he wants the police to think. Might be someone in the medical field or a person knowledgeable about butchering. I'd check out the slaughterhouses myself. I hope you're not dealing with a serial killer and slaughtering is their signature." Alfred flinched.

Duffy just stared at the medical examiner. He had the same fears. The puzzle just kept getting more and more bizarre. They also found a girlie magazine in each one of the bags dating five to seven years ago. He'd never heard of a case anything like this before.

Alfred saw Mike was dissecting possibilities in his mind. He snapped him out of it.

"Your victim was a very beautiful girl. Could she have gotten mixed-up in prostitution? Parents and friends are usually the last to know. Possibly a trick gone awry?" Alfred continued in his pursuit.

"Maybe a customer got mad and decided to make a grotesque example out of her. Could someone have been stalking her at school? The news did a good job of broadcasting. Your killer probably has access to a television and knows the authorities are all over this." Alfred was astute.

"Unfortunately, we don't have motive or any witnesses. No substantive clues leading us anywhere or to anyone. Jennifer's family was together throughout graduation up until reporting their daughter's disappearance. Their alibi is airtight.

"We haven't found her buddies yet. Who knows where they are and what they're doing. Certainly not their lame ass parents. I'm hoping they can explain why Jennifer didn't join them on their private escapade. These girls are as thick as thieves from what the parents said. They wouldn't have just abandoned their friend. Just more blanks to fill in," Duffy groaned.

"Okay, let's figure this out." Duffy organized his thoughts.

"Our killer is probably under 5' 10". We still don't know where the girl's murder took place. The body bags had to get to the dumpster by car so it could have been any place. We know the killer does Jennifer in between 6 and 8 p.m. What does the murderer do then? Just wait around until dark to get rid of the body bags? The parking lot is routinely patrolled so the killer has to figure that into their timing unless they just happened to drive by and saw the empty dumpster." Duffy was stumped.

"I don't think the dumpster was a random choice, Mike. The killer is way too thorough."

"Let's move on to Abbott. What can you tell me about him?"

"Not much, but my guess is they were both killed by the same person. Time of death approximately 9 p.m. A perfect strike across the left jugular, again by a right-hander. The hit on the head was pretty powerful. I'd say that came first. I think Abbott was just a hapless victim. No other evidence." Alfred said expressionless.

"There has to be evidence we're overlooking, Alfred."

"Mike, Decatur isn't Chicago. The community thought it was immune from the crimes of the big cities."

"Not anymore. Thanks a lot for all your work, doc."

"You have my blessings." The coroner held out his hand.

CHAPTER 27
BACK AT POLICE HEADQUARTERS

NATALIE WAS STILL REELING from the scene at the morgue. She remembered hearing about Mike Duffy's ruthlessness from her mom. Natalie's amnesia was her savior back then.

"Rick, pick up line 2, Mike's on the phone."

"Thanks, Brenda."

"How are things going with the Lawsons?" Duffy inquired.

"Not good. It's going to be impossible getting any coherent information out of either of them tonight. They're pretty distraught."

"I heard identification was difficult," Duffy commented.

"Paralyzing," Lombardi replied.

"Thanks for driving them to the morgue and back to headquarters."

"Sure. On the way back they were pleading with me to find the monster that killed their daughter. It made me even more determined to find the sick bastard that did this," Lombardi said defiantly.

"I pray to God we do before anyone else shows up dead," Duffy replied.

"What did Alfred have to say?"

"He believes both murders were committed by the same person. Not surprising. He'll keep working on it. Unfortunately, we're still in the dark as to motive, location of Jennifer's murder and any hard evidence. Did you have any luck going over the Miller surveillance tapes?"

"Yeah, a very busy day just as Stan Miller said. There was a parade of people racing around buying food for parties. I've also been looking over the pictures the Lawson's took at graduation and there are a couple of girls pictured with our victim that were in Miller's at the time Abbott was killed," Lombardi continued.

"Emily Martin was the one who asked the clerk for the salsa. She walked in about 2036 hours and looked over what was left on the shelves. She shopped for a while, yapped with other shoppers, and at 2104 hours, headed over to the counter to check out. She obviously asked the cashier about the salsa and jabbered for a couple of minutes contending with several interruptions from other customers.

"Norma gave us a pretty good picture of what happened. Everything in the video seemed consistent with her statement. The checkout counter gave Norma a clear visual across the back parking lot. She stopped talking with Emily and turned to look outside left toward the Mexican restaurant. I watched the expression on her face change when she looked out the window. She was definitely spooked. She looked toward the back of the store apparently looking for her boss.

"At 2110 hours, she pretended to remember something, spun around and dialed the cops. Next, the verification call came from us. Norma finishes the cash transaction with Emily at 2116.

"At 2117 hours, Natalie Grant came in just in time to take a grocery bag from Emily. Nothing appeared odd, suspicious, or inappropriate between the two girls. Grant is tall, built, and attractive. Looked like she was going to a big shindig the way she had her hair all done up, not a hair out of place. They both appeared cheerful. The two squad cars entered the Main Street entrance into the parking lot just as Natalie Grant walked into Miller's.

"Clearly the girls had no idea what was going on outside. The surveillance camera was focused on the front of the store and some of the parking lot. There were several teenagers standing outside blocking most of the view of the front parking lot for a good 20 minutes before the cops arrived. Loads of motorcycles with riders hanging around, too. Quite a few cars came and went through the exits during that time period. It was difficult to see exactly what was going on with all the pedestrian traffic. Once the cops flew by, everyone's attention quickly turned toward the back lot.

"Natalie and Emily exited to the left side of the building out of view of surveillance. They split before the exits were cordoned off. There are two primary ways to approach Miller's. Since it sits apart from the rest of the shopping center, the parking lot encircles it along with two exits. The main entrance being from Main Street and the other off Wood Street. Surveillance doesn't cover the Wood Street entrance and adjacent parking.

"Someone could easily walk from behind the convenience store and not be seen by either one of Miller's cameras if they came from the Wood Street side. A person could also walk up from the mall and bypass the cameras completely. We don't know what direction Emily approached from. Natalie parked on that same side so we couldn't see when she got there. She could have been sitting in the car waiting for Emily the whole time. There's no other perimeter surveillance on property or off that covers that entrance.

"About an hour before Emily arrived, the surveillance tape showed four motorcycles pull up. Two with chicks as passengers on them. Two of the guys were all muscled-up, tattoos, crew-cuts, you know, marine types. Nothing looked suspicious. Miller sure wasn't wrong about this being one of his busiest days of the year." Lombardi was done.

Duffy shot back with orders.

"Tomorrow let's have Stan Miller and Norma look over the tapes to see if we can ID some of them. There are a couple motorcycle rallies in town this weekend. See if these guys are locals, anything that could possibly fit our hypothetical killer or killers?

"Get our informants out snooping. See if anyone is talking, bragging. The hookers might be of help, too. Alfred and I discussed prostitution as a possibility with Jennifer. She was no virgin. And we can't forget the slaughterhouses. I want a list of grocery stores with their own meat departments."

Lombardi had the police report in hand. He'd been busy.

"There was a visa card given to Jennifer by her mom. We've learned she bought some stockings and a pair of shoes in Sander's Department Store. She was alone. Both transactions were rung up at the same cash register. The charges went through at 1824 hours. No other transactions were noted by the credit card company. The sales clerk said she came in by herself and left alone with two bags under her arm."

"Well, that tightens up the time of death. What about the store's surveillance cameras?"

"There's one at the front door and one located by the restroom on the second level. Sander's depends more upon a couple of plain clothes security. They also utilize sensors on their most expensive items which trips the alarms at the door if they haven't been removed at the cash registers. One of the security people was on break while Jennifer was in the store. The other one didn't see her at all. She was caught on surveillance tapes coming and going but wasn't seen talking with anyone other than the salesperson. She walked out at 1840 hours. I've got the tapes here," Lombardi finished.

"Damn, I was hoping that would have been a break for us. Running into a friend or someone familiar. Girls stop and gab. We'll review the tapes later. Someone had to have been meeting her at the shopping center or lying in wait. Neither of Jennifer's shopping bags has shown up so the killer either has them or disposed of the items elsewhere."

"Mike, I got to have a talk with Jennifer's brother, Jeffrey. Apparently, he told Natalie that his sister was getting a new car for graduation. Her parents were going to surprise her with it at dinnertime. If Natalie told the rest of the girls it would be easy to see why they weren't too worried about Jen not showing up for the party."

"They also could have been pissed off none of them got a new car and just split. What did you get for graduating high school, Rick?" Duffy pried.

"My first wind up watch."

"Well, I got a handshake and a lecture from my dad informing me about my new responsibilities. How many kids get new cars from their parents on graduation day? No one wants to hear their friend bragging if all they got was a hug and a kiss. It's past 2300 hours and the Grant house is still dark. We've got a car stationed out front and another patrolling the area. The parents of the girls are also being interviewed, but no one knows where they are so far. Seems the original plan was a sleepover at Grant's, but clearly there is a pre-party party." Exhaustion was kicking Duffy.

"Mike, how long 'til you're back at the station? The boys are in the lab trying to put IDs to the prints they lifted. Matching them up is the biggest thing we've got going at this point."

"I'm on my way there." Duffy yawned.

CHAPTER 28
DRUNK AND ROWDY

NATALIE WAS NOW HEADING into that dark corridor where her memory corrupted. She'd spent the better part of her adult life using imagination to fill in the vacant spots. Finally here, she felt shivers of revelation as she progressed forward. The party was in full swing.

Patrick shouted, "Hey everybody, I think we have enough whiskey in us to strip in unison and jump into the lake."

Everyone was pretty tipsy so the call was easy. Patrick set the mark.

"On the count of three, all you skinny dippers take off your clothes." Everyone stripped without vacillation.

"Go girls go! Let's beat them in."

KT and Emily sprinted into the dark, wet void. After plunging in, KT asked Em if she was okay.

"Yeah, I think I'm good. I'm kind of light-headed. I sure drank a lot of whiskey."

KT stayed next to her. "Alcohol will do that to you." KT was feeling the booze, too.

Emily swam farther into the lake. She seemed unconcerned about any danger.

"Don't go too far. Stay close to everyone," KT warned.

"Who's swimming this way?" Emily squinted.

"It's Aidan. I guess he's not interested in Natalie, after all." KT wasn't surprised.

"Wow, I feel really weird." Emily's body was experiencing the combined effects of the drugs and booze.

"Keep it together, here comes my brother."

"Hey, Em, want to take a swim with me across the lake?"

Emily thought Aidan was adorable. "Sure, why not."

She gathered up all the energy she had left. "I'll race you over."

"Okay, you're on. Let's go, hotshot." Off they went.

KT was alone now and mad. Colin hadn't tried once to strike up a conversation. Maybe Patrick hadn't told him she was his for the asking. It occurred to her that flirting with Dylan might make Colin jealous and, consequently, interested in her. But she had to get Natalie out of the picture. As well, if she hinted to Patrick that Natalie was attracted to him, he could keep her occupied so she could make her move. She paddled over to Patrick.

"Hi, brother."

"Hi, sis."

"Having fun?"

"Yeah, sure."

KT gave him a story. "Don't give up, Patrick. I know Natalie thinks you're really cute. She told me so."

Patrick didn't buy it. In fact, he told his sister that Natalie was a teasing bitch. His ego was still wounded. But KT wouldn't have her chance dashed. She finally admitted her real intent. He questioned why she didn't propose this scheme to Aidan. After all, the original plan was to get Aidan and Natalie together.

KT pointed her finger across the lake.

"That's the reason. Aidan's interest is somewhere else. He's completely into Emily and she appears to be receptive."

"I saw him swim off. Now I know why," Patrick smirked.

"Where is Natalie, anyway?" KT asked.

"I saw her run off into the water with the twins. Liam, Dylan, and Colin are entertaining them."

"Well, I think it's time for you to go and help preoccupy my best girlfriend. I need to spend time with Colin without interference. I've got to find out why he's been ignoring me."

"So you think Natalie may have something to do with it? He doesn't even know her. We've never discussed anyone but you, KT. I don't get it either. He told me he thought you were a fox." Patrick was surprised.

"Well, I don't need her around complicating the situation. She knew I really wanted to be with Colin," KT pouted.

Patrick agreed to help.

"I'll do my best, but you're on your own with Colin. He's really smart and may figure this one out. Let's go take a swim."

KT quickly approached Colin and began her scheme. She needed to get him alone.

"Hey, Colin, want to race me across the lake? I bet I can beat you," daring him.

"Well, a challenge from a lady O'Neill. I could give you a three minute head start and still beat you," Colin bragged.

"Hey, buddy, is this competition open? Can anyone race?" Dylan wanted in.

"I don't know, Dylan, you'll have to ask Ms. O'Neill."

"Is it, KT?" All eyes were upon her. KT would now have to shift to Plan B. She'd make Colin jealous. The tease knew how to make men hunger.

"I'd love to race you across the lake, Dylan. Colin talks big, but he's chicken. He doesn't want to get beaten by a girl," KT laughed.

"I'm not chicken, KT, there's nothing chicken about me at all," Dylan boasted.

"We'll see about that." KT was all go.

"Anyone else up for the competition? What about you, Patrick?" Colin asked.

"I think I'll stay out of this one." Patrick wanted as far away as possible. He swam over to Natalie. As if on automatic pilot, she took off for Colin.

"Count me in guys," Natalie piped up.

"Okay, we've now got Natalie in the race. Is anyone else up for competitive water sports? Or are the rest of you fools too drunk to race?" Colin challenged.

"Well four makes a race, two per team," he announced.

"Dylan, I want you on my team." KT said as she appeared next to him.

"Fine with me, KT." Dylan was thrilled.

"Okay, Ms. Grant, I guess you're stuck with me," Colin grinned.

"I'll suffer through it." Natalie stifled a smirk.

They lined up.

"Patrick, give us the signal."

"Okay, on the count of three…1-2-3 GO!" They took off.

Dylan and KT shot out in front. Natalie fell behind. She called out to Colin to slow down and join her. Natalie's hands searched under the water until she found him. Colin got so aroused, he choked.

"You're crazy, you do know that."

Natalie giggled. She pushed herself up against him.

"I thought that's what you liked about me. This is going to be a quickie. We'll need to swim extra fast to catch up to them," she said as she fondled him.

"Don't stop!" Colin groaned.

KT and Dylan had reached the other side of the lake. It was a clear victory. The two paddled around looking for Colin and Natalie. Dylan spoke first.

"I thought they were swimming neck-n-neck with us?" He was dumbfounded.

KT smelled a rat. She was boiling mad at Natalie. It was time to show Colin what he was missing. KT would see to that.

Her whole demeanor changed toward Dylan. He was now her weapon. She smiled at the lucky guy who would have the honor of screwing her. Dylan wouldn't complain. She had nothing to worry about there.

"Dylan, come over to me. I want to kiss you."

"In a heartbeat." He swam underwater and popped up right in front of her.

"I was hoping you'd be attracted to me. You are one sexy chick." His head was spinning.

"You really turn me on. I couldn't wait to get you alone." KT caressed his chest.

"You feel so strong and hard everywhere." Her hands explored under the water.

"What do you say. Want to play?" KT wasted no time.

"Are you sure? Colin and Natalie can't be far behind." Dylan said hesitantly.

"Stop talking about Natalie and Colin. Don't you want me?"

"Of course, I want you. I thought you had the hots for Colin?" Dylan was confused.

"Doesn't a girl have a right to change her mind?" KT said coyly.

"Absolutely! But I don't play second fiddle." Dylan felt her hands massaging him.

"I can definitely get into you now." Dylan's hands moved passionately over her breasts. He wanted desperately to get laid.

KT stopped him. She didn't want him coming too soon. He'd have to work for this. And she had something much bigger in mind.

"Not yet, wait! Let's crawl up that flat rock."

"Huh, now? Between you and the booze my head's spinning and my dick's throbbing. What's going on here?" Dylan was puzzled.

"The rock is wet and smooth. It'll be more sensuous," KT insisted. She swam to shore.

"You're in for it now, KT." Dylan followed her out of the lake.

"You want to be an exhibitionist? Fine, let's get on the rock and let everyone see us going at it. I'm game." Dylan didn't care.

KT made sure she got high enough so the others would get a good eye-full. Dylan crawled up right after her. She taunted him higher. She then told him what she wanted. Kneeling on the rocks she had him enter her from behind.

"Isn't this better? Show the world how much you really want me."

Dylan pushed hard. He couldn't wait any longer. He was starting to lose his erection. The booze was messing with him.

KT screamed. "Don't stop, Dylan. I'm almost there."

Out in the water Colin saw what was going on.

"Natalie, I think we better turn around and head back. Emily and Aidan are on the shore and he's all over her. KT and Dylan are wrapped around each other on the rocks screwing their brains out."

"What? KT and Dylan are screwing? That bitch is trying to make you jealous. No, we're not turning around. I'm going to show her what I really think of her games." Natalie was livid.

Colin held her by the arm. "I don't care what she does or who she does it with. Let's head to shore now! You told me you guys had to leave by midnight and we're way past that. Enough is enough!" Colin was unyielding.

Natalie finally relented and started swimming back, but she was bound and determined to get drunk. Natalie would have it out with KT when Colin wasn't around. He didn't need to be a part of their problem. Colin tried his best to calm her down on their return swim. She never heard a word.

Dylan was still trying to satisfy KT, but just couldn't perform anymore. Then, out of the darkness, they heard a shriek.

"HELP ME! Somebody, please, help me!" Aidan was terrified.

Then, the air stilled. Dylan and KT stopped and listened. Suddenly alarm set in.

"Aidan, is that you? It's Dylan, I'm over here on the rocks with KT. What's the matter?"

"We need help, now! Please come over here fast!" he pleaded.

Emily had passed out and Aidan was cradling her when Dylan arrived. He could see she were really bad off. Dylan's pounding adrenalin had temporarily cleared his head. He asked Aidan what happened.

"Emily complained about being out of breath and cramped up half way across. She went under a couple of times. I had to grab her and pull her onto shore. She mumbled something about a kid trying to drown her. Then she passed out. I've been trying to get her to wake up, but she won't come around. I tried mouth to mouth, but it didn't work. She's not responding to anything. She's barely got a pulse. The alcohol and those pills she took are poisoning her. We've got to get her to the hospital right away." Aidan was frantic.

"Is there a way to drive a car around the lake and come to this side?" Dylan asked.

"Yeah, get KT."

Dylan yelled, "KT, get over here fast! Something's wrong with Emily!"

"With Emily? NO! I'm coming!" She bolted over the rocks.

"Aidan, what happened?" KT knelled down beside Emily's pale, limp body.

"It's gotta be her meds and the whiskey. She's barely breathing."

"Dear Lord, she's so cold." KT was speechless.

"We need a car over here ASAP." Dylan knew KT could swim faster than he could. He was sick to his stomach.

"Swim back as fast as you can and get help! This is serious."

She took off.

While Emily's emergency was ongoing, Natalie and Colin arrived on shore. Natalie grabbed the bottle and started slugging down the Jameson. Colin gave up. He just sat and stewed. The party was going down the tubes fast.

Deidra was the first to see.

"Melanie, look out into the water. I think that's KT. She's yelling something and waving her hands."

"What's she saying?" Melanie strained to see.

"Something's wrong! Something's *very* wrong!!" Deidra ran over to KT as she staggered out of the water. She was trying to catch her breath. Everyone gathered around her but Natalie.

"Emily's passed out on the other side of the lake. We need to get her to the hospital fast." She was still gasping.

"Natalie, did you hear me? Stop drinking that damn whiskey! Our friend's in trouble and needs us!"

Natalie ignored her.

"This isn't a joke. I'm dead serious! We need to leave right now. Someone has to drive to the other side of the lake and pick Em up." KT's alarm finally registered.

Colin spoke first. "Dylan had the keys to his car. I don't know where he put them. Natalie, let me drive your car over. I'll go pick Emily up."

Under the circumstances his offer was reasonable. Natalie was drunk. She could barely get her words out.

"You don't know how to get there, Colin. I know this lake. Round up the others and meet me at the hospital."

Natalie's mind went into autopilot even though her body wasn't onboard.

SITTING IN THE CHAPEL, Natalie started to tremble. Her memories were flooding in, pushing against the faulty levy. She knew the end of her journey was close at hand. She had to break through this barrier. A frightening flash burst into her thoughts. She now remembered getting into her dad's car and all that followed.

God, don't let anything happen to Emily. She doesn't deserve it. I'm so dizzy. I've gotta keep a clear head. She drove on sheer adrenalin.

Colin flew into action and mobilized the group. Worried that Natalie wasn't up to handling the emergency, he berated himself for letting her go in her inebriated state. He confronted KT as they worked feverishly to pack up.

"You really need to get your act together. I saw what you did up on the rocks. So whatever you plan to do with Dylan don't hurt him because of me. Just to set the record straight I'm falling in love with Natalie. Call it chemistry, destiny or love at first sight, all I know is she's the right girl for me." Colin's words were knifelike.

"You've made your point! This won't have any effect on our friendship in the least. Guys come and go and when Natalie's done with you, we'll laugh about this." KT lashed back.

"You really are a mean, vicious person, KT. I hope Dylan has a strong heart because you'll junk him like a piece of trash. Natalie isn't like you. She's warm, loving and has a heart of gold." Colin's words seared into KT's heart.

"Are you quite done, Colin? We have a friend who needs help."

"Yeah, we're done."

CHAPTER 29

COPS ARRIVE AT O'NEILL FARM

AS THINGS RAPIDLY UNRAVELED at the secluded lake, just down the road two patrol cops were sitting in the O'Neill driveway wondering where the family was at this late hour.

"It's past midnight. No cars around. Where is everyone--in bed?" Deputy Lucille Lewis was a tough, experienced cop.

"It sure is dark around these parts. Are you positive we've got the right place, Lucy?" Deputy Tommy Sinclair was her rookie partner.

"Yeah, the address is right. I guess we better go wake up the dead."

"I'll stay out by the car," Sinclair remarked.

"Listen, we've had two homicides go down tonight. I'm not going anywhere without a gun protecting my back."

"Lighten up, Lucy. We're just running down girlfriends of Jennifer Lawson's. We have no reason to suspect anything is wrong out here."

"Don't assume this quiet farm is innocent, Tommy. Who knows, all five missing girls could be dead and cut up into tiny pieces inside this house. There's a crazy murderer on the loose. God, I hope we don't find the girls in garbage dumps all around town," she grimaced.

"Got it, Lucy, point well-taken."

"I'll knock, you stay off to the side. If everything is fine I'll have you go round to the back and check things out there."

"Great, no one's answering the door." She pounded even harder.

"No one's here, Lucy."

"Sure seems odd this time of night. Go check the back." He disappeared, then returned shaking his head no.

"Tommy, my radio's going off in the car. Stay alert." She headed over.

"Deputy Lucille Lewis here."

"Hi, Lucy, it's Mike Duffy. What's going on at the O'Neill farm?"

"Hi, Mike. We arrived here ten minutes ago and it appears they're not at home. The lights are out and no one's answering the door. The gates were open so we pulled right in. No cars in the driveway. There's a farm truck parked off to the side that's cold to the touch.

"There is no evidence of foul play, at least outside. Tommy just checked the back and signaled everything looks normal. No vandalism. How are you guys making out?"

"Nothing solid yet. We have cops watching all the girls' homes. We've spoken with the Stuart family. Apparently Melanie and her twin sister Deidra were dropped off at Eisenhower High School after dinner around 2045 hours. by their mother Rachel for a school-sponsored function in the gymnasium. The parents believed they would be going to Natalie Grant's for a sleepover afterward. They haven't heard from either daughter since. We called the school and found there was no function. So we know these two girls lied to their parents. The Stuarts are quite upset and very concerned about their daughters.

"We also located Emily Martin's parents, Amanda and John Martin. They got a different story but with the same lie. Emily told her parents she was spending the night over at Natalie's, too. She was supposed to walk there right after dinner. The Martins haven't heard from their daughter either since she left around 1900 hours.

"That only leaves Natalie Grant and Caitlin O'Neill. We've got someone at the Grant house but no one's home there either. I want you and your partner to stick around the farm for another hour. If they don't come back, return to the station. I'd hate to think we have any more homicides out there. Fortunately, we've had no positive IDs from the hospitals or urgent care centers. There are lots of cars out looking for them. We'll find them."

"Mike, girls celebrating high school graduation are going to want to hang out with boys. They all told their parents lies so they could duck out. I'll lay you odds they're with guys partying."

"Yeah, that's pretty likely. KT has three older brothers who go to Notre Dame. Maybe they have part in this," Duffy added.

"Logic says the brothers would try to make their sister's graduation. Don't you think?"

"We've checked on that. No one we've interviewed saw the O'Neill boys at commencement. Only Caitlin's mother and younger sister attended."

"That seems odd that her father wouldn't show. I grew up with the Irish. They never miss out on an opportunity to celebrate. It's in their blood. There's got to be a good explanation why he wasn't there. Family comes first. Her brothers would have to make an appearance. Coming from Notre Dame is a good distance and maybe they planned to celebrate tonight."

"That's a whole lot of people to be gone at this time of night," Duffy remarked.

"We'll keep a lookout and check back with you if anyone shows up or if we find anything suspicious. If nothing happens we'll return to the station by 0100 hours."

"Good talking to you, Lucy. Be careful. We don't know what we're dealing with."

"Will do, Mike."

The conversation ended.

CHAPTER 30

LEAVING WHISPERING LAKE

NATALIE FLEW AROUND the lake. She would rescue Emily at any price. In a drunken state, she still found the way.

"Natalie, over here." Dylan frantically waved her in. She skidded to a stop.

"What happened?" she screamed.

"You need to ask Aidan."

Natalie saw it wasn't good. Aidan explained the situation.

"We've got to get her to a hospital now. Help me carry her to the car." They moved fast.

"Leave the window down so she can get some air. Cover her with that blanket. I'm taking her to Macon County Hospital. Meet us there."

Natalie thought as she sped away. *Em, I won't abandon you so don't you abandon me. Why did you drink all that damn whiskey on top of your pills? You're too smart to mess up like this. Hold on, I'm going as fast as I can. The booze is really messing with my vision. OH, NO…a deer!*

TIME MOVED IN SLOW MOTION as everything converged on that dark, lonely road.

"What's that up ahead, Patrick?" KT was nervous.

"Natalie's car's in the ditch!" Patrick saw the whole scene at once.

"Wait, KT! Don't open the door. Let me pull over first." Patrick yelled.

"My friends are in that car. We need to get to them. Girls, grab your flashlights!" KT and the twins jumped out.

Patrick ordered, "Liam, get our flashlights, too. Aidan, snap out of it. Set the flairs on the road. We may need them."

Patrick led the rescue.

"Holy shit! The car rolled. There's the deer she hit." Patrick and Liam moved quickly.

"Liam, flash the light inside."

He reported. "Natalie's trapped, pinned against the steering wheel. Emily's not inside the car." They tried unsuccessfully to open the jammed doors.

"I smell gasoline. We need help. Where the hell are Colin and Dylan?" Patrick shouted.

KT panicked. "Where's Emily? Deidra, Melanie, help me find Em. Spread out." The girls feared what they would find.

Melanie called, "KT, Emily's over here by the tree. I'm scared to touch her. Is she dead? She's got blood all over her."

"Step back, Melanie. Let me get to her." KT knelt down.

The twins stood frozen. “Please tell us she’s not dead.” Melanie sobbed.

KT cradled Emily in her arms. Tears streamed down her face as she rocked her lifeless friend.

“Oh, my God, she is dead! What do we do, KT?”

“We need,” she stammered, “we need the police and paramedics. Deidra, go get Aidan. One of us has to drive back to our farm for help.”

“GOD’S punishing us! We never should have come out here. Emily’s dead and we’re all to blame!” Melanie crumpled to the ground.

“Please calm down. This is hard enough without your hysterics.” KT tried to pacify things.

“Emily didn’t want to come. We pushed her and now she’s dead and who knows if Natalie is alive or dead. We abandoned Jennifer, and we don’t even know what’s happened to her,” Melanie raged on.

“Enough! I take full responsibility. Does that ease your conscience?”

“KT, you need to talk to Aidan. He’s sitting on the ground by the flairs shivering. I couldn’t tell him about Emily. Patrick and Liam are still trying to get Natalie out of the car.” Deidra pleaded.

KT nodded. She gently placed Emily on the ground.

“Get a blanket from the car and cover up Em. I’ll go to Aidan. Melanie, I loved Emily, too. I’m sorry I screamed at you. We need each other more now than ever, I’ll be right back.” They hugged.

“Aidan, listen to me. No one is blaming you or holds you responsible. Please don’t fall apart on me. I can’t do this alone. I need to tell you something very painful…I’m afraid...”

“NO! You’re lying to me. Get out of the way.”

He pushed free of KT and raced over to Emily. She was covered with the blanket. Aidan became hysterical as he collapsed beside her. “Please, NO! She can’t be dead! Emily!”

Dylan’s car was racing up the road when they saw the accident scene.

“Stop!” Colin jumped out of the car and started running.

Dylan tried to follow but became sick. Colin prayed as he ran past the flairs.

“We need help!” Patrick was overwhelmed.

“Patrick, where’s Natalie?” Colin’s fear was palpable.

“She’s pinned inside and we can’t open the doors. She’s unconscious. We need to get this car turned over fast, but it’ll take all of us to do it. There’s gas everywhere. Where’s Dylan?”

“He’s by his car puking.”

“Get him!” Patrick demanded.

Colin ran to Dylan and grabbed him by the shirt. “We need you!”

They raced back.

“Liam and Dylan, go to the back end of the car. Colin, help me in the front.”

"Where's Aidan?" Colin asked.

"He's in shock, forget him. On the count of three…everyone push. Stand clear." The car righted.

"Patrick, give me your flashlight. Natalie, wake up. Natalie!" Colin couldn't rouse her.

Dylan looked inside. "Where's Emily?"

"She was thrown. She never had a chance. The girls are with her now." Patrick said quietly.

"No." Dylan slumped to the ground.

"Don't break down, Dylan. We need to get Natalie out. She's unconscious and bleeding." Colin crawled into the backseat.

Seeing the situation from inside, he directed. "We need a lot of hands, but be careful."

They did as they were told. The seat slowly eased backward. He got his hands around Natalie and released her seatbelt. They all moved in unison.

"We're running out of time," Patrick warned. "The gasoline smell is stronger!"

"I know, I know!" Then Colin vowed, "Hold on Natalie, I'll get you out and when I do, I'll never leave you." Tears streamed down his face.

CHAPTER 31

DECLAN AND SIOBHAN

DECLAN WAS FURIOUS. He slammed his car door leaving John Callaghan's. He had enough on his plate. Siobhan should have suspected shenanigans.

"Are you going to talk to me or just give me that cold Irish shoulder of yours the rest of the drive home? I've told you before never act disrespectfully in front of our kin and friends. It's unacceptable, Siobhan. What did you expect? You made me feel like it was my fault Caitlin lied to you."

"Lower your voice. You'll wake up Darcy." She was asleep in the back.

"Everything that goes wrong around here seems to be my fault. I know I disappointed our family today, and I'm truly sorry for that. It's not just this family I'm responsible for. I have workers and their families depending upon me and 160 acres of crops. Are you listening to me, Siobhan?"

She wasn't. She was busy watching what was going on up the road. Siobhan gasped. Now Declan saw, too. There were huge flames belching out of a car in a ditch and their four children were standing on the road in front of them. Siobhan's eyes widened.

"Our kids! Beep the horn!" Her distress grew.

"Patrick sees us," Declan said.

Patrick ran up to the car.

"Dad, we need help." Patrick was frantic.

"Whose car is that? Is anyone hurt?" Declan's own fear showed.

"Yes, KT's best friend Natalie is unconscious. We pulled her out just before the car caught on fire. She hit a deer and flipped… and, and, Emily Martin…is dead. Dad, please come."

Declan acted. "I'm calling 911 now."

He grabbed his cell phone as they both got out of the car.

"911. What is your emergency?"

"This is Declan O'Neill. There's been a terrible car accident off of Eagles Pass Road in Macon County. It's on a private road just north of the O'Neill farm, my farm. We need the paramedics out here right away. We have a girl unconscious, and I'm afraid to say another girl is gone. The car is on fire. Please hurry!"

Meanwhile, Siobhan tried to comfort her son as he told her what happened.

"There's a girl dead back there, Mom, it's Emily. She was thrown from the car. She's gone. I have her blood on me." Patrick cried like a baby.

"Oh, Patrick, I'm so sorry, son." Siobhan cried as well.

"Everyone get as far away from the car as possible. It might explode," Declan shouted.

"Over here, Dad," KT yelled.

"Are you hurt?" Declan trembled.

"No, but Aidan's in terrible shock. He was with Emily when she passed out at Whispering Lake. Natalie was driving her to the hospital when she hit a deer. The car flipped and rolled. Natalie was pinned in, but Emily was thrown out and landed by that tree. The guys rolled it back over and pulled Natalie out just before it caught fire. Colin is holding her now. Dad, it's just terrible." Declan embraced his daughter.

After she consoled Aidan, Siobhan ran over to where Colin was holding Natalie. The scene was nightmarish.

"Colin," she shook him gently. It's Siobhan O'Neill. Please let me help you."

"No need, Mrs. O'Neill. I've got Natalie safe in my arms. I have to protect her until the paramedics get here. I promised."

Minutes later the police, fire and paramedics arrived.

"Clear the way. Son, we'll take over from here." Colin reluctantly released his hold.

A female officer approached Mr. O'Neill and asked, "Are you the one who called 911?"

"Yes. I'm Declan O'Neill. This is my son, Patrick."

"I'm Deputy Lewis. What happened here?"

"One of my daughter's friends, Natalie Grant, was trying to take another friend, Emily Martin, to the hospital and they hit a deer. The boys pulled Natalie out. The other girl was thrown from the car. She's over there. Unfortunately, she didn't make it."

"Were they the only two passengers in the car?" The deputy was writing.

"Yes," getting confirmation from Patrick.

"No one else is hurt?"

"No." Patrick responded.

"I'm going to ask you all to move way back there and stick around. We'll need statements. The kids smell like they've been drinking. We're going to have to do sobriety testing in a little bit. Just sit tight."

A shocked Declan asked, "How did you get here so fast? I just hung up with 911."

"We were down the road. My name is Deputy Lucille Lewis and this is my partner, Deputy Thomas Sinclair. Dispatch notified us right after the call came in. I'm assuming these are your children and the other missing teenagers from Decatur? The Macon County police have been looking for them for hours."

"What do you mean the police are looking for my kids?" O'Neill was stunned.

"Why don't we just take care of the accident first, then we'll talk about the other situation." The two deputies walked away.

"Radio for backup, Tommy, and let Mike Duffy know we've found the missing girls. Not the kind of celebration night these kids were expecting. One girl seriously injured and another bound for the morgue. Make sure no one leaves the scene under any circumstances." Her instructions were clear.

"What's going on here, officer? There's been a horrible accident; yes, but…"

O'Neill was cut off.

"Mr. O'Neill, we have a bunch of buzzed teenagers, a fatality, a badly injured girl, and a vehicle on fire. I've asked you to stand back. This isn't a request, it's an order!" Deputy Lewis turned away.

O'Neill spun around to his wife, "Siobhan, what the hell happened today? Why were the police looking for our kids?"

"I don't know. All I know is Caitlin was getting together with her friends to have a sleepover at Natalie's for a graduation party. The boys had plans with their own friends. It didn't even occur to me that they would have planned to go to Whispering Lake together." Siobhan was beside herself.

"Even at your age, Siobhan, you're still naïve. It's apparent the girls had more on their minds than just a sleepover. It's also apparent our kids lied to us. They were drinking, a lot by the looks of it. Drinking and driving! Plus, some of the girls are underage.

"I can only pray Natalie comes out of this thing okay. That poor girl dead, I can't even imagine how her parents are going to take this. Siobhan, I'm so sorry for not showing up today." Declan clung to his wife and broke down.

Deputy Lewis returned.

"Mr. O'Neill, things are under control. Why don't you give me your statement now?"

"Sure. I was at a neighbor's for an emergency meeting this evening because a farm worker and friend of ours was killed on the expressway today. We had to discuss that and the drought. My wife, Siobhan, and daughter, Darcy, arrived later and stayed with the wives in the house. We were on the way home when we came upon the accident. We called 911. That's about it."

"Mr. O'Neill, we have questions pertaining to other matters, but we will address them back at the station. That's why we were at your place earlier."

"Excuse me, Deputy Lewis, we need you over here," Deputy Sinclair interjected.

"I'll be right there." She redirected to the O'Neills.

"Mr. & Mrs. O'Neill, wait here. We're not done." She walked off.

The accident scene changed rapidly. The fire was put out before a bigger disaster occurred.

"The paramedics are heading out and the Fire Captain needs to speak with you."

"Okay, roundup the teenagers, Tommy. We'll do the field test, then take them down to headquarters. I'm going to release Mr. & Mrs. O'Neill and their younger daughter. We'll let the detectives deal with them later." She went over to the Fire Captain.

"Hi, Lucy. What a mess." Captain Gus James stared at the blackened shell of a car, his sun beaten face covered with grunge from the ordeal.

"Yeah, pretty miserable scene, Gus. One young girl dead and another severely injured. Thanks for responding so fast. We're lucky there's no wind. This area would have gone up like a tinder box." The smell of smoke choked the air.

"It's a miracle they got that girl out in one piece before the fire lit. It took some fast thinking and ingenuity to free her safely," Captain James acknowledged.

"A lousy situation, but luckily someone was thinking clearly. Only smart thing these kids did all night. It sure sobered them up fast. They even put out flairs. I guess fear can motivate people to do some pretty heroic rescues," she concluded.

"Think we're done here. Anything else you need from us?"

"No, Gus. Your men did a great job. Here comes backup up and the coroner." She said goodbye and headed for the coroner's car.

"Hi, Lucy, looks like you've got your hands full. Where's the body?"

"Hi, Alfred, she's over by the tree. She was ejected during the crash. Her name is Emily Martin. From what her friends tell us, Emily supposedly OD'd on pills and alcohol, then blacked out. The driver, Natalie Grant, was taking her to the hospital and hit a deer. The other parties followed behind in two cars. Grant was extricated by her friends. She hasn't regained consciousness and is being transported to Macon County ER now.

"All the kids stink of booze. They must have had one hell of a party. They're all being taken to the station. I have to go finish with the parents. The victim's waiting for you, Alfred."

"They always are!"

CHAPTER 32
INVESTIGATION BEGINS

EVERYTHING EXPOSED ABOUT the investigation came from police reports, newspaper accounts, and television interviews. Natalie learned names and details. In a small town like Decatur, everything about a high-profile murder was known except for well-kept secrets.

"Captain McKenzie, Detectives Duffy and Lombardi are here to see you, sir." Brenda stood at the door.

Mack McKenzie stood 6'3" with strong facial features and a lanky body. At 55, nothing surprised him.

"Show our dedicated detectives into my office."

"I'll go get them." Brenda disappeared.

"Come on in and sit down, boys. Tell me you've got a crack in this case. Your call about finding those kids gave me mixed messages, Mike." Mack McKenzie leaned forward.

"Well, Mack, let me just say we've got a lot of company here at the station; the Stuart twins, the O'Neill kids and a couple of their friends. I'm not sure if we've just gotten a lucky break or if it's a whole lot stickier and more complicated." Duffy looked exhausted.

"Deputy Lucille Lewis and Deputy Thomas Sinclair were watching the O'Neill farm waiting for the family to come home when a 911 call came in at around 0115 hours. They responded immediately. There was a fatal accident just down the road from the farm.

"It seems that an intoxicated Natalie Grant was driving fast trying to get an unconscious friend, Emily Martin, to Macon County Hospital when she hit a deer, lost control and flipped the car. When the uniforms arrived on scene they found the whole group of them." Duffy took a pause and sipped some coffee.

"According to the reports, the kids pulled the Grant girl from the car just before it burst into flames, but Emily Martin was ejected and didn't make it. She's over at the morgue now. Natalie Grant was knocked unconscious and transported to Macon County Hospital by ambulance. We have an officer at the hospital. They're waiting for the neurosurgeon on call to get over there and evaluate her.

"Declan O'Neill, his wife Siobhan and daughter Darcy were also on scene, but they arrived after the accident occurred. They'd been at a neighbor's." Duffy finished the coffee and continued.

"We still have no clues as to who killed Jennifer Lawson. This was the group of girls that were invited over to Natalie Grant's for the sleepover tonight. But it turned out to be a boozed up graduation party free-for-all at Whispering Lake on O'Neill's property.

"I know it seems farfetched, but it is difficult for me to believe that someone outside of this loop killed Jennifer Lawson. Maybe one or more of these girls had a secret vendetta or jealous rage against her. Possibly a boyfriend got between her and one of these other girls." Duffy speculated.

"May I interject?" Lombardi put his two cents in.

"Teenaged girls can be very dramatic and amped-up because of raging hormones, but they just don't hack up their friends or enemies."

"Rick, if they can hold a knife, they're capable."

"Okay, boys, someone did this. Let's just find out who the culprit is." McKenzie's impatience showed.

"We've got the girls in separate rooms, the guys, too. Mr. & Mrs. O'Neill were driving home from the Callaghans' farm which we've confirmed. Declan O'Neill had been with the Callaghans from 1500 hours on. His wife Siobhan and their daughter Darcy arrived there sometime after 2100 hours. They left around 0100 hours, came upon the accident and called in the 911 emergency.

"Neither of them had been drinking and Darcy was asleep in the backseat. We had nothing to hold them on and let them go. They know they're on notice to come down to discuss other issues with regard to the murders. We have their statements." Duffy was bleary-eyed.

"Here's what we know so far." He laid out the facts.

"You know the accident that happened on the expressway today? Well, the farm worker that caused the whole disaster and got himself killed was employed by one of the neighboring farms. So the farmers got together for an emergency meeting to discuss the accident, its ramifications, and the current drought.

"O'Neill runs this group. As well, Maggie Grant, Natalie Grant's mother does bookkeeping for John Callaghan who hosted the event tonight. She was there getting financial papers up-to-date for Mr. Callaghan and his bank for Monday. Callaghan had left a telephone message for Grant that he needed her assistance tonight. That meant the girls planned sleepover party at the Grants would be unsupervised.

"The O'Neills and Mrs. Grant both left the Callaghans at about the same time, 0100 hours Maggie Grant went the opposite direction toward home so she never saw the accident. She was notified of the accident by the police who were doing surveillance at her house. One of our deputies escorted Mrs. Grant to Macon County Hospital to be with her daughter. Emily Martin's parents have already been notified and have gone down to the morgue to identify their daughter. That accounts for the whole group of them." Duffy was physically spent.

"Mike, we'll put a task force together first thing in the morning so you'll have strong backup and field support as well. Just put a wrap around this case before any other bodies show up in garbage bags or we have an entire city in mass hysteria. What else do you have?"

"I've assigned Ray Barlow as my point man to stay on top of all the meatpacking facilities within a 150 mile radius. He's got ten good men with him, but the big slaughterhouses are up to 250 miles away. So we're grateful for the support."

"Tell me more about the kids," McKenzie asked.

"The kids claim they didn't know anything about Jennifer's whereabouts. They were together throughout the evening. They left the Grant home figuring Jennifer had changed plans because of the new wheels she was getting for graduation. That passes muster as we know from Jennifer's brother that he spilled the beans to Natalie about the car.

"We may never know what Natalie Grant has to say if she doesn't come out of this. If Emily murdered Lawson or knew anything about it, that's a closed door now. I wonder if Emily's death could be tied into this somehow? Emily may have been manipulated into OD'ing on the meds and booze if she knew something and someone wanted to shut her up."

"That would be hard to prove assuming Emily brought her own meds along and they were all drinking voluntarily. Her girlfriend was rushing her to the hospital for Christ's sakes. If Emily's death isn't accidental, but a homicide Decatur's citizens will worry there's a serial killer on the loose for sure. What else?"

"We're also checking out the recently released William Smith. It might be coincidental, but law enforcement and mall security for the shopping center both received calls about him right after graduation. Could just be concerned citizens worried about his reappearance in town. We'll find out," Duffy stated.

"That piece of worthless human flesh. Yeah, everyone's up in arms over his release." McKenzie remarked.

"There were a couple of rough neck guys heavily tattooed seen over at Miller's Convenience Store just an hour before Abbott got killed. In fact, the parking lot was filled with Harleys. We're running checks to see who these guys are.

"Hard to believe no one saw or knows anything about either of these murders. Those bikers had to be all over that parking lot cruising. Maybe Abbott made a presence over there and scattered them. You could see them smoking weed on the tape. He had to have smelled it. Maybe he threatened someone. Of course, we're in every scum hole checking out the word on the street. If there's any news out there we'll hear about it." Duffy was confident.

"Since the kids all tested over the legal limit for drinking we decided to keep them overnight. We separated them in some vacant offices to sleep it off. The tank is full for the night anyhow. Half of them are sick to their stomachs so getting coherent information seems unlikely. Tomorrow morning should be better all around. I need to go home and catch a few winks. Is that okay with you, Captain?"

"Sure, go home, recharge yourself. See you boys bright and early."

"Good night, Captain."

"Good night, detectives."

CHAPTER 33

THE BLACKBIRDS' OMEN

KT HAD CONFIDED in Natalie all through their lives. Some of the stories she shared about her family were shocking. Natalie had no idea how the O'Neills would factor into the murder, but she knew they did.

Back home, the O'Neills faced their own demons. The house was quiet and Siobhan had just returned to bed from checking on Darcy. Slipping back under the covers, Siobhan purged her deep-seated anguish to her husband.

She admitted feeling deep regret about sending Liam off to live with her sister Brigit when he was young. But she had been close to a nervous breakdown after a hidden miscarriage. She'd started taking anti-depressants before she knew she was pregnant with Darcy. Now she blamed herself for Darcy's mental retardation.

Siobhan cried out. "Will Liam ever forgive me? I should have been the one to leave. And, my sweet Darcy, I didn't know I was hurting her."

Then Siobhan prophesied. "We have dark days looming in front of us, Declan. This is a different kind of drought, one that water can't relieve. This one will suck the life right out of us."

Holding his distraught wife, Declan had other struggles to think about. Though he feels her despair, he also feels another heavy responsibility. It was always about the land.

His ancestors struggled, starved, and died for this new earth. He had to find a way to save it. He twisted inside.

"If I can save the crops we'll have hope back in our lives. If I let them die, our life as we know it will perish. Even the blackbirds will leave us in the end. You just take care of our children and see to it our family stays together. I will take care of our property."

After Siobhan finally fell asleep, he slipped out of bed and went downstairs to call Finn Sullivan. The sun was coming up.

"Sorry for the early call, but we need to get together as soon as possible. I've made the decision to tap into Whispering Lake. We've got to get things ready out there. We'll need pipes, lots of pipes, and generators and pumps. But, we'll need to be quiet about this. Whispering Lake will only be available to our nine farms."

"The clans realize the burden is on your shoulders, but we're all in this together." Then Finn paused. He had other concerns.

"Declan, what really happened with our kids last night? I've heard about the accident and that girl who died. John Callaghan called me at 1:45 this morning after the cops interrogated him about you and Siobhan being at his house last night. They questioned him about the Grant woman, too. John said her daughter Natalie was the driver. Colin called from the station but told me not to worry. Said he was okay. I'm grateful nothing happened to my boy or your kids. Can it get any worse, Declan?"

"Every time I think it can't, it does. I'm thankful, too, that none of our kids were hurt. Siobhan and I didn't sleep very well last night. I don't know how much more of this I can take. We've already had several deaths associated with the lake. It's time for Whispering Lake to save lives now."

"You're not the only one who gets up with the crows. I spoke with Ian McCloud just minutes ago. He'll review my policy. He was confident the truck was covered regardless of its driver and said Farmers would stand behind me.

"Sonja and I spoke briefly last night. She wants a simple funeral. Said that Manas would want it this way. She has no problem with him being buried at the old cemetery but doesn't want any long drawn-out testimonials. She asked if we could put one of our medallions and some turquoise stones into the casket to protect him in the afterlife. I said, of course."

"Good. So tomorrow it is. You handle the funeral arrangements. Please ask Christopher, Ross, and John Graham to dig the grave by the big tree. I wish I could help more, but I'm up to my neck in everything else I'm dealing with. Make it for 1 p.m."

"Sure, no problem."

"Unfortunately, I need to go down to the Decatur Police Station first and clear up any potential problems or misunderstandings before any accusations start flying. After that, I need to take a walk around Whispering Lake and commune with the waters again." It was ordained.

CHAPTER 34
DECATUR POLICE STATION

SATURDAY MORNING, 8 A.M.

THE TWO DETECTIVES met at the station. Bright and early, the still isolated kids were waiting, not knowing what to expect. Mike Duffy decided to interview the O'Neill boys and their friends first. Duffy would interview the three brothers while Lombardi got his shot at Colin Sullivan and Dylan Maguire. They would then interview each girl separately. By then, they hoped to know more about any match with the sneakers and fingerprints.

"Hello, Patrick, I'm Detective Mike Duffy." Duffy started off the interrogation.

"You helped keep things together at the accident site with fast thinking and good instincts. An impressive job son, but I have to ask you some questions. You're not being accused of anything. We're trying to solve these murders so it's essential we know where everyone was yesterday. We need a clear picture of what happened with you, your brothers and friends. Can you give us complete details from the time you left South Bend to the time you were taken to the station? You're of age and we're not required to have a parent present. Are you willing to cooperate?"

"I'll help you the best I can. My brothers, Liam, Aidan, and I were scheduled to leave South Bend around 3 p.m. and go home for KT's graduation celebration."

"What were your plans?" Duffy asked.

"Two close friends from college, Dylan Maguire and Colin Sullivan caravanned with us. KT had seen a picture of Colin and went crazy over him. I thought he would make a great graduation gift for her. After dinner we were going to sneak out to our lake for a private party."

"That's real brotherly of you," Duffy said sarcastically.

"So you and your brothers left for home in a caravan at 3 p.m.?"

"No, my friends were half an hour late. We left at 3:30. I gave Dylan a map and directions to the lake if we got separated. We figured we could make it to my family's farm in 3 ½ hours. We stayed pretty much together 'til we hit the I-72. It turned into gridlock in no time, and we got separated in the heap of traffic. I noticed our gas tank was almost on empty. So we bailed and pulled into a gas station. That's when I turned on the news and heard about the fatal accident."

"What happened then?"

"It was about 6:30. We filled up and decided to go across the street to a convenience store to buy the beer for the party and make a pit stop. The can at the gas station was out of service. We got directions from the attendant on how to get around the mess taking some back roads. We eventually got back on course and arrived home about 8 p.m."

"What about your buddies?"

"We figured they'd just head out to the lake. None of us had cell phones."

"What happened when you arrived home?"

"As soon as we walked in the front door my mother grabbed me and pulled me aside. I heard all about Manas dying and the drought. An emergency meeting was called and Dad wouldn't be home for the celebration dinner. I didn't see KT at first which struck me as odd. Finally, she appeared and I could see she was pretty upset. We talked, and I assured her that Colin and Dylan were still coming. She perked up and went upstairs to call Natalie and fill her in."

"Move on to the party at Whispering Lake," Duffy prodded.

"We finished dinner and I drove my mom and Darcy down to John Callaghan's farm. He's one of the farmers that's part of the group my dad's involved with. The emergency gathering was being held in his barn. Mom stayed with the wives in the house while the meeting took place. Mr. Callaghan tried to get me to attend. I'm also a member, but I just wanted to party. I slipped away and went back home. I picked up my brothers and KT and took off for the lake."

"What happened at the lake?" Duffy was writing.

"We arrived after KT's friends. Dylan and Colin weren't there yet. Natalie had slipped away to change into clothes KT had brought for her. We hadn't even met. She was gone a long time. The girls got nervous that something happened to her. So Aidan, Liam and I said we'd go on a search and rescue mission.

"We found her all right, skinny dipping at the far end of the lake. When she saw me, she surfaced buck naked and flaunted herself right in my face. A real tease. I came on to her, but she cut me off and split to go get dressed. It really ticked me off. Liam saw my situation and left.

"I went back to the group. Natalie showed up dressed like a vixen. Then Colin and Dylan finally arrived. I hung out with Deidra, Melanie and Emily drinking beer. Eventually everyone started swigging the whiskey. Emily asked me if it was okay to mix the booze with her pills. I said one drink shouldn't hurt. I had no idea she was taking Valium.

"Finally, everyone was bombed and we all stripped naked and ran into the lake. KT was pissed off because Colin was coming onto Natalie. She swam over to me and asked if I would help her out. She wanted me to move on Natalie but that was a no-go. So her little plan backfired.

"Someone suggested we team up and race across the lake. Aidan and Emily were clearly into each other and took off alone. Then Dylan and KT teamed up and so did Colin and Natalie. No one else was interested in racing. I know my sister. She would stop at nothing to make Colin jealous. I knew she had something up her sleeve.

"The rest of us swam back, got dressed and sat by the fire to warm up. Pretty soon Colin and Natalie came back alone. Natalie was pretty ticked and started drinking a lot. I knew KT had made her point.

"A while later I saw KT running out of the water screaming hysterically that Emily was unconscious on the other side of the lake. Natalie grabbed her clothes and a blanket and took off in her car like a bat out of hell.

"Not long after, Aidan and Dylan swam back saying Natalie was heading to the hospital with Em. KT and the twins packed into my car. Colin and Dylan drove together, but they didn't leave when we did. Dylan was puking.

"Deer roam our area at night and I doubt Natalie knew that, but I don't think it would have made any difference. She was really drunk and had to be flying! We got to the main road in probably three minutes and came upon the accident.

Natalie's car was on its side. She was pinned in. Emily had been thrown out. There was no time to think--just act.

"I worried about the car catching on fire and exploding. Colin and Dylan showed up four or five minutes later, but it seemed like an eternity. Colin, Liam and I righted the car. Then Colin climbed into the backseat, released Natalie's seat beat, and we pulled her out.

"A minute later the car caught on fire and it was all smoke and flames. Dylan ran off and tossed his stomach again. KT was on the ground holding Emily in her arms. Aidan just sat there dazed. The twins were by Emily crying and holding on to each other. It looked like a war-zone.

"Then I saw my parent's drive up. I ran to them crying like a baby. The cops came soon after my dad called 911, then the fire department and paramedics. That's the whole story. When can I go home?" Patrick was drained.

"We have to keep you for a little while yet, but thank you for being straightforward with us. Do you have that gas receipt and receipt from the convenience store where you purchased the beer?"

"Sure. They're in my glove compartment."

"Good. Once we check out everyone's story we'll release you." Duffy stood up.

Down the hall, Colin Sullivan was being interviewed by Detective Lombardi. Colin had already agreed to help. He knew his legal rights. Lombardi started the questioning.

"Let's start with yesterday from the time you stopped on the I-72 because of the car accident. Did anyone see you on the road who could attest to the fact you were there?"

"I asked some man in a yellow Volkswagen about the accident and he told me the mess had been cleared up. I was returning to our car at the time. Other than him, no one."

"What time did you get to the lake?" Lombardi hammered away.

"I don't know. Definitely after 9 p.m. We tried to follow the map but got lost once we turned onto that private road. I was so bummed that I grabbed a bottle of Jameson out of the trunk. Dylan and I finally took off on foot to look for the lake. We ended up sitting down under a tree and drinking. Dylan passed out so I went to find it alone.

"I heard something and it turned out to be Natalie slipping on some leaves. Seems she left the group to change into clothes KT had brought for her. Do I need to tell you what happened between the two of us?"

"I think so." Lombardi had no feeling for this guy.

"Well, Natalie and I hit it off right from the start and got together. I've never felt like that with anyone else…and now she's struggling for her life in the hospital. I need to get over there as soon as possible." Colin's eyes watered.

The door opened and Duffy poked his head in.

"Rick, can I have a word with you?"

Lombardi excused himself.

"The O'Neill brothers have an airtight alibi. I have receipts for gas and beer that put them too far away for any chance of committing Jennifer Lawson's murder. The gas station and convenience store clerks corroborated Patrick's story. All three brothers took the polygraph and passed. They were still riding caravan and in view of their buddies at 6:30 when they hit the I-72, so that pretty much clears all five of them. What have you found out from Colin Sullivan?" Duffy was curious.

"Well, so far, not much. He claims he and Maguire got lost when they got onto Eagles Pass Road. Sullivan and Natalie Grant hooked up. He admitted that. He's pretty broken up over Grant."

"Finish up the interview and poly him and his buddy. We have to interview the girls now. I'm sure they're a part of this somehow." Duffy headed down the hall.

While Lombardi was getting the polygraph set up for Sullivan and Maguire, Duffy called the crime boys. He was anxious to get the reports. Unfortunately, they weren't ready.

A while later, Lombardi appeared.

"Well, Sullivan and Maguire passed their polygraphs. The girls are up."

They got ready for Melanie Stuart. She was brought in.

"Melanie Stuart, I'm Detective Mike Duffy and this is my partner, Detective Rick Lombardi. You recently turned 18 so we don't need to have your parents present. Is this fine with you?"

"Yes." Melanie squirmed in her seat.

"We understand that you and your friends had a difficult time last night. Not the kind of high school graduation celebration anyone would bargain for. We're investigating the murders of Jennifer Lawson and James Abbott, the security guard at the mall and need to fill in some blanks. Please tell us exactly what happened to you yesterday from the time you woke up 'til the time you were picked up on Eagles Pass Road last night." Duffy started the interrogation.

"I can't believe Emily and Jennifer are gone. Can you please tell me how Natalie is doing? Is she going to be okay?" Melanie looked ghostlike.

"We can tell you she's alive but in serious condition. Can we get on with our questions?" Duffy showed no sympathy.

"Deidra and I got up around 9 a.m. We had breakfast with our parents and got ready for graduation. We planned on going to school around 2 p.m. so we could be there an hour before commencement started. We left at 1:45 p.m. with our parents." Melanie started shaking.

"Did you see Jennifer when you got to school?"

"Not when we first got there. Mom cornered Ms. Greer, our guidance counselor, for a private chat. Dad and Mr. Gilroy, the principal, went right into a debate about the upcoming election, so Deidra and I went to find our friends." Melanie fidgeted.

"Did you see Caitlin or Natalie at that time?" Duffy pushed on.

"No, Natalie wasn't there yet. I didn't see Caitlin either. You mean KT, right? That's her nickname."

"Continue, please."

"My parents got themselves seated in the stands. The entire graduation class had to line up then. That's when I saw the rest of our group. Emily was talking with Natalie. Jennifer was chatting with KT. We went through the program, graduated and got our diplomas."

"What happened then?"

"Natalie mentioned there was going to be a slumber party at her house to celebrate and she'd call us later with the details. We took a couple of group photos. We've all been together since grade school. I'm feeling really sick to my stomach. Can I take a break please?" Melanie's face was bilious.

"Sure, Melanie. We'll send for you when we need you." Both detectives stood up. They led her out.

"What do you think, Rick?" Duffy asked.

"Her body language was defensive. She's definitely hiding something. Did you notice her tennis shoes?" Lombardi was observant.

"Let's get her sister in here and see if their stories match. Why don't you do this interview, Rick. I told you these kids weren't above reproach. I can always smell a liar. Stick with me kid, it'll age you, but you'll earn your stripes. Furthermore, I agree with your assessment of Melanie," Duffy smiled.

Deidra was escorted into the room. She was noticeably more controlled than her sister.

"Deidra Stuart, I'm Detective Rick Lombardi and this is my partner, Detective Mike Duffy." The preliminaries were started.

"Sure ask me all the questions you want. I have nothing to hide. How's my sister doing? Melanie doesn't do well in tight, confined spaces. Is Natalie okay? Is she still unconscious or did she wake up? Has anyone told her about Emily and Jennifer yet?" Deidra rattled on.

"Young lady, we're the ones that are supposed to be asking the questions. We will answer yours if you promise to answer ours honestly and completely. Do we have a deal?" Lombardi waited.

"Yes, Mr. Detective Rick Lombardi, we have a deal," Deidra said sarcastically.

"I've never been called that before." It was to be a game of wits with this girl, Lombardi sensed.

"Your sister is okay and Ms. Grant is still in surgery." Lombardi was done playing her game. "Now it's your turn."

"Yes, sir." Her sarcasm disappeared.

They began. Her comments mirrored Melanie's, Duffy wasn't surprised. Then they got to the end of graduation.

She continued, "Just before we left, Natalie told us about the slumber party she was having. We said we'd talk later on after we got home. Melanie and I left with our parents at 5 p.m."

"Did you see Jennifer before you left?"

"Maybe. There were so many people, I can't remember if I saw her or not." Deidra stiffened.

"Okay, let's get to when you, Natalie and your sister spoke about your plans for last night."

"Natalie called right after we got home. She said we should meet at her house and sneak out to Whispering Lake for a party.

"We told our parents we were going to a school sponsored event and would walk over to Natalie's afterward. We had our mom drop us off at school, then we hurried over to Natalie's and waited for her and Emily to return from getting snacks." Deidra shifted her gaze.

"What time did your mom drop you off at school?"

"About 8:45. We were supposed to be at Natalie's by 9."

"So she dropped you off at 8:45 p.m.?" Lombardi reiterated.

"Yeah." Deidra squirmed in her seat.

"Approximately how long did it take you to walk from the school to Natalie's house?" Lombardi pushed.

"I don't know. We were talking. We didn't check our watches." Deidra's eye fluttered involuntarily.

"What streets did you take?"

"We walked straight up Sycamore to Maple, then left on Maple to Pine and down Pine to Juniper. The same way we've taken for years. Why does it matter how we went?" Deidra thought she could outsmart the detective.

"So you've been taking that way for years?" Lombardi set the trap.

"Yes."

"Then why don't you know how long it takes? Are you sure, in your rush to get to Natalie's, you and your sister didn't consider going another way? Like maybe take a shortcut through the parking lot at the Decatur Shopping Center? You could have easily saved yourselves some time cutting through there. Come on, you've got to know all the shortcuts."

"Of course we know the shortcuts. They're great during daylight, but our parents taught us to never walk in parking lots after dark. We don't take any chances," Deidra smirked. She saw it coming.

"I bet you don't. That will be all Ms. Stuart. Thank you for your time." Lombardi finished.

"Can I see my sister now?" Deidra asked.

"Not yet. When we've finished our interviews and checked out your stories we will let you both go home." Lombardi and Duffy got up.

"I hope it's soon." Deidra's fabrication worked. She was confident.

"One last question? Did you girls bring a change of clothes for the sleepover; pajamas, extra shoes, things like that?" Lombardi said pushing his chair in.

"Sure. I saw to it we had all of that. I packed our duffel bags."

"An extra pair of shoes for each of you?" He shot back.

"No. Just for Melanie. She's the slob. I'm the neat freak. I never get my shoes dirty enough to change them."

"Thank you, Ms. Stuart. That will be all for now." They escorted her out and returned.

"I'm curious, Rick. Why didn't you comment on her tennis shoes? I know you looked down at them. The size looks like it could be a perfect match to our bloody shoeprints. Melanie was wearing the same tennis shoes."

"I just wanted to see how much information Deidra was willing to give up without being put against the wall. Did you take a good look at their physiques? They're both small-framed. I don't think they could hoist a potato sack let alone three body bags." It was an obvious assessment.

"We'll ask Mrs. Stuart if there's a pair of tennis shoes missing. Take note. We need to do a match on their sneakers. Too many coincidences are popping up for something not to click. It's far-fetched with the disarticulating, but maybe both sisters killed Jennifer and had someone else throw her body bags into that dumpster. We do have the third-person theory to consider. Some muscle to help them. We'll need to see if we have a match on fingerprints, too." Duffy saw some light.

"I agree they're both lousy liars, but I'm still not convinced these girls are our killers. Too many screw-ups and they don't fit the profile."

"No argument there. The dumpster scenario is confusing. There's a link here somewhere, I'm sure."

Duffy patted Lombardi on the shoulder. "You did such a good job with Deidra, I think you should interview Ms. O'Neill."

They walked back into the room and called for Caitlin O'Neill. She sat. They began as with the others.

"Detectives, I haven't stopped shaking since I held Emily in my arms. I still can't believe Jennifer was murdered like that. Maybe Emily could have made it if Natalie wouldn't have been so drunk. She would have missed that deer and everything would be okay now.

"But how can I stay mad at Natalie when she's fighting for her life? The party at Whispering Lake was my idea. I convinced everyone to go. I'm sick to my stomach over all this."

"Caitlin, we understand how you're feeling, but we still have two unsolved murders to deal with."

"Two? Oh, that's right, the security guard."

"Please start with yesterday morning."

"Yes, okay." She straightened in her chair.

"Call me KT, that's what everyone calls me. When I woke up at my usual time, 5:30 a.m., I got a surprise. My sister Darcy is mildly retarded so my mother keeps her away from almost everyone. We can never leave her alone."

"KT, you're wandering."

"No, not really. The thing is, Darcy wasn't in her bed yesterday morning. This has never happened before. I ran around the house looking for her, but she wasn't anywhere. Then I ran outside and saw Darcy walking through the cornfields."

"Why is that so strange?" Lombardi folded his arms.

"Because my sister is terrified of blackbirds and they're always in the fields. Darcy's scared to death they're going to attack her and rip her eyes out. When I reached her, she seemed to be in a trance and was singing riddles to herself. I grabbed her by the shoulders and she looked at me with scary eyes. She said the blackbirds told her to go into the field. She kept repeating these words…

"Blackbirds hear my Irish song
Blackbirds know what's going wrong
Death and disaster will rule this day
Blackbirds warn, get far, far away."

"It scared me. I yelled for my mother. She came running out the front door and scooped Darcy up and took her back into the house. That's how my graduation day started, being plagued with blackbirds and omens."

"You think Darcy had a premonition?" Lombardi was curious.

"Detective, my family is Irish Catholic, but my father and other farmers in our community still practice the old pagan ways of Ireland. Yes, I think Darcy had a premonition and I'm a believer, too. I wanted the entire family to be together for my graduation but there was always something going on with the farm that stopped my dad from showing up for my school functions. I hoped graduation day would be different. I was wrong."

"Did you resent him for that?" Lombardi leaned in.

"No. My mother told me there were major problems due to the drought and my dad couldn't make it. Our farm is in trouble. I thought about Darcy and her premonition and I started to get scared again." KT's eyes grew wide.

"What happened next?"

"My three brothers weren't going to be able to make it back in time from South Bend for my commencement ceremony, but we still planned on having a family celebration dinner. My mother, Darcy and I got dressed and left for school around 2 p.m. When we got there I saw Jennifer, so I left my family at the bleachers. I needed to have a conversation with her alone.

"There was this guy at school named Scott Ryan. At one point Jennifer and I were kind of fighting over him. But I met someone else so told Jen she could have him with no interference from me. She said she was sorry that the whole thing happened. Why would anyone want to hurt her?" KT looked dazed.

"So you had your talk. What happened then?" Lombardi pressed for more.

"Jennifer and I hugged each other. I'm so grateful we were able to make peace. How could I have ever known that such an awful thing would happen to her just hours later? I'm afraid whoever did this to her will come after me next. Do you think I'm in danger?" KT's voice quivered.

"At this point we're working hard to keep you all safe. Did you speak with anybody else at the graduation before you left?" Lombardi was insistent.

"Sure, lots of people. The twins caught up with us for last minute pictures before everyone took off. We left the school grounds around 5 p.m. and drove straight home. All I could think about was Colin Sullivan, Patrick's friend from Notre Dame. He and Dylan Maguire were driving in from South Bend to party with us. I really had my mind set on Colin. In fact, I even told Natalie I had dibs on him."

"Tell us about that conversation with Natalie."

"Natalie called as soon as I got home to ask if she could borrow some clothes for the party. I told her sure. We talked about the party, but kept it a secret from our parents."

"How were you planning to get to Whispering Lake?"

"That was the problem. My brothers had a car, so did their friends. But Natalie didn't want six girls piling into a car with a bunch of guys because her neighbors are pretty nosy and it would get back to her mother. She figured she'd ask her mom to borrow the car for the night.

"Well, I got another call from Natalie telling me her mom had to go to work and wouldn't be back till late. Her dad's old car was still in their garage. She figured she could sneak it out and that's how we'd get down to the lake."

"Then what?"

"My mom came up to my bedroom. I heard all about Manas dying, the emergency meeting my father had to attend, and that my celebration dinner would be delayed. I was really disappointed and had to get out of there. I said I would be back in a couple of hours. Mom was so frazzled dealing with everything, she didn't question me.

"I got my bike and rode over to Heaven's Door and caught a bus to the Decatur Shopping Center. I wandered through Sander's Department Store for a while. Then I thought I saw Jen and tried to find her, but she was gone."

"Did you see the security guard, James Abbott?"

"Not then."

"But you knew him?" Lombardi said accusingly.

"Sure, everyone did." KT seemed unfazed.

"Did you see anyone else at the mall that you knew?"

"No. I was wearing dark sunglasses and wasn't in a conversational mood. I had been crying a lot."

"Do you know what time it was when you left?"

"I remember seeing the clock above the exit. It was 6:35 p.m. I decided shopping wasn't any better than being at home so I jumped back on a bus. It was really crowded. There were two screaming kids. I couldn't wait to get off. In fact, I got off early and bummed a ride from some stranger back to Heaven's Door."

"You know that's dangerous."

"Yes, I know," she said patronizingly.

"You said you thought you saw Jennifer in Sander's Department Store?" Lombardi repeated.

"Yes, but I wasn't positive it was her."

"What time was that?" Lombardi was tightening the noose.

"Maybe five minutes before I left the mall, so 6:30."

"Do you have any proof that you took that bus ride? Any kind of receipt? Would the bus driver remember you for any reason? Did you notice the bus number? Talk with anyone?" Lombardi machine gunned his questions.

"I don't remember the bus number or talking to anyone. I had exact change so I didn't talk with the driver. It was a tight push getting on the bus in the first place. There were no seats so I was stuck standing right in front of those bratty kids."

"We can check the bus schedule and find out which bus you took. Do you recall the exit you got off at? The name of the person who gave you the lift, and the type of vehicle?"

"Yes, Third and Main. No introductions were made. The man talked on his cell phone most of the way. The car was some kind of black sports car. I didn't pay attention. I was still so bummed out."

"What time did you make it home?"

"Around 7:20. But nobody knew I was there. I was still feeling sorry for myself and decided to walk into the cornfields.

"It was dark when I heard my mother calling me. My brothers were finally home and dinner was on the table. Just knowing they were home helped. I called Natalie to let her know everything was still a go. She didn't answer so I left a message. I smelled the food and my appetite returned and it was finally time to celebrate."

"What time was that?"

"It was 8:35."

"How did you know the time?"

"Cause I couldn't take my eyes off the clock. Anyhow, dinner was great. Just after dessert, Mom got a phone call and asked Patrick to drive her and Darcy down to the Callaghan farm."

"What did you do then?"

"After they took off, I cleaned up the kitchen. At 9:45, Natalie and the rest of the girls called. I heard all about Jennifer being missing. That worried me some, but I was so excited about meeting Colin I passed it off as no big deal. I thought she might have met up with Scott Ryan because of our conversation at graduation. That made sense to me.

"The girls and I talked about whether to go to Whispering Lake or not. We decided it couldn't hurt to just take a couple of hours and celebrate. I wasn't sure I'd get another chance with Colin. Then Patrick came back from dropping off Mom and Darcy."

"What time was that?"

"I'm guessing it was a half an hour after I had talked with my friends."

"Whispering Lake sits on O'Neill property. You weren't concerned in the least that someone, maybe a farmhand, would see or hear you and alert your parents?"

"No, that thought never crossed my mind."

"Why?" Lombardi further asked.

"No one goes out to that lake at night. No electricity. That's why it seemed like such a good idea."

"Why don't you tell us what happened once you arrived?"

"Em and the twins were already there setting things up. Dylan and Colin hadn't arrived yet which bothered me. Natalie disappeared into the woods to change into some sexy clothes I had brought along for her and left on the table. I figured she split without saying hello first because she wanted to meet my brothers looking hot. Emily became worried when she didn't show back up. My brothers went searching for her.

"Apparently Natalie went skinny dipping and they found her naked. Liam and Aidan said she really tormented Patrick, so they came back alone. Natalie walked up minutes later all smiles telling me how much she loved my clothes. That's when Dylan and Collin arrived. I didn't get the reception from Colin I had hoped for. He was focused on Natalie and she was flirting back." KT pouted.

"They brought plenty of whiskey and everyone started doing swigs. Pretty soon we were all feeling the booze and ditched our inhibitions. Patrick suggested we go skinny dipping so we stripped and ran into the water. I wanted to get back at Natalie and make Colin jealous so I took off with Dylan," she stared past the detectives.

"Emily's emergency changed everything. I raced back across the lake to get help. Natalie was drunk. I guess Natalie and Colin saw Dylan and I having sex so she was real bitchy to me. Finally, the reality of Emily being in danger hit her and she took off in the car to get her. Natalie knew the way around the lake because she used to fish there a lot with her father.

"After she split, I got a verbal lashing from Colin. He basically called me a slut. Everything backfired in my face. Do I need to tell you about the accident?" KT was emotionally drained.

"That won't be necessary." Lombardi saw her state of mind.

KT was excused, shown to a room and was given a polygraph test.

"What do you think, Mike?"

"I think Ms. O'Neill has answered our questions as completely as she chooses to, just leaving out some pertinent facts."

"Go on." Lombardi wanted to hear Duffy's reasoning.

"Come on, Rick, the girl's trying to set up an alibi. She says she went to the same stinking shopping center where James Abbott and Jennifer Lawson were found dead, but no one saw her to corroborate? Why mention she "might" have seen Jennifer if you are trying to distance yourself from her? How about getting off the bus early to take a ride from some imaginary stranger? Then taking a stroll through the cornfields after an "omen" where, again, no one saw her. Looks like she's trying to cover her tracks and doesn't know exactly how," Duffy said suspiciously.

"I disagree. I think Ms. O'Neill is telling us the truth. Let's wait for her polygraph results," Lombardi countered.

"The polygraph can be beaten, even by an 18 year old. You know that. The way I see it, she did see Jennifer, approached her, took her somewhere private to "talk" and did her in. Somehow, she knew where to dump the body without being seen, then circled back and finished the job. I think she was hiding behind those sunglasses for a different reason. She didn't want to be recognized."

“Oh, you think she had time to do all that chopping and bagging? Let’s drag the twins into this. Maybe they had the things ready for KT,” Lombardi fired back.

“How do you verify cornfield time? Come on, she could have come back to the farm around 8:15 p.m. and had the twins finish up by dumping the body bags. That would explain their shoe prints at the dumpsters. Maybe one of the twins did in Abbott ‘cause he saw them,” Duffy challenged.

“Well, we know Jennifer was killed somewhere between 6:45 and 8 p.m. and Abbott was killed around 9 p.m. KT’s alibi is tight at 9 p.m. or do you think her entire family is covering for her? The twins’ alibi is tight between 6:45 and 8 p.m., the time Jennifer was murdered. Remember, they were having their celebration dinner and were dropped off at 8:45 p.m. at school. Or do we have the entire group of them, including their parents involved in this twisted murder?” Lombardi retorted.

“As far as I’m concerned all these kids’ statements have holes in them. We have one sick fuck running loose and no one is safe until we arrest the bastard that did these murders. Everyone’s on my radar until proven otherwise.” Duffy was unyielding.

“Okay, Mike, let me get this straight. What you’re implying is that it’s possible the O’Neill brothers could have escaped that nasty accident and got themselves home much earlier than we’ve been led to believe. That they called home on the way to let the family know they avoided the brunt of the traffic.

“KT and Jennifer have secret plans to meet over at the shopping center after graduation to discuss their mutual love interest. The girls get into a nasty argument. Jennifer says things to KT that deeply disturb her. KT pulls out a switchblade and stabs Jennifer in the chest. Scared to death KT tells her brothers what she's done.

"They concoct a plan to chop Jennifer up so the murder is so gruesome no one would ever suspect a girl was involved. She has three brothers that may have gathered all those things that we found in the body bags and without any problem hoist the bags into that dumpster. They would protect their sister no matter what.

"You see this as plausible? But where in the hell did they chop the body? Where's all the blood that would have come gushing out of a cut up corpse? There should have been blood in their car, it was clean. We used Luminol for Christ's sakes. Besides, both cars looked like they hadn't been washed in a week. Plus, the boys would have had to ditch their clothes and weapons way before they ever got out to that lake.

"We can do all the hypotheticals you want but with no murder weapon or hard evidence we've got squat. We still don't even have a motive or a murder scene. All we have are a few bloody shoeprints and smudged fingerprints. I want the psychopath that chopped up Jennifer Lawson put away no less than you. I just don't see Caitlin O'Neill as being our murderer.

"The expressway accident didn't occur until 5:20 p.m. Most likely Jennifer's murder was already thought out. If so, no way could those boys have been involved. We've already decided the two murders were committed by the same person. KT was sitting at the dinner table while Abbott had his throat slashed." Lombardi was red in the face.

"Damn it, Rick, I can see the holes in my theory. There are flaws in every scenario we've come up with. We're running out of suspects, but someone is guilty as hell." Duffy was exasperated.

They went to check on KT's polygraph results. It was clean, as Lombardi had expected. Just another blow to Duffy's case. They needed to regroup.

"Let's take a break and go over to the hospital and see what's happening with Natalie Grant. I'd also like to check with the parents about these stories before their kids talk with them. We should know more about the sneakers and the twins' fingerprints by then."

CHAPTER 35
MACON COUNTY HOSPITAL

SATURDAY MORNING, 10 A.M.

EVEN THOUGH a shocking murder investigation was under way, the suburban area of Decatur seemed oblivious. Residents were mowing their lawns and the smell of freshly cut grass permeated the air. A heavy odor of diesel fuel drifted as trucks going to and from the farmland reminded Duffy that things weren't as they appeared.

As they drove up, Macon County Hospital looked like any other community hospital. Inside the stark and antiseptic hallways, doctors, patients and visitors moved about lost in thought. No one noticed the two detectives walking through.

"There's the information desk."

"Detectives Duffy and Lombardi here. A Natalie Grant was admitted through emergency around 1:45 a.m. We understand she's in the ICU. Where is the waiting room?"

The receptionist pointed down a corridor through the double doors to the left. She then presented them with visitor badges.

"Much obliged," Duffy smiled.

Duffy saw an attractive, middle-aged woman with deep auburn hair and hazel eyes sitting alone.

"Excuse me but would you be Maggie Grant?"

"Yes, I am. Who are you?"

"I'm Detective Mike Duffy and this is my partner, Detective Rick Lombardi, homicide, Decatur Police Department. We're sorry to bother you at this time, but we need to have some very important questions answered. We heard your daughter was out of surgery and resting comfortably in the ICU, but there are two homicides we're dealing with and we'd like to ask you some questions. Can you please help us to figure out what's happened here, Mrs. Grant?"

"Call me, Maggie. I may not have any answers for you. My world is upside down. My sister, Mary Ann Hollister, is on her way here from Minnesota to be with me. Since my husband's death five years ago my sister and friends are all I've got besides my two kids. My best friend Amanda has always been there for me. She's Emily's mom. I don't even know what to say to her. I can't believe Emily is gone." Maggie Grant was suspended in disbelief.

"Maggie, please tell us exactly what happened yesterday morning being very careful about times." Duffy tried to be sensitive.

"I took the day off from work because of Natalie's graduation. I work for Caterpillar full-time as a secretary. Besides Natalie, I have a younger son, Kevin. We had breakfast together and went to graduation around 2 p.m. After it was over we mingled a bit. Natalie chatted with friends and took a lot of pictures. Kevin stayed by me. We left the school grounds shortly after 5 p.m. and came straight home. I didn't schedule a graduation dinner because, frankly, I didn't have the time to put it together. I told Natalie we would celebrate on Sunday." Maggie stared out.

"Please continue, Mrs. Grant."

"Kevin had plans to go over to his friend Gary's house for the night. I haven't told him the severity of what's going on with Natalie. Andrea Reynolds, Gary's mom is dropping him off over here later on today. She's been a true godsend.

"When we got back from school Kevin went to his bedroom, packed his overnight bag, and then walked over to their home. Her husband Bill is a radiologist at this hospital and was here last night. Once he heard it was Natalie they brought into emergency, he called Andrea."

"Maggie let's get back to when you got home from graduation after Kevin left. What happened then?"

"I turned the news on the radio. Then I listened to my telephone messages. I had received a call from John Callaghan at 2:30 p.m. He was aware that Natalie was graduating so I knew it must be very important. He said he needed me to come over and work with him on a financial statement he had to give the bank on Monday. It was crucially important and couldn't wait. I had his financials at my home. Being his bookkeeper, I knew I had no choice.

"I called John back and told him I would be there as soon as possible. He apologized for the intrusion and last minute imposition. As I hung up the phone I heard a news flash. They told about the terrible multi-car accident with a fatality on the expressway with heavy delays expected. I knew I had to leave right away.

"Natalie was upstairs talking with friends on the telephone making arrangements for a sleepover. I called up to her to come downstairs, explained the situation and asked if she would be okay with her girlfriends unsupervised. Natalie assured me everything would be fine. She did mention the girls had a surprise for her. Natalie said not to worry. I trust my daughter, Detective." Maggie started to cry.

"What time did you leave?'

"5:45 p.m."

"Are you sure?"

"Yes, I saw the time when I got into the car. I finally got over to John's home and we started working. Then he got the word someone he knew from a sister farm was killed in that crash. Because of that and the drought, Declan O'Neill scheduled an emergency meeting which John offered to host. He asked me to be patient. Everything got terribly delayed. There were people coming and going all evening.

"I found myself sitting with their wives waiting to get back with John. Siobhan O'Neill was one of them. I had never met KT's mother in person until last night. She yelled at me for not being home to supervise the girls' party. It got ugly. Siobhan picked up the phone and called my house and got the answering machine. The woman was enraged. It was past 11 p.m.

"When I arrived home I was shocked to see the police in front of my house. They told me Natalie had been taken to the hospital and said they would escort me. They didn't tell me about Emily. When I asked why they were there, I was told about Jennifer Lawson and the security guard being murdered. I couldn't believe it. When I called Amanda to tell her what had happened to Natalie one of Amanda's friends answered the telephone and told me the news about Emily. I was mortified."

"Just a few more questions. We want to make sure Natalie wasn't set-up in these homicides in any way." Duffy switched gears.

"Why would you think that? Jennifer was one of her best friends. They've known each other since childhood. And that security guard, just because she knew him doesn't mean anything. Everyone knew him. What you're saying makes no sense." Maggie was staggered.

"We're in the midst of this investigation and need to check out anyone with a close connection to Jennifer Lawson. Natalie is the only girl left that hasn't been interviewed. Of course, Emily's death will be investigated, too. No one is accusing your daughter of any wrongdoing. Until we figure out why Jennifer was murdered we're not sure what's true and what's fabricated. Natalie could be used as a fall guy because she can't defend herself right now. That leaves opportunity for the bad guys to frame her." Duffy tried to moderate things.

"You've got to be joking. The only thing I don't know is how she got my late husband's car started. It had been sitting in the garage for five years. Anyhow, my daughter was trying to get Emily to the hospital to save her. I heard Emily mixed Valium and whiskey and then overexerted herself swimming across that lake. She's always been a fragile girl. Natalie would never do anything to hurt any of them." Maggie shook her head.

"You're sure there were no secrets, jealousies, or difficulties these girls had between them? Do you know if Natalie has a diary?" Duffy kept going.

"There are no secrets, detective, no secrets at all. You're welcome to check over her bedroom. I know of no diary. Natalie keeps everything in her head. Her memory is amazing."

"What size shoes does Natalie wear?" Duffy was insistent.

"She wears the same size I do, a 7 ½ . Why do you ask?"

"It's just part of our investigation. Does Natalie wear tennis shoes?"

"She had to for P.E. What kid doesn't? Natalie does ballet so she has ballet slippers. She runs every day and has two pairs of running shoes. I'm tired of answering your ridiculous questions." Maggie stood up.

"Okay, we can stop here. If we need to check Natalie's room, we'll let you know. You have our heartfelt wishes that everything turns out well for your daughter. If you remember anything, or want to contact us here are our cards. Please don't hesitate to call. Goodbye."

The detectives left the hospital in silence and returned to their car.

"Well, Rick, what do you think of Maggie Grant's responses? Do you think she's covering up for her daughter?"

They sat in the parking lot assessing the situation.

"Don't think so. She held onto her cross for dear life—definitely the God-fearing type. A responsible, hard working woman caught between the roles of good parent and loyal employee. I can see why she felt obligated to go off to Callaghan's and leave her daughter in charge of the party. Natalie was known for being responsible. Why worry?"

"Yeah, can you believe that! Responsible enough to sneak out a car, get herself drunk and almost killed, and get her friend a front row seat at the morgue. All these parents are a line-up for dumb and dumber."

"No argument there," Lombardi agreed.

"The time frame seems reasonable with her answers. Abbott's murder happened around 9 p.m. when the girls were supposed to be meeting at Natalie's. They all seem to have airtight alibis, but I still feel they're connected in this thing somehow. There's something very unsettling about these girls," Duffy grimaced.

"Somewhere there has to be some evidence we're overlooking or some slip-up on the killer's part that we're not seeing. It's highly unlikely a 17 or 18 year old girl is going to cut up a friend by herself. She'd need an accomplice. It's too gruesome and technically difficult. We have to take a closer look at other relationships surrounding Jennifer. Maybe Jennifer wasn't so innocent or had an enemy or two." Duffy questioned.

"A conspiracy theory would involve too many lies and cover-ups for someone not to screw up somewhere," Lombardi analyzed.

"Unfortunately, the longer it takes to interview these people the harder the murderer's trail will be to follow. We have mediocre evidence at best, no murder weapon, smudged fingerprints, and matching shoeprints. God, we need a break. That's the bottom line, Rick."

"Whoever walked around in that dumpster didn't like the thought of touching anything. Sounds like we're dealing with a female rather than a male here--small fingerprints, small shoeprints. We're agreed?" Lombardi waited.

"Maybe, maybe not, we can't rule out a guy at this point. The partial fingerprints on those crates are large. They're probably from the people who handled them before they were tossed into the dumpster. Damn bloody footprints destroyed any chance for fingerprint ID's on the stacked crates. Wonder if that was intentional?

"Someone on the outside must have helped their buddy out. The person on the outside threw the crates they were standing on back over. They were mindful of that. Rick, people in panic don't think, they run. It's all about flight. Nothing equates here." Duffy was baffled.

Lombardi gave another supposition.

"The twins standing on the crates inside and outside would definitely make them tall enough to at least get their arms interlocked while one of them crawled up the inside of that dumpster. It's odd to imagine why anyone would do this knowing there was a chopped-up body in there. The Stuart twins just don't impress me as the brave type going into a dumpster with three body bags and rats. Even if their shoeprints match up many other things don't."

"Joel's perceptions are still clawing at my mind, that maybe someone went into that dumpster without knowing there was a body in there. Every scenario we've come up with is shaky. The only thing that does make sense is that we might have one hell of a bizarre, twisted coincidence," Duffy acknowledged.

"Yeah, that thought has occurred to me, too," Lombardi agreed.

"If that's the case, Rick, I'm afraid the bloody shoeprints aren't going to incriminate. We need solid evidence. You have heard of dumpster diving. Why is it not conceivable that some kids thought it would be fun to jump into that dumpster to look for treasures, found the body bags, freaked out and scrambled for it?"

"Then explain to me, if they were really freaked-out, why just use your fingers to move around the dumpster frame? Kids that would be base enough to go into a dumpster looking for things aren't worried about getting their hands dirty. Their prints would be everywhere. Wiping away the evidence wouldn't be a concern. As well, who's using logic when you're next to a corpse and feeling trapped? I'd put my hands on anything to get the hell out of there," Lombardi was steadfast.

"Guess the twins are smelling more and more like dumpster runners. There's definitely a connection even if they're not the murderers. Yeah, bring up rats and see how Melanie responds," Duffy snickered.

"Where are we headed? Who's our next interview going to be with?" Lombardi asked.

"I think we should pay a visit to Melanie and Deidra's parents and hear their rendition of yesterday's events. We have to check the twins' stories out before we start making any accusations. These girls might opt out of the polygraph. My guess is the Stuart twins' are swinging by their necks in this."

They took off.

CHAPTER 36

RACHEL STUART'S INTERVIEW

A WHILE LATER, the two investigators pulled up to the Stuart home. Duffy rang the doorbell. A pleasant looking woman opened the door.

"Hello, I'm Detective Mike Duffy and this is my partner, Detective Rick Lombardi, Decatur Police Department. Are you Rachel Stuart?"

"No, I'm Chantal Girard, Rachel's sister. Please come into the living room and have a seat. I'll go upstairs and get my sister."

"Don't get too comfortable, Rick. I have a feeling this interview is going to be over rather quickly. Take a look at the walls. Those are pictures of politicians. Recognize that guy?" Both detectives stared.

"It's Senator Paul Simon, with I'm guessing Russell Stuart," Lombardi replied.

"Yep. Must be Stuart. Here he is with Mrs. S. and the twins."

"Who *is* this guy?" Lombardi was intrigued.

"Melanie said her dad was a local big shot and a journalist. She wasn't kidding. He apparently has some very good connections in high places."

"He sure does." They both observed up close.

A short, thin woman with cropped brown hair dressed in a blue pantsuit came walking down the stairs. Even from a distance her heavy makeup was obvious.

"Hello, I'm Rachel Stuart. What can I do for you?"

"Mrs. Stuart, we'd appreciate a bit of your time. I'm Detective Mike Duffy and this is my partner, Detective Rick Lombardi. We don't mean to bother you, but we need your help. It's in the best interest of your daughters that we get some background information."

"I didn't know my girls were in need of my assistance. I've heard all about what happened to Jennifer Lawson and Emily Martin. I've called over to the hospital to see how Natalie is doing, but I can't get any information. I just want my girls home, can't you understand that? When will you release them?"

"As soon as possible, Mrs. Stuart. There have been two homicides committed within the past 24 hours that we believe were perpetrated by the same person or persons. We're trying our best to solve this case and keep your girls safe. As I said these questions are in their best interest." Duffy was uncomfortable.

"Well, if you put it that way. What do you want to know?"

"Just tell us what happened at home before you left for graduation; the times you did things and anything unusual, no matter how small, that might have occurred."

"My husband went for his morning run, the twins got up and did their daily chores, and we all left together for graduation at 2 p.m. I wanted to get to school early so I could talk with the girls guidance counselor about Melanie. Deidra got into Penn, but Melanie didn't. Anyhow, we got to school and the girls took off to be with their friends. I spoke with Ms. Greer for about 15 minutes privately. I was hoping she would talk with Melanie about Illinois State. It's a very good school. My husband was close-by having a conversation with Mr. Gilroy, the school principal."

"Did you see Jennifer Lawson?" Duffy inquired.

"Yes, I saw everyone. The graduating class was fairly small so we all know each other from attending school functions through the years. I heard about Billy Smith, that sex offender. I think he's the person that did these horrible things."

"Mrs. Stuart, we aren't accusing anyone of anything at this point. We're just trying to get all the facts and see where they lead. Killers make mistakes, and I'm sure they've been made here." Duffy hoped he was right.

"Can we get back to our interview? What happened next?"

"We left around 5 p.m. and drove straight home. I went into the kitchen to start dinner. The girls went upstairs to their bedroom. I was fixing the salad when I heard the phone ring. It rang once and was answered upstairs. I assumed it was for the girls. Natalie had mentioned the sleepover at graduation and Deidra and Melanie said they wanted to go.

"A few minutes later they came racing downstairs into the kitchen. I heard all about the celebration in the school gym starting at 8 p.m. The call was apparently from Natalie and she said everyone was going and they'd go back to her house afterward.

"They asked me to drive them over to the school parking lot instead of Natalie's house. I said fine. After we were done with dinner, they grabbed their overnight bags and I dropped them off. The lot had several cars parked in it and I saw kids all around. I kissed the girls goodnight and told them to have a fun time. I told Deidra to call when they wanted me to come get them from Natalie's the next morning." Mrs. Stuart's posture was defensive.

"Was there any doubt in your mind that they may not be telling the truth?"

"Not at the time. They're very responsible. I let them have their own rein. I try to see myself as being progressive." Her left eye started to twitch.

Duffy tried to keep her on track.

"Let's get back to your recollections of yesterday. Their overnight things, what was packed?"

"I didn't pack their duffel bags, they did. Deidra handles all their clothes for sleepovers. They always dress exactly alike. Yesterday they wore their dark blue slacks with matching blue blouses. I believe that pretty much sums up what I recall." She looked down at her watch.

"Mrs. Stuart, can we please go upstairs into your daughter's bedroom? Both girls own two pairs of tennis shoes, right? We need to see if they are still in the closet or if the girls packed them."

"I don't understand? Why do you need to know about their shoes?" She appeared flummoxed.

"We're just checking out their story. It's protocol." It was, in fact, the main reason why they were there.

"Fine, then follow me." They walked behind her up the stairs into the twin's bedroom.

"See how organized their closet is? Oh, there are a lot of shoeboxes in there. I guess I need to go through them. You'll have to be patient." She bent down and began the search.

After rummaging through all the boxes, Mrs. Stuart re-evaluated the situation and stood up.

"I can't find any tennis shoes at all. The girls had to be mistaken. It's hard keeping track of everything they have and what needs to be replaced. Melanie is much harder on her shoes than Deidra. She probably tossed away her old pair. I'm sure Deidra just missed that. When everything looks the same it's easy to do." She was pleased with her analysis.

"Do either of the girls keep diaries or journals?"

"Not that I know of. Two girls sharing a bedroom isn't a haven for privacy." Mrs. Stuart hadn't a clue.

"Well, I think we're done in here. Mrs. Stuart, thank you." Duffy heard what he had anticipated.

Rachel Stuart was glad it was over. She led them out. Duffy small talked as they descended the staircase.

"I do want to mention those are some pretty amazing pictures on the wall in the living room of Mr. Stuart with Senator Paul Simon."

"Oh, yes, Mr. Simon used to be in newspapers, too, and they met a while back when Russell was doing reporting. He has quite a library of signed books as well. If you come back I'm sure Russell would love to share them with you."

"By the way when can we get to speak with Mr. Stuart?" Duffy inquired.

"Russell went to work today because I pushed him to go. I know he will be exhausted later on. Russell didn't sleep a wink last night."

"What about tomorrow?" Duffy asked.

"I'm sorry, but Sunday is out of the question. It's God's day. Don't you both go to church?" She acted shocked.

"I keep the faith, Mrs. Stuart. I just wish everyone would. Unfortunately, murder doesn't take Sundays off and neither can we. I'll give Mr. Stuart a call sometime after dinner. How about 8 p.m. Regrettably, this isn't a social call and can't be delayed for any reason."

"That will be fine. I'm going to try and get dinner on the table early this evening. I doubt seriously that Russell will be in a good mood when we pick up our daughters. They'll have plenty of explaining to do. Russell is definitely the disciplinarian in the household."

"I think we've taken up enough of your time, Mrs. Stuart. Tell your husband we'll be calling him. Thanks again."

The detectives were relieved to be out of there. They knew the twins had lied. The radio was going off in the car. Lombardi ran to answer it. Duffy waited with anticipation.

"We've got our proof. Melanie's partial fingerprints and shoeprints are a match! They're examining their duffel bags right now," Lombardi reported back.

Duffy slid into the driver's seat. He felt a sense of uncomfortable satisfaction sweep over him. He couldn't wait to get back to the station and fry those girls.

Lombardi picked up the conversation.

"Mike, I can't argue the facts, but there're a lot of conflicting points here that still need resolving. I'm just not convinced yet." They sat in the car with the motor running.

"I do believe Rachel Stuart is a bit of an eccentric, but I doubt she planned a celebration dinner that didn't include her star graduates. Being in two places at one time--even for twins, that's a stretch."

Lombardi turned up the AC. He was sweating bullets.

Duffy joked. "I guess we know what Russell is working on right now."

Lombardi responded in a mocking voice. "Yeah, headlines! Read all about it!"

No matter how this went down those girls were in for it big time with their father. Then the seasoned detective turned to his younger partner who was obviously bothered. This was still Lombardi's first murder investigation. *What an opener*, Duffy thought. He then summed up the case for his partner. Lombardi was all ears.

"This killer doesn't want to get caught. They chose a neutral spot where foot traffic and car traffic moves day and night. No surveillance cameras on the perimeter of the lot. Pretty easy to slip in, do the security guard and hightail it out of there. They picked their time to dump the body bags in the dumpster, then scrammed. The person who butchered Jennifer Lawson has covered up their steps extremely well. We didn't find any prints on or near Abbott. They must have been wearing gloves which makes me think that the whole dumpster situation is going to unravel."

Lombardi took it all in. He knew what that meant to the Stuart twins. Duffy continued.

"The killer is too smart to make all those mistakes at the dumpster. The way I see it, they did away with Jennifer Lawson and dumped her into that dumpster before the twins even got in there. That's the coincidence I was talking about earlier. Any killer who's thought out a murder to the extent this person has wouldn't make those kinds of mistakes, not a chance."

Lombardi chimed in. "So Melanie and Deidra stumbled onto something they weren't prepared for. We now know their prints fit, but I agree they probably had nothing to do with the killings. So let's go back to the other three girls, Caitlin O'Neill, Natalie Grant, and Emily Martin. Regarding Natalie, it's a 50/50 shot whether she'll come out of this thing alive and mentally all there. KT has an ironclad alibi. Emily's at the morgue. Unless there's a wild card entry, we're back to nothing."

"We never *left* nothing, partner. That's what the killer gave us, absolutely nothing!" He put the car in gear. "I'm anxious to hear what Melanie and Deidra have to say about their gymnastics at the dumpster." They drove off.

CHAPTER 37
MELANIE'S INTERROGATION

SINCE THE DETECTIVES now had proof that the Stuart twins were lying, Duffy called Captain McKenzie. Things were coming together, but the answers only created more questions.

"Hi, Captain, Duffy here. We just finished interviewing Rachel Stuart at her home. As expected the twins lied about the tennis shoes. Rick just spoke with forensics and got confirmation. Hank says we have a match on the bloody shoeprints with Melanie Stuart's tennis shoes. Her fingerprints matched the prints that were lifted off the inside of that dumpster. The other shoeprints outside the dumpster are most likely from Deidra. We're checking out their duffel bags, I'm sure we'll find something to support our findings."

The Captain listened. However, he'd already been updated. The lab informed him of the results the instant the report came through. Mack McKenzie worried though. He knew that the evidence they had wasn't worth squat. He thought before answering.

"We now can place the sisters at the dumpster. Unfortunately, it's still only circumstantial—not conclusive. Prints don't lie, but how could they be eating dinner and, at the same time, be involved with killing their girlfriend? Got an answer for that one, detective?"

Duffy knew he was in the hot seat. He anticipated McKenzie's response before making the call. McKenzie didn't make Captain for nothing.

"I also doubt the Stuart twins are involved with the murders, too many inconsistencies. I'd like to sit down and talk with them. They lied about being there, Mack. Why didn't they report Abbott's murder? I don't want our investigation to unravel, but we can't make any mistakes either."

"I'll keep a lid on it, but you better get back here fast." McKenzie knew how jaws flap around the station.

"Thanks, Mack." They hung up.

Duffy was working against the clock. They headed back to the station. This time the twins would be interviewed in the interrogation room otherwise known as "the box". They had spared them this earlier.

They stopped to grab a cup of coffee on their way.

Lombardi spoke. "I still don't think between the two of them they could throw a sack of potatoes into that high dumpster even with adrenalin pumping. It took both of them on crates just to get the one out. Remember, there were no prints anywhere on the body bags. There was no evidence left on Abbott. Why the hell would there be prints only leading back to these girls?"

Duffy sipped his coffee. Lombardi continued with his latest analysis.

"It seems to me our murderer has found two scapegoats to take the fall. What if the real murderer dumped the body bags but then decided to come back. Maybe they realized they left something that would incriminate them. In the meantime, the twins are taking a shortcut through the parking lot trying to save time getting over to Natalie's. Abbott's checking out the parking lot, the girls saw his car patrolling and didn't want to be seen. They decided to hideout in that dumpster. Only Melanie got in with Deidra's help, Deidra couldn't without aid. She was stranded outside."

"What about Abbott, Master Sherlock Holmes?" Duffy smiled.

"I'll take that as a compliment." Lombardi continued with his premise.

"Well, if the killer did, in fact, return to the lot for something, he would have come across Abbott. Not taking any chances, does him in. Maybe saw the twins, maybe not. Not his problem right now. The security guard was. Picture this.

"Our murderer sneaked back into the parking lot and approached Abbott from the shadows. Abbott stopped his car to see what the problem was. If the murderer had pulled a gun and threatened Abbott, he would have stayed in his car and took off. Nope, Abbott wasn't afraid of this person. He got out of his car to greet and perhaps help find something the murderer said he'd lost. Once Abbott's out of his car looking down, the assailant took him by surprise. Bashed him across his temple, then slashed his throat. Convinced Abbott isn't a problem any longer, makes his getaway."

"What about the girls?" Duffy interjected.

"Maybe they were already out of there before Abbott's murder. Or, maybe Deidra saw the murder actually happen while Melanie was still in the dumpster. That could explain the shoeprints in the dirt. She was hiding from the killer," Lombardi concluded.

"Well, if Deidra saw the murder she may be able to identify the killer. If Emily killed Abbott and Deidra recognized her, she would have confronted her or tried to stop her in the act. These girls were close friends. On second thought, if that's what happened, they would have reported the crime to their parents or the cops. They definitely wouldn't go to a party knowing their friend was a murderer. Not a chance. Unfortunately, that still leaves the question what were they doing by the dumpster?" Duffy was confounded.

"Or, maybe that's not what happened at all. Is it possible that Deidra was too busy trying to get her sister out of that dumpster and didn't see the murder actually take place? Maybe they saw Abbott afterward and freaked out, then made a run for it. The dumpster is hidden in the shadows and the murderer might not have seen them because of Abbott interfering. The killer doesn't have time to go back to the dumpster and leaves that one detail untied." Lombardi recognized a slip up.

They reached the interrogation room.

Inside, Melanie is frightened out of her wits. She knew her situation wasn't good. The room was cold, smelly, and there was only a small table, four folding chairs and an overhead light.

The two detectives walked in. Neither was smiling.

"Melanie, hello, I'm Detective Lombardi. You've already met Detective Duffy."

"Why am I in here?" Melanie was shaking uncontrollably. "Am I in trouble?"

"We have reason to believe you and your sister are somehow involved with the murder of your girlfriend Jennifer

Lawson. I'm going to have to read you your Miranda Rights. Do you know what they are?"

"Yes, but I haven't done anything wrong! Kill Jennifer? Me, Deidra, that's crazy! This is about the dumpster, isn't it?" She froze.

Like a tape recording, Lombardi spewed out her rights.

"Do you understand your rights?" he asked.

"Yes," she blurted.

"Do you want an attorney, Melanie?" Lombardi asked sharply.

"If I didn't do anything wrong do I still need to have one?" She was terrified.

"That is your decision. If you didn't do anything wrong, you shouldn't be afraid to tell us what really happened. We know you've lied to us." Lombardi was curt.

"I'm sorry I lied, but we had no idea what we got ourselves into. I want to tell you everything that happened last night, but I'm completely innocent and I don't need an attorney."

"Okay, Melanie. I'm going to let you know that we have proof that you and your sister were in and around a particular dumpster that's at the far end of Decatur's Shopping Center's parking lot. So why don't we just start with when you arrived at the parking lot?" Lombardi sliced to the core.

"We lied to our parents. They had no idea we were going to Whispering Lake and we didn't want to get caught. We were supposed to meet at Natalie's at 9 p.m. We fibbed about a school event so our mother would drive us over to the high school. If she would have driven us over to Natalie's she would have wanted to speak with Mrs. Grant and we knew she wasn't there. That would have caused a problem. It seemed like a good plan at the time."

Lombardi reiterated, "Tell us about the parking lot."

Melanie complied, "Well, first I hurt my arm cutting through the bushes when we left the high school. Since we were already late, Deidra decided we should cut through the parking lot to save time. I told her I didn't want to walk there at night. She insisted.

"My arm was bleeding, and I was worried my blouse would get stained so Deidra suggested we head over to the dumpsters so she could get out a band aid and fix my arm. Just when we got there we saw Mr. Abbott, the security guard driving through the parking lot doing patrol. He was moving real slow shining his flashlight on all the parked cars. Mr. Abbott knows our mom so we couldn't let him see us. She goes over to that shopping center a lot. Deidra was afraid if he saw us he'd tell on us. So Deidra decided we should hide in the dumpster until he went by.

"This was all her plan. I didn't want to go into that big, dark, smelly thing. She conned me into going in first. She gave me a hand up and pushed me over. The bottom was all sticky and gross I couldn't see anything. We had thrown our duffel bags over first. I couldn't see where either one landed because it was so dark.

"Deidra couldn't get in by herself so I was stuck in there all alone. Then she said she saw Mr. Abbott's car was getting closer and needed to hide. I couldn't tell what was going on outside. Then, I heard her whimpering. She said Mr. Abbott was on the ground not moving. I was completely freaked.

"My eyes started to adjust to the dark, that's when I saw rats scurrying around. I could see their big ugly eyes staring at me. I was already a wreck about Mr. Abbott, now I was surrounded by disgusting rats. I started screaming to Deidra to get me out. They were clawing some garbage bags at the far end of the dumpster. I was glad. I just wanted them to stay away from me.

"I wasn't able to climb out by myself. So Deidra sent over some crates for me to stand on. I finally saw our duffel bags and tossed them back over. It was a balancing act on those crates, they were so wobbly. Deidra grabbed me and four-armed me so I kicked off of the crates and climbed up the side of the dumpster wall 'til she pulled me over.

"My sneakers were covered in something, but it was so dark I couldn't tell what. I leaned on Deidra and changed into an extra pair of shoes we had brought along. I put the dirty ones into the side pocket of my duffel bag. That's when I saw Mr. Abbott. His head was at a weird angle. He looked dead.

"Deidra said she didn't see what happened to him, 'cause she had her hands over her eyes and ears while she hid. We were afraid someone was still out there and would kill us if they thought we saw them kill Mr. Abbott. Deidra took the crates and tossed them back into the dumpster to cover our being there.

"Deidra thought it would be smarter and safer not to leave together. It wasn't that far a walk to Natalie's. We both looked pretty scruffy. I needed to find a place to change my dirty clothes. I got up to a street light and saw blood all over me. I panicked.

"I ran over to a vacant house I saw across Main Street, took a garden hose on the side of the house and washed myself off. Luckily I had a change of clothes. Deidra had also packed a small towel which was a Godsend. I didn't even want to think about all that sticky stuff in the dumpster. The blood washed out of my clothes okay, but it wasn't coming out of the sneakers. I needed to get rid of them.

"Detective, I wrapped my tennis shoes in the towel and threw them into a storm sewer on Pine Street and ran to Natalie's house. I got there before anyone else. There was a note on the front door from Natalie saying she and Emily would be back soon from getting snacks and gas, just to be patient they wouldn't be long." Melanie coughed.

"No time on it?" Lombardi fired back.

"Not that I remember. When Deidra came I was hiding in the bushes, still scared someone was going to kill me. Deidra said she saw Natalie and Emily over at the gas station. She was going to change her clothes there, but switched plans because she didn't want to be seen. The mechanic had the hood up checking things. They were sitting in the car talking and laughing so Deidra knew they hadn't seen her. She backtracked around and came to Natalie's from another direction."

Melanie asked the detectives for a drink of water. Her throat was parched from talking. Brenda showed up in no time holding a glass and a full pitcher. She took a sip and continued her saga.

"I noticed Deidra had some blood on her sleeve right where I had leaned on her. She thought it was from my cut, but the cut was on the other side. She got creeped out and ran to change her clothes in Natalie's side yard. That's when I told her about all the blood on my stuff.

"Deidra tried to minimize things, but I knew she was scared, too. I told her I was going to use Mrs. Grant's washing machine and say I started my period and had an accident. She gave me her stained blouse to wash. All we wanted to do was forget the entire nightmare. We had just graduated and everyone wanted to celebrate. Can't you understand that?" Melanie pleaded.

"We're investigating murder here not rationalization for your conscience, Melanie. What happened then?" Lombardi showed no mercy.

"Pretty soon Natalie and Emily came back all smiles. Natalie saw my wet duffel bag and asked me about it. I told her it was my time of the month and I had washed up on the way over. Wet clothes were inside. I asked if I could use her mom's washer and dryer and she said yes."

"Where are those clothes now? Are they still in the washer or dryer?" Both detectives perked up.

"Yes, the clothes should be in the washer. I put the duffel bag into the dryer for a few minutes and took it with me. I figured I'd dry the clothes when we got back."

"Good. We'll have that checked." Duffy nodded at the one-way mirror.

"But Jennifer and KT still hadn't shown up. So Natalie decided to check her answering machine and that's when we heard about Jennifer not arriving home, and KT's brothers getting home late because of some major car accident. KT said that she would be going straight over to the lake instead of coming to Natalie's. Jennifer's parents called several times. That's what bothered Natalie the most. We didn't know where Jennifer was either so we weren't sure if we should wait for her. We remembered that sex pervert Billy Smith was out of prison and worried maybe he got her."

Melanie began to sob. "I think you know the rest." She drank some water.

Duffy and Lombardi were silent for a moment. Then Lombardi spoke.

"Melanie, this story sounds believable. We'll have to check on a few things, and we'll send someone out to retrieve your shoes from the storm sewer. Hopefully, there's a catch basin and a filter that would have held back your shoes. Also, we'll need to know the location of the house where you changed your clothes and a description of the clothes you left in the washer at the Grants."

"The house had a For Sale sign out front. It's on Main Street right across from the shopping center. The storm sewer isn't far from Natalie's house. It's at the corner of Pine Street and Juniper. I left a pair of blue pants and two blue tops in the washer."

"If what you're telling me is the truth, it still leaves us with a killer or killers out there somewhere," Lombardi said with apprehension.

"I'll swear on a Bible. Yesterday happened just the way I said it did down to the very last detail." Melanie stared directly into Lombardi's eyes.

"I have just one more question. I see you don't have pierced ears. Does your sister?"

"No, a long time ago Deidra had hers pierced, but she got constant infections so she stopped wearing them."

"Well, I think that about does it. We need to polygraph you now. I want to believe you, Melanie, I really do."

CHAPTER 38
DEIDRA'S INTERROGATION

DEIDRA SAT in the interrogation room staring at the one-way mirror. She knew what it was. She wondered how many cops were watching her. She tapped her fingers on the table and tried to be calm, but deep inside she was scared to death.

"Hi, Deidra, I'll remind you, I'm Detective Duffy. You're in big trouble Deidra and so is Melanie. We've got a positive ID on you and your sister's tennis shoes and fingerprints at a murder scene. Your duffel bags are a problem for you, too. We have reason to believe you're involved with both James Abbott and Jennifer Lawson's murders in some capacity. I will have to read you your Miranda Rights before we go any further."

"Murders! I haven't murdered anyone and neither has Melanie."

Deidra knew she had been caught lying, but how did they find out? She and Melanie were very careful to cover their tracks. Her mind raced back to the dumpster scene. What had she forgotten? She never even heard Duffy read her, her rights.

"…Do you understand your rights?"

"What? Yes, I understand my rights." She sat still.

"Deidra, you're just being held at this point. The district attorney hasn't formally charged you and your sister yet. We know you lied and that Melanie was stuck inside the dumpster. Her prints show a match. You were on the outside. What actually happened out there, Deidra?

"I'm not convinced you had anything to do with the murders, but the evidence is compelling. I'm not the enemy. We're just looking for the person or persons who killed your girlfriend and Mr. Abbott in cold blood. Do you want to help us?" Duffy softened his approach.

"We didn't kill anyone!" Deidra's face animated.

Her story mirrored her sister's.

She continued, "I know we look puny, but our dad taught us how to defend ourselves. We've done wall climbing before. Since I couldn't get in by myself and Mr. Abbott's car was getting closer, I ran around the back of the dumpster and hid. I crouched down and covered my eyes and ears, but I never heard the car get closer. So I decided to peek around and see where he was. That's when I saw him lying in the parking lot with his flashlight shining on his face. I freaked out. I saw blood and knew he was dead.

"I ran back to Melanie and told her what happened. At first she didn't believe me. I yelled at her to crawl out, but the dumpster was so tall she couldn't reach the top. I needed a plan to get her out of there fast. That's when I saw a metal rod lying on the ground. I used it to hook some crates that were piled up high on the other dumpster.

"I was terrified whoever killed Mr. Abbott would come to kill us, too. Then all of a sudden she started screaming. She saw rats running around. I finally got the crates down, threw some over to her to stand on and piled a couple up for me to stand on, too. She found our duffel bags and tossed them back outside. Melanie grabbed hold of my arms and crawled out. My sister was already freaked about Mr. Abbott so the rats just finished her off.

"We had no idea that Jennifer was in there all cut up. I still can't believe it. I know now we made a horrible mistake not going to the police. That's the entire truth, detective." Deidra trembled.

"Did you honestly think you and your sister could get away with that stunt at the dumpster? People on the run don't tidy up after themselves, Deidra. They haul ass. You are definitely compulsive. You had us going with the dumpster walk, I'll give you that. By the way do you own gold hoop earrings? I notice you don't have anything in your ears."

"No, I don't. When I was 13, I had my ears pierced. I kept getting infections so I finally gave up. The holes closed back up. Why?"

"Do you recognize this earring? Know who it might belong to?" He held the earring out to Deidra.

She shook her head no.

"It looks like you and Melanie got yourselves smack between two homicides. You're lucky you're alive. The way I see it, you slipped through the gauntlet. Yeah, I believe you. Let's go see if the polygraph does."

Brenda came in and escorted Deidra out.

The two detectives sat and waited. The boys were already following up on Melanie's leads. They were now convinced the twins were being truthful. That unfortunately made the case more problematic. The word came back Deidra and Melanie passed their polygraphs. They were back to square one.

"How about getting a bite to eat, Mike?" Lombardi was beat.

"I could use a sandwich. I haven't eaten a solid meal since we were notified about Abbott's homicide yesterday." Duffy agreed.

They walked over to Hannah's, the local diner down the block, sat down at a booth and ordered grilled ham and cheese sandwiches and coffee. Duffy's cell phone started ringing.

"Mike Duffy, here."

"Mike, its Carl Brewster and Joel Cohen."

"We've followed up on the storm sewer and retrieved a pair of girls' tennis shoes and a towel stained with blood. We took two blue tops and one blue pair of pants from the Grants' washer. It was a harder go at the house on Main Street. When we pulled up the gardeners were there. The lawn's been freshly mowed and they had just finished dumping mulch all over the flower beds in the front and back. They said they were pushing hard to get the property fixed up because the owners needed a fast sale.

"We examined the garden hose. Didn't see any obvious traces of blood anywhere. Nothing was on the walls of the house. We checked all around. The gardeners had been using that hose and the entire area was completely wetted down. All the gardening mess was being sprayed toward the drain, so whatever evidence might have been there was long gone. There were several empty containers of various toxic chemicals and sprays that would have eliminated evidence of blood residue if any was there.

"None of them said anything about seeing blood. We used the luminal on the gardener's gloves, on the hose and ground, but came up negative. Do you want us to turn this place into a potential crime scene and rip up the backyard?" Carl was out of breath.

"Based on what you've just told me it sounds like a dead end. The bloody tennis shoes prove Melanie wasn't lying. So does her polygraph." Duffy was discouraged.

"Honestly, Mike, we can't wait to get the hell out of here. The place is making me sick. I have allergies. What do you want us to do now?"

"Well, that isn't the kind of news I was hoping for. The shoes definitely help the twins out, but damn those gardeners." Duffy was pissed.

"You might as well come back in." They hung up.

Where do we go from here? He thought.

CHAPTER 39

EVERYONE'S RELEASED

INSIDE THE STATION everything was buzzing. Parents were arriving and the assembly of party animals was getting ready to leave. Duffy and Lombardi returned to the precinct.

"Captain, can we come in?"

"Sure. Hope you enjoyed lunch. The group's being released. The Stuarts are here waiting for their daughters. I heard that when old man O'Neill comes to get his kids, he wants to talk with us. What's the next plan of action?"

"I think after we say our goodbyes and have a chat with Declan O'Neill, we'll pay Alfred another visit. We're no further along even though we've cleared the Stuart twins. We still can't tie any of the other kids to either of the murders. At least we've retrieved Melanie and Deidra's clothing from the Grants' dryer. As well, the tennis shoes matching the shoeprints we lifted at the scene were extracted from the sewer.

"Unfortunately, we weren't able to confirm her story at the property where she changed her clothes. The boys didn't find any traces. Apparently gardeners working there had done major drain repair and re-landscaping using chemicals and sprays that would have obliterated any blood evidence.

"We already had proof Melanie was telling the truth so we didn't pursue ripping up the yard. Killing Abbott, as an independent act, makes no sense. What could be their motivation? We're still missing vital evidence and a murder weapon." Duffy felt demoralized.

"What about the Grant girl? What have you learned? Is she the missing link?" McKenzie asked.

"Natalie Grant's in ICU, stable, but still unconscious. Who knows what we'll find there. Maybe another dead end. At least she made it through brain surgery. It could be weeks, maybe months before we'll know if she regains her memory.

"She's the only one of the girls we haven't been able to interview. Mrs. Grant said Natalie and Jennifer had been good friends since childhood. It seems pretty farfetched to imagine Natalie killing Jennifer and then going off to party with her other friends like nothing happened. She almost died trying to save Emily, so the girl's got a heart.

"Detective Betty Andersen briefed me about her interview with Ms. Greer, the guidance counselor at Eisenhower. They were all good students. Not a troublemaker in the group." Duffy paused.

"Mike, the murders appear to be leading away from the kids. Maybe the murderer heard about these kids having a party and set this whole thing up for them to take the fall."

"They kept the party to themselves, Mack. We've got to get inside the head of this killer. There's always a good mask to the truth. I'm sure it's going to be a humdinger."

"You're getting philosophical in your old age."

"Psych 101, buddy, head of my class. If they have a conscience there's generally a psychological trigger. That's our homework. Before they leave I'd like a word with each of our hung-over suspects." Both detectives stood up. "Plus, I'm looking forward to meeting the famous Russell Stuart," Duffy added with a smirk.

"His cronies are all the city officials. I've met him before. Likeable guy,"

"We'll see about that. You didn't interrogate his two girls," Duffy said sarcastically.

"You don't get to sit in my office and shoulder the blame for whatever goes wrong around here. No conviction is my conviction. Want to change jobs?" McKenzie cocked his head.

"I guess I'd rather deal with the crooks. At least they don't parade as politicians," Duffy chuckled.

Lombardi joined in, "I'd rather meet with Billy Smith. Stuart's not going to be so cordial with me. I don't want to hear him haranguing about this being my first case and how I botched it with his daughters."

"Thicken your hide. We're destined to be targets for witnesses, suspects, family, and friends, and let's not forget, co-workers. It's part of the job description." McKenzie stood up.

"Okay, go say goodbye and keep me posted. Scram."

"Will do, Captain." They turned and walked out.

"Put your best smile on, partner. Melanie, Deidra, wait up. Detective Lombardi and I wanted to say goodbye to you. You must be Russell Stuart. We finally get to meet in person. I'm…"

A short, thin man, clearly a genetic prototype for the twins interrupted. His face flushed.

"Detectives, I have nothing to say to either one of you. My girls have had quite enough of the Decatur Police Department! What a way to remember graduation day for my daughters—spending the night at police headquarters. One girlfriend brutally murdered, another one overdosed and dead, and a third in critical condition in the hospital. A security guard they knew slashed to death just yards away. They'll have nightmares forever.

"Do your homework first before making accusations. We were all together at our home during the time Jennifer Lawson was killed. Anyone with half a brain could see the situation at the dumpster was a sad coincidence. They were terrified by your inquisition and had no idea what was really going on there. Lying isn't murder! You haven't heard the last from me. What a story this is going to make on the front page of my newspaper. Good bye."

"Guess our mugs aren't going on Mr. Stuart's hall of fame wall," Lombardi joked.

"That is a shame," Duffy laughed.

"Hey, O'Neills, hold up. Detective Lombardi and I want to thank each of you for your co-operation with us throughout this investigation."

"Detectives, I think I can speak for my family. One good thing came from this crisis. We learned how important family is no matter what." Patrick had aged.

"Crises can have that effect on people," Duffy replied.

"Patrick."

"Dad!"

"I see you all survived your "sleepover!" Your car's been cleared and is in the back of the station. Take your siblings home, no side trips, that's an order!"

"Yes, sir."

"Detective Mike Duffy? Declan O'Neill here. Could we have a private talk?"

Duffy was taken aback by O'Neill's rugged good looks and thick Irish accent. His blue eyes were penetrating. Duffy asked him to wait in his office which he indicated to the left. The detectives weren't through saying their goodbyes.

"Dylan, Colin, it's your lucky day. There were no actions brought against either one of you by the Martins, the Grants or the O'Neills. The accident upstaged your crime of driving under the influence and contributing to the delinquency of minors by providing them with alcohol.

"As far as I'm concerned you're both accountable for what happened to Emily and Natalie. The whiskey and pills may have caused Emily's death, but you brought one of the weapons—and alcohol is indeed a weapon. Natalie's in ICU. You set the play in motion. Not being charged doesn't mean you are morally vindicated. We still have a double murder to solve, and if either one of you Don Juans has anything to contribute on that matter we'd appreciate a phone call. Here are our cards. Good day, gentlemen." The lecture was over.

The frustrated investigators turned around and slowly walked back to Duffy's office.

"You just sounded like Father Duffy. I thought you were going to take them by the hands and drag them first to AA, then into a confessional," Lombardi joked.

"They had it coming. If it wasn't for those two testosterone amped males we wouldn't be going down to the morgue again. This double homicide might have been a whole lot easier to solve as well.

"Now we have to consider the leader of the pack, Natalie Grant. What's her alibi? Her mother was gone all evening at the Callaghans'. Her brother was at a sleepover. All we know about Natalie's whereabouts is that we saw her on a surveillance tape joining her friend in Miller's Convenience Store just after the uniforms arrived at the back lot. Too bad their surveillance doesn't pick up the side parking area. Not being able to see where she was parked, how do we know how long she was sitting in the car? Did the two of them even come together? What about that hairdo and getup?"

They stood outside Duffy's door contemplating their next move.

"You have any sisters, Mike?"

"No, just a nosy sister-in-law."

"I do. They can stand in front of a mirror toying with their hair for hours. Natalie Grant had plans to meet new guys and wanted to look her best. Remember, KT claimed Natalie had asked to borrow a sexy outfit. That explains her still wearing workout clothes."

"Makes sense. Outside of the dead and severely injured who's left to suspect? The parents all have alibis. What about that boy Jennifer and KT were fighting over?" Duffy asked.

"Scott Ryan was home sick in bed. Apparently, the entire family has been down with the flu." Lombardi was on top of things.

"Let's go see what the Irish Godfather of Whispering Lake has to say for himself."

They walked in and closed the door behind them.

"What can we do for you, Mr. O'Neill?" Duffy asked.

"I thought it only right to come down here and have a talk with you considering the accident as well as that free-for-all party my kids and their friends had on my property. My wife is pretty naïve and takes our kids word for everything. I'm not such an easy target. My kids know better than to give me some cock 'n bull story. I would have seen right through it.

"I've been completely inundated lately with trying to keep our farm afloat because of this damned drought. Plus, I'm dealing with the death of Manas, one of Finn Sullivan's key employees. Finn is Colin's father. You probably know all about that fatality on the expressway yesterday. Well, Manas was the person who caused the accident. We're having his funeral tomorrow so you see my priorities yesterday were already spelled out for me. I had no idea what was going on under my nose."

"Mr. O'Neill, we believe the person who killed Jennifer Lawson was also responsible for killing Abbott. Except for you, your entire family was together having dinner. We're still following up on your daughter's statement. Patrick had receipts from a gas station and convenience store during the time frame Jennifer Lawson was murdered. They were too far away to have been involved. When we checked out Patrick's story we didn't need to interview Aidan or Liam. We just had them all take a polygraph." Duffy changed his tone.

"We're still trying our best to solve a double homicide which might have some connection with KT. We have to stop this guy. We don't want any more bodies showing up in dumpsters. Maybe you could shed some light."

"Please call her Caitlin. It's her proper name and I prefer it. I came down here to help if I can. I have nothing to hide and have no problem answering your questions." O'Neill didn't waiver.

"Thank you. Are you familiar with Caitlin's girlfriends? Have you ever met any of their parents?"

"Yeah, sure I've met Caitlin's friends through the years, though she rarely brings her friends out to the farm. Having a sister who is retarded is difficult to explain. My wife Siobhan frets over it, but that's life. Still, I think I've met them all at one time or another."

"So you've met Jennifer Lawson." Duffy asked.

"Yes, I have, long ago after an accident at the lake. My heart goes out to her parents. They must be going through hell. Who would do such a terrible thing?" O'Neill's blue eyes squinted.

"We're working on it, sir. So you haven't had any recent contact with Jennifer?"

"No. I wish I could tell you more, but I never have time to get involved in my daughter's goings on because of my crazy work hours. I've been feeling the weight of the world lately. Our crops are being devastated by this drought. My wife's all over me because I didn't attend Caitlin's commencement or celebration dinner. Now this. I've got enough Irish guilt to last me an eternity."

"What about any of the other parents. Do you know any of them personally?"

"How do you mean?"

"Do you go out socially with any of these girls' parents?"

"No, don't socialize. Of course I know about Bernard Grant, Natalie's father. He died in a boating accident at Whispering Lake. He owned Grant's Hardware and Tool Shop in Decatur before John Callaghan bought it."

"What about the boating accident? Can you enlighten us?"

"Sure. I was at the farmers' market when it occurred. The explosions were heard by a couple of my workers. They jumped into our truck and headed out to the lake. They found Natalie and Jennifer walking on the road and picked them up.

"After seeing the carnage at the lake, they brought the girls directly over to my house and called the police. I got a call, too, and came home fast. That was the first and only time I met Jennifer. It was a God awful thing that happened to that man. Where is this going?"

"Mr. O'Neill, we just want to get all possible motives out on the table."

"Motives indicate suspicion. You detectives have no idea about my family or maybe you think by digging into our past it'll help you solve this murder. I'm going to set you straight. Maybe a bit of background about my heritage might help to explain things you cops may already be digging into. It will help you to understand us."

"Go ahead, Mr. O'Neill."

"We're descendants of nine clans that came here to escape the famine in Ireland in 1847. The Irish call that year "Black '47" as being the worst year of the plague. A man by the name of Richard Barrett originally owned all the land we have our farms on today. There are 960 acres. Barrett fed, clothed, and even built cabins for each of the clans at different locations on his property. When he died, widowed and without heirs, he made good on a promise he made to them. He granted each of the nine clans 100 acres.

"Because of all the extra help the O'Neills gave him, they were granted the biggest and the best piece of land where his own farm sat, which included Whispering Lake. As a result, we sit on 160 acres. We were also charged with the role of leadership. Barrett, with the help of my ancestors and friends, built up a giant farming business that made a good living growing corn and soy beans."

"Mr. O'Neill, while your story is interesting, what in the dickens does all this have to do with the investigation?"

"Give me a chance, I'm coming to it. Our clans share a Celtic heritage and honor ancient beliefs that have been handed down from our forefathers. The Irish weren't welcome in a whole lot of places back then and coping with a negative stereotype and prejudice kept the clans united, but segregated from the rest of the community.

"Our people are Irish Catholic, but we're also nature worshipers and observe the old Irish ways. Traditional practice involves rituals that surround nature so if you come by any of our farms you'll see wrought iron and white river rocks that form the triskelion patterns on the fences, gates, and driveways. We believe this symbol protects our land. Detective, this is our legacy. It's all about the land.

"I heard how that girl was murdered. We don't do human sacrifices or cut up animals so I'll save you the time wondering. We're peaceful people. You might call our group a coven, but we're not devil worshipers. Our ancestors combined several practices to honor and respect nature. We don't murder.

"Last night we were driving home from an emergency meeting. We're in a devastating drought and all our farms will face perilous consequences if we don't do something to solve the water shortage quickly. Plus, with Manas getting killed in that expressway accident I decided we needed to meet. John Callaghan made his barn available, even though we have a gathering hall at Heaven's Door. We've held regular meetings there for 139 years ever since our ancestors built it. I was sure things would get around to this so I thought I'd save you the gas coming out."

"Very interesting, Mr. O'Neill."

"Please call me, Declan."

"Back to the question. Do you know any of the parents personally?"

"Well, like I started to say, Bernard Grant sold us farming equipment, tools and supplies. I'm going back several years ago, but I don't recall the exact date. Grant sold us a small engine part that was for our Allis-Chalmers tractor, but it was defective. Normally, my foreman takes care of all supply matters. I don't get involved.

"Well, we needed to fix the tractor that day so I decided to return the faulty item myself. When I got there, Maggie Grant was manning the store. Bernard was out having lunch with customers. How much of this conversation is private, detectives?" O'Neill's face reddened.

"I can't promise you anything you say is private if it relates to a murder. All pertinent matters can be brought up in court. If you plan on saying anything that is self-incriminating, you might want to consider getting yourself a lawyer," Duffy suggested.

"No, no. This is personal and sensitive, that's all. I said I would help and I will. Well, we got to talking and I noticed Mrs. Grant had bruise marks on her neck. They weren't in a place that normally gets hit unless you're smacked by a hand or choked. She saw me staring and tried to hide them.

"I guess when two people are suffering emotionally they are drawn together. My wife had lost our fifth baby late in her pregnancy and wouldn't let me touch her. The doctors said she was in clinical depression. I had lived with this rejection for many months by the time I met Maggie Grant. I don't think I need to fill in the blanks. We hung on to each other for about two months, but knew it wouldn't go anywhere. She could never leave Bernard, and I was hopeful Siobhan would emotionally return to me so we ended it.

"Her children never knew anything about the relationship nor did mine. My wife was wary. Her Irish intuition must have told her it was time to start holding me again because she did. I love my wife and have never strayed since.

"I never got to know Bernard. Frankly, I didn't want to. I wanted to punch him out for what he had done to his wife. Maggie said he'd stay in his tool shed for hours on end drinking and tinkering with things. I was glad. At least during those times I knew she was safe. But Maggie still stayed by his miserable side until that explosion ended his life. She claimed Bernard was an excellent father and provider. He just drank too much and had a bad temper from time to time. Yeah, I never believed that.

"The boating accident was investigated and was just that, a terrible accident. There was a leak in the gas can and he must have been passed out from drinking and a fire erupted. That small boat of his probably went up like a torch. Those girls were with him on the fishing trip that day. Jennifer apparently got a stomach ache and Bernard put them both on shore so they weren't on the boat fortunately.

"The girls were only 13 years old at the time. A pretty horrifying experience to watch your father go up in flames like that. Natalie idolized him from what Maggie said. She loved going fishing and spending time on the lake. They were really close. The newspapers headlined, "Fatal Explosion on Whispering Lake," with a picture of those two terrified girls holding hands down at the station. I'll never forget it. It's hard to believe she's fighting for her own life now."

"What happened to Maggie Grant after the accident?"

"There was no large insurance policy if that's what you're wondering. Bernard and Maggie had a good savings and that's how she managed everything the first six months. She tried but just couldn't handle the shop and raising two children by herself. That's when John stepped up, bought the business, and hired Maggie part-time to do the bookkeeping. She also started working as a secretary over at Caterpillar during the day. She's a real hard worker. Never remarried. I think she still grieves for her husband."

"Maggie Grant was free then and available. Wasn't the attraction still there?" Duffy intimated.

"I did call her from time to time just to see if she needed anything. She always refused help. Anything else, detectives? I have a lot to do regarding this drought and the funeral tomorrow. Plus, I need to have a soul searching conversation with my children." O'Neill stood up.

"Declan, we really appreciate your truthfulness and candor. We'll leave your personal comments right here. I don't see why any of that has to surface. We would like you to take a polygraph test just for the record." Lombardi and Duffy both rose.

"Not a problem. I wish I could help you more. I just can't imagine what could push anyone to go that berserk and do what took place yesterday. Where do I go to take the polygraph?"

"An officer will take you down the hall. Thank you again."

Declan O'Neill was led away. Now there was a whole new set of circumstances to consider.

"What do you think, Rick?"

"At least now we're getting a better picture of these people. I'll go back and check out the accident report with Bernard Grant. I'd like to see that picture of Natalie and Jennifer." Lombardi was upbeat.

"That was pretty interesting info about the clans. O'Neill was smart to step up and beat us to the punch. He knew our digging would find out about them sooner or later. Well, it's time to visit Alfred again. Let's see what was in Emily's system that ended her short life." They walked out.

CHAPTER 40

BACK TO THE MORGUE

GOING TO THE MORGUE is not for the weak of heart. Lights flash across Natalie's mind and she sees Emily's stiff body lying on a cold, metal slab.

"We have to stop meeting like this, Alfred. What are the odds of seeing your favorite forensic pathologist for three different autopsies, which are somehow related, within 24 hours?"

Alfred responded, "What are the odds of me working the crazy hours your case is demanding? I'm not even sure if I have a wife anymore."

They got down to business.

"We received the results from the toxicology tests done on Jennifer Lawson. Clean like I thought. Emily, on the other hand, had quite different results. Another beautiful young woman meeting an untimely death, but this time we have a lethal combination of Valium and alcohol poisoning---the classic cocktail to end up here in the morgue. She had enough of both in her system to push her body into a spiral of arrhythmias, coma and cardiac arrest. She probably had an early sense of euphoria and detachment and figured more was better. Don't these kids read WARNING labels, especially when they're in bold print? Just stupid!" Alfred was holding onto a scalpel.

Duffy shared what he had learned from the parents, that Emily was prone to panic attacks and had a long history of anxiety and phobias. The bottle of Valium they recovered from Emily's shoulder bag was half empty. He looked to Alfred for help.

Alfred Sweet's School of Forensic Pathology was now in full session. He continued.

"First, the meds do what they were supposed to do. In all likelihood, she felt real calm at first, like you say, then probably figured why not keep the euphoria heightened and took more."

Duffy interjected, "What I need to figure out is what really happened. Was this an act of stupid negligence or intentional? Was she hell-bent on committing suicide, just having a good time, or coaxed into having the mixture that would send her on a one way ticket to the morgue? Could she have had knowledge of the murder, maybe someone found out and fed her the stuff to eliminate her. Is it possible that she knew the identity of the killer and was drinking herself silly because she couldn't handle the truth?"

"You're over-thinking this, Mike," Lombardi jumped in.

"Over-thinking might actually help us stumble onto what really happened unless you have a better alternative. I'm waiting."

"Okay, let's say we're back at Miller's. Could Emily and Natalie have murdered Jennifer together? Did Natalie drop off Emily at Miller's and leave to dispose of the body bags? All she would have needed was a few minutes to do the dirty deed. Mrs. Martin said Emily left home right after dinner, around 7:15. Emily could easily have met up with Natalie somewhere, found Jen and killed her."

"I'm not necessarily disagreeing with either one of you. We have to look for a common denominator that caused three deaths in one evening. Having no solid leads, evidence, witnesses, or suspects is unacceptable. We've got to find out the root cause that has triggered this. Damn case has me stumped," Duffy conceded.

"Rick's right. You really do have to stop your bellyaching. This is how I see it. Emily was 17 years old, at her high school graduation party with a bunch of older guys and wanted to feel free, uninhibited, and not a prisoner of her own phobias and fears. So she ignored her good common sense and just went for it. The whiskey took away her inhibitions and clouded her judgment and along with the meds, depressed her system.

"We understand she attempted to race across a lake with some guy named Aidan. She was already feeling the toxic effects of the combination, making her dizzy, disoriented and extremely fatigued. Her companion saw her struggle and swam back to help.

"He dragged her out of the water as quickly as possible. The victim then lapsed into unconsciousness and coma. Her body didn't have the ability to fight back. Simply put everything in her body wound down until her heart stopped and she died. The boy tried to revive her, but it was too late.

"The car accident didn't kill her. Based on her liver analysis I estimate time of death around 0045 hours. When I examined her at the crash site there was vomit in her mouth. During autopsy I also found vomit in her lungs which caused her "drowning" commonly seen with comatose victims of acute alcohol poisoning. The driver was rushing her dead friend to the hospital," Alfred declared.

"The boyfriend claimed he felt a weak pulse. Maybe he was so messed up, drunk and all, he just imagined he did, or was he feeling his own pulse if he used his thumb," Duffy stated.

"Yes, her death was sooner, not later," Alfred said with conviction.

Lombardi's pager went off. Mike looked at his partner and nodded for him to go. Lombardi excused himself and turned to leave.

Alfred cleared his throat.

"The morgue is always open, Rick. Stop by anytime. I won't give you a cold shoulder." Alfred was always the proverbial comic.

Lombardi kept walking. "Meet you outside, Mike."

"Sure, I'll just be a little while longer."

Alfred responded, "No one around here complains about my sick sense of humor. In fact, they all listen politely. Okay, back to our victim. Based on my physical examination and chemical analyses, cause of death is due to ingestion of a lethal combination of alcohol and Valium. She died of cardiac arrest secondary to aspiration and asphyxiation.

"As for the injuries she received from the accident, she was thrown through the open passenger window. We know she wasn't wearing a seat belt. She sustained multiple fractures, extensive head trauma and massive internal bleeding. Upon arrival, her skin was blue-tinged and pale from both bleeding out and the alcohol poisoning.

"As I stated in my call to you, it appears at this point you're not dealing with a vehicular manslaughter case. Possibly suicide, but most probably just recklessness and stupidity. Lethal combinations of alcohol and drugs are way too underrated by teenagers." Class appeared over.

"Alfred, I almost forgot. Does the victim have pierced ears? Was she wearing earrings when she arrived?"

"Yes, she did have pierced ears. She was wearing silver hoops. They're with her personal effects. Need them?"

"Nope, but what I do need is a girl with a missing gold hoop earring. Natalie Grant, the driver of the vehicle spent several hours in the O.R., craniotomy, and is in the ICU now. We're heading to the hospital after we pay another visit to our waning group of suspects. We'll check back with you later on for the final reports. Thanks for playing devil's advocate."

"No more bodies today, please! Hopefully, that girl recuperates just fine. Who was the neurosurgeon that did the surgery?" Alfred asked.

"Don't know yet, but when I do I'll let you know."

"Hopefully, Dr. James King was the one on call. He knows what he's doing. But even then, it's iffy. Outcomes are hard to predict.

"If this girl is one of your suspects be prepared for a roller coaster when her memory returns. The loss of memory for events prior to the injury could linger on for weeks, even months depending upon the severity. There are cases of permanent memory loss, Mike. You'll know soon enough, I'm sure, once she regains consciousness. Let me know what the doctor says." Alfred was finished.

Duffy was done in. "Thanks, doc. See ya."

"What took you so long in there? Getting comfortable around stiffs?" Lombardi was being a smartass.

They left the morgue and climbed into their car. The day was slipping away and they were no closer to finding out who murdered Jennifer Lawson and James Abbott. However,

Alfred cleared up any confusion they had about Emily's overdose.

Lombardi spoke. "Russell Stuart called and I wasn't about to hush him. Can you believe it! He wants us to come over to his house tomorrow at 4 p.m. Mrs. Stuart said that Russell doesn't discuss anything other than family matters on Sunday. Not only doesn't she know a thing about her two daughters, she hasn't got a clue about the man she's married to either."

"Rick, I need a sugar fix. Let's go to the donut shop. We can talk about Billy Smith. I still think he's a waste of time, but what the heck. We're getting to the bottom of the barrel."

"Unfortunately, we are. Even the tattooed guys we located from Miller's had verified alibis up to the time they were seen on those tapes." Lombardi shared more bad news.

"Damn, not one lousy lead warmed up this investigation. Still feel that newbie enthusiasm?" Duffy's cynicism was showing its ugly head.

"We're just in a momentary sandstorm, Mike. Once the dust settles the air will clear and a whole new picture will present itself. I keep telling you we've already seen the clues. We just haven't recognized them yet, that's all."

What a dreamer, Duffy thought.

CHAPTER 41

INVESTIGATION CHANGES DIRECTION

DUFFY NEEDED TIME to recharge. He hadn't had a decent night's sleep in almost a week and his fatigue was getting the better of him. Maybe he'd see things differently after having a sugar surge. They pulled up to Mrs. Swenson's Donut shop.

"Mike, you've got to be kidding. You might as well dive into a vat of fat."

"You'd be surprised how many clues become crystallized while I'm eating jelly doughnuts. Sugar is my mental springboard," Duffy grinned.

"Okay, it's your cholesterol," Lombardi surrendered.

They got out of the car and went inside. They sat down with donuts and coffee at an outside table. Duffy was committed to solving this puzzling case. He opened up the conversation.

"The killer made a mistake and Abbott paid for it with his life. Why in God's name would someone be so careful about not leaving any prints, but blatant about leaving messages and empty trails, like the condoms and girlie books?" Duffy shoved some donut into his mouth.

"This psychopath has outplayed us so far. However, there was no way to know Melanie and Deidra would change course and walk through that parking lot. The killer must have dropped off the body bags minutes before the twins happened along. Whatever the killer was going back to do wasn't important enough to chance another encounter and risk getting caught," Lombardi deducted.

"Ironic, isn't it? A perfectionist forgot something? Guess no one's perfect," Duffy mused.

"Maybe we're approaching this from the wrong angle?" Lombardi's eyes sharpened.

"Go on." Duffy pressed.

"What about all these parents' pasts, and their kids, for that matter? We now know KT's father had an affair with Natalie's mother. Maybe Declan was wrong and someone did find out? These kids have known one another for years. Kids talk. We know Maggie Grant works for John Callaghan. Are we sure there's nothing going on between the two of them?"

"Rick, everyone has deep dark secrets."

"Adults aren't the only ones who pry and gossip. Kids do it, too. I lived it. Growing up in an Italian neighborhood was prep school in soap opera 101. It is conceivable that the secret got out and really upset someone and pushed them over the brink. We need to do a thorough background on each one of them. Something tells me the murder motive is buried deep in someone's past." Lombardi was reinvigorated.

Duffy liked the new slant. It made sense. He jumped right in.

"Let's go out to the Callaghan farm and have a chat with the man. Maybe bookkeeping wasn't the only reason he got Maggie out there last night. She never remarried. Why? She's an attractive woman. Maybe Declan was just a fling, but John Callaghan turns out to be something quite more. He's catholic, married, so divorce is out of the question. He hires her to do evening work at his home. It sounds pretty convenient if you're carrying on an affair right in front of everyone.

"It's also pretty noble coming forth and buying a business because you feel badly for the widow and her family. I'm not used to people being that altruistic.

"Maggie Grant takes off on her daughter's graduation night to go to work for him? She'll leave six girls alone, unsupervised? For a responsible parent to run off like that doesn't make sense unless her values were skewed by an affair. Maybe Maggie had something far more important on her mind. It was past midnight when she headed home."

Duffy paused to swish down some coffee. He wasn't done.

"We'll deal with Callaghan first and see where that leads us. We can stop off at the hospital on the way back. I want to check on Natalie's condition and have a chat with Mrs. Grant if she's still there. We still need to see Billy Smith, too. The devil is in the details, and I think we're getting warmer."

CHAPTER 42

JOHN CALLAGHAN'S FARM

"THIS REALLY IS God's country," Lombardi said as they drove onto Eagles Pass Road. The ride was only 30 minutes, but they were in another world. The farm sat on good size acreage, but the house was quite modest. They drove up.

A simply dressed, middle-aged woman answered the door.

"Hello, is John Callaghan at home? Detectives Mike Duffy and Rick Lombardi, Homicide Division, Decatur Police Department. We'd like to have a word with him."

"Detectives, please come inside. I'm Mary Callaghan." Her gray eyes had an iridescent effect.

"Marguerite, please go and see if Mr. Callaghan's still home. John was supposed to work on funeral arrangements this afternoon. They may have already gone to pick out the casket. We've had a death of a long-time employee from one of our sister farms. This weekend has been filled with way too much tragedy." She seemed reflective.

"Excuse me, Mrs. Callaghan, Mr. Callaghan will be right in." Marguerite left.

"Here comes John now. I'll leave you three alone. Good day, detectives."

"Hello, I'm John Callaghan, may I help you?" A tall, lanky man with graying hair and a black mustache extended his hand.

"I'm Detective Mike Duffy and this is Detective Rick Lombardi. We're here about the two murders that were committed yesterday. The police called you for confirmation regarding the O'Neills' presence here last night. We're hoping you might be able to give us a little more information."

"Sure, what can I do for you?" Callaghan appeared apprehensive.

"Mr. Callaghan, we're trying to understand the relationships between the group of six girls involved in the case and their families. We've met with Declan O'Neill and he was very helpful, but we still have a few gaps to fill in." Duffy wanted this guy to squirm.

"Am I being accused of something and need to contact my attorney?"

"We're not accusing you of anything, Mr. Callaghan. Of course, you can call your attorney if you have reason to believe you need one," Duffy replied.

"Well, I don't, but you've come to my home unannounced and that puts me on alert, that's all."

"Can you explain the relationship you have with Maggie Grant?"

Callaghan's face went brick red. His response was emphatic.

"Maggie Grant is my employee and trusted friend and there is absolutely nothing going on that's inappropriate." He shook his head.

"It just seems odd that you bought her husband's business out of the goodness of your heart and also gave her a job," Duffy submitted.

"I bought that business because I believed it was a sound venture call. But I admit there was a facet of guilt. Bernard was very good to his customers and as a gesture of appreciation I allowed him access to Whispering Lake to go fishing. Even though the O'Neills own the lake, all the clan members use it. How sad that he lost his life there.

"Maggie was left with two kids to take care of and I felt somewhat responsible. I knew Maggie did the bookkeeping for the business. It just made sense to keep her on part time. Maggie is a valuable asset. She generally works here one night a week, her choice. As long as she gets the work done I don't care when she shows up. In fact, she often does the work at her house.

"As for her being out here last night, fine, you want to know all my problems so I'll tell you. My farm is facing ruination because of this damned drought. The hardware store is still plugging along, but our accounts receivable are seriously delinquent. I've almost drained our entire savings account. I contacted my bank about a loan on the property and they requested current financials on everything by Monday. They've already done an appraisal on the farm.

"I felt badly about it being Natalie's graduation day, but my back was against the wall. She was on her way over when I got the news about Manas and the emergency meeting. Everything got delayed and she had to stay very late. It was a zoo around here last night.

"Siobhan got into it with Maggie about leaving the girls unsupervised and it just kept getting worse. That fatal accident down the road was the last straw. I became convinced that Darcy's premonition about the blackbirds was coming to pass."

"Premonitions?" Lombardi and Duffy eyed one another. They saw a connection with KT.

"Yes, premonitions! I believe in them. When Siobhan arrived she told me KT found Darcy wandering in the cornfields muttering a poem she claimed was from the blackbirds. Siobhan feared it was an omen because of Manas' dying. You'd have to know that girl Darcy to understand the significance. She'd never go out into the cornfields willingly. She's terrified of blackbirds.

"They were warning us through her. What else could it mean? Siobhan didn't even know about the other deaths when she told me this." Callaghan's eyes widened.

"Would you be willing to take a polygraph to support what you've said today?" Lombardi asked.

"Of course. I'm just so stressed over my financial security, the farm, and everything else." He was sweating.

"Go down to the station and tell them to call Mike Duffy regarding a polygraph on you. We appreciate your time." They turned and left.

Outside, the heat was oppressive. Callaghan wasn't wrong about the drought. It had major ramifications. The detectives tossed around Callaghan's statements.

"His anxiety was palpable, Mike. He's definitely covering up something, but what?"

"What did you expect, Rick? A sworn statement saying he was guilty of everything we implied?" Duffy was now sweating.

"If he is lying, why isn't he afraid of taking a polygraph?" Lombardi wondered.

“Everyone’s guilty of some sort of temptation, Rick. All I know for sure is that we have three corpses down at the morgue that can’t tell us what happened to them and another person in ICU. Those are the only facts I can count on, nothing else. I can’t depend on blackbirds to show us the way. Let’s get over to the hospital. Maggie has to know some secret truths she’s not telling. It’s not likely, but maybe Natalie has come out of it and can enlighten us.”

CHAPTER 43

MACON COUNTY HOSPITAL

THE DETECTIVES REVIEWED the conversation from their earlier visit, then laid out their plan for Maggie Grant. Mike Duffy wanted a private conversation. Rick would entertain any visitors she might have so he could talk to her alone. They arrived at the hospital a short time later.

"What if she isn't ready to spill her guts about her relationships? What if John Callaghan is telling the truth? Where are we then?" Lombardi asked.

Meanwhile, they grabbed visitor passes and headed down the corridor. Duffy spoke in a hushed tone as two doctors and a nurse went by.

"This woman is somehow involved. Her husband had a freakish accident and died, two of her daughter's friends are dead. Her daughter is here. Some way Maggie Grant is part of this melodrama. Hold your tongue, there's the group."

"Hello, Mrs. Grant, how is Natalie doing?" Duffy inquired.

"She's out of surgery and stable. The doctor will come out and see me soon." Maggie seemed relieved.

"That's good news." Duffy asserted.

"Detectives Duffy and Lombardi, this is my sister, Mary Ann Hollister, and my son, Kevin."

After the introductions, Duffy asked if he could have a word with her in private. She agreed.

"Rick, would you please stay with Mrs. Grant's family. If the doctor comes, get us immediately." Duffy turned to Maggie.

"How about a cup of coffee? I noticed a coffee pot just down the hall."

"That's sounds good." Maggie got up.

They walked to a quiet sitting area and sat down. Duffy began the conversation.

"First, I want to thank you for giving us access to your home. We found what we were looking for in the washer and checked over Natalie's room. We took only a couple of things and left your home undisturbed. We did go into the garage and your late husband's shed. It looked like it hadn't been entered in some time.

"Mrs. Grant, we're hitting a wall every which way we turn. Is there anything you can share that might be helpful regarding these girls or their families?"

She paused, "What in heaven's name was in my washer that was of interest to the police?"

"Verifying a story. One of the girls said she left some dirty clothes in your washer. We have to check every lead."

"Detective, I'm a loner. I don't meddle in other people's business. Outside of Amanda and a few friends from work I generally keep to myself. I go to work, come home, and take care of my family. That's my routine. That's my life. I go to church Sundays. I don't even date." Maggie sipped her coffee.

"Why is that, Mrs. Grant?"

She just stared at him.

"That's an odd question, but I'll answer it. When I married Bernard I married him for life. Granted he wasn't an easy man. Many times I wondered if I had made the right decision. We both came from Farmington, a small town in Minnesota. We started seeing each other in high school. He stayed local and I moved to New York to attend Columbia University.

"I met Amanda and John Martin in my sophomore year and spent most of my free time with them, but I didn't date. I had Bernard waiting for me at home." Her body language was that of a weary woman.

"Mrs. Grant, I understand these may be sensitive questions, but we are investigating a double homicide and your daughter is the only one of the girls we haven't interviewed. Think really hard. Could there have been any jealousy or secrets any of these girls might have harbored? Maybe with KT, Jennifer, the twins, or Emily?"

"Not that I am aware of."

"Was there anything in your personal life that Natalie would have shared with Jennifer?"

"What are you implying, Detective Duffy?" She stiffened up.

"Was there an affair that either you or your husband could have had that your daughter may have found out about and shared with any of her friends?" He looked her straight in the eye.

"Are you joking with me? This is unbelievable."

He leaned in and spoke directly. “No, I’m not, Mrs. Grant. We’ve interviewed other parents, one being Declan O’Neill. Affairs go on all the time. Our only interest, bluntly, is in any evidence that may lead us to the person who committed these murders. We are obligated to dig in every corner, no matter how uncomfortable.”

“What did Declan say to you?” Her face flushed.

“He had nothing derogatory to say about you if that’s what you’re asking. He tried to help us understand his relationships with the girls’ parents.” Duffy was tactful.

Maggie stared out into space.

“It was a dark time in my life. Bernard was having difficulties and took his frustrations out on me. He became abusive and knocked me around a few times. My children never saw any of it. He’d get drunk sitting down in that tool shed of his and the abuse would start when he’d come up to bed. It was typically after midnight so the kids were asleep.” Her eyes glazed.

“Did you ever report this to the authorities or seek medical attention?”

“No, where I come from you keep your dirty laundry private. Every time it occurred I rationalized it was because of the alcohol and his deep depression. Declan O’Neill showed up at the store one day to return something. I had spoken with him on the telephone prior, but this was the first time I had ever met him in person. His blue eyes bore through me. He saw some bruises I had gotten the night before at Bernard’s hand. When he questioned me about them, I completely fell apart.

“Detective, despair is a lonely feeling and when you sense someone somehow understands your misery you’re drawn to that person. Declan had his own pain. We became each other's confident at first, then slipped over the boundary. I didn't want to destroy my family or his, but I knew if I continued that's where it would have gone. Declan felt the same way. I can't imagine that either of my children knew what was taking place. We were very careful.

"Bernard was so caught up in his own suffering he never asked where I was if I came home late. I only represented pressure to him. Bernard and his mother always had that contentious relationship. He hated his older sister. I actually believed he loathed women in general. But he liked having Natalie around which made me glad. He used to take her to Duluth to visit her grandparents. His dad was a decent man and I felt he was a good influence on Natalie as well. Kevin was always a momma's boy and didn't like spending time with his dad. They were like water and oil together. At least Natalie enjoyed the outdoors and fishing.

"As for Declan, he never saw his kids until dinner time, if then. His work hours were long and tiring. He could leave for hours on end and no one would question where he'd been. That gave us freedom to meet. He owns a cabin on the outskirts of Heaven's Door. That's where we went to be alone. One day we just realized that neither of us could leave our spouses so we ended it. Do you have any other questions?" Maggie looked drained.

"Finally, can you please tell me about your relationship with John Callaghan?"

Maggie was incensed. He had no right digging into her life. Grudgingly, she answered him.

"One affair doesn't make me a whore, detective. There is nothing to say about my relationship with my boss. Unless you can produce some valid reason why you believe

I'm responsible for any of these horrible murders I have nothing else to say to you." Mrs. Grant stood up.

Lombardi interrupted, "Excuse me, Mrs. Grant, Dr. King has just come out to speak with you about Natalie."

"Detective, I apologize for snapping at you. Let me talk with the doctor now. We'll continue our conversation afterward. I want this all put behind me as soon as possible." Maggie Grant walked off.

Dr. King and Mrs. Grant moved to a quiet area. She motioned to her sister and son to join them. They sat as he explained the surgery.

"A craniotomy was performed to relieve the pressure on her brain and control the bleeding. Her head was partially shaved so don't be shocked when you see her." Maggie and her sister held onto each other.

The doctor went on to describe the intricacies of the procedure. When he was done, he assured Mrs. Grant that everything went well. Natalie would be kept sedated so she could rest. Maggie had a time taking it all in. She was overwhelmed with the medical terminology. She looked at the doctor.

"All I want is my Natalie back to the way she was," she choked.

"Your daughter is young and healthy and has a good chance of full recovery. These things take time. When she is fully awake we'll know more. As with any head injury we always have to watch for complications. She should be out of ICU in a few days if she doesn't develop any problems.

"Just be aware she's been through quite a shock and it takes a while to recover. At this point it's up to Natalie's body as to how fast she will recuperate." His beeper was going off.

Dr. King told Maggie he would be checking in on Natalie twice a day. If she had any concerns she could call his office any time to reach him. He tried to be reassuring.

Maggie thanked him, again and again.

Duffy and Lombardi watched from a distance. It was clear Maggie Grant was suffering. There was no point in continuing the interview. After the doctor left, they moved in. Duffy spoke up.

"Mrs. Grant, I think we're done for today. Again, please accept my apologies for upsetting you. Here's my card. Good day."

CHAPTER 44

BILLY SMITH'S INTERVIEW

MIKE FILLED RICK IN about the interview when they got back in the car. It wasn't pretty.

"I wonder if Kevin knows about his mom's affair with Declan O'Neill. He sure as hell could have witnessed the abuse she took at the hands of his drunken asshole father. Kids don't sleep that deep and if Declan saw her bruises so did her kids. He never spent any time with his dad, could've hated him, and hated his mom for not standing up for herself." Lombardi despised abusers.

"We'll have to find that out. I guess it's time to go pay Billy Smith a call. At least we know he checked in with his parole officer. Let's make this scumbag our last interview for today. We've got an interesting day facing us tomorrow when we show up at Manas' funeral. Wonder what we'll find out there. I can't wait for the interview with Russell Stuart afterward."

They drove off toward Decatur and pulled up a street they had canvassed the night before. Smith lived with his mother only four blocks away from the Decatur Shopping Center. They parked, got out and approached the old, decaying three story house.

"You knock on the door, partner." Duffy stood off to one side.

A disheveled looking woman appeared wearing an old, tattered bathrobe. Her hair was messy and wrinkles crowded her sun damaged skin. Hard living showed its wrath.

Like mother, like son, Duffy thought.

"Hello, we're looking for William Smith. Detectives Rick Lombardi and Mike Duffy, Decatur Police Department here to see him."

"I'm his ma, Beatrice Smith. I know why you're here. My son ain't had nothin' to do with 'em murders. He's been right here with me. Billy never goes no further than our porch. He knows his path now is with the Lord Jesus." Her breath smelled of cheap wine.

From somewhere upstairs, a voice rang out, "Momma, I'm comin' right down."

The infamous Billy made a grand entrance wearing a black t-shirt, worn jeans and cowboy boots. He was tall and stick thin. Lombardi noted outside of pockmarks from adolescent acne he was a fair looking guy.

"Guess you were right, Momma, you said they'd be payin' me a visit. So you think I sliced up two people right here in my neighborhood to announce Billy's back? You dicks know I only did young pussy. I was here all day with my cat helping her bring little pussies into this damn fucked-up world. Sorry I cussed, Ma. I can tell ya every program I watched all day and all night. The pizza guy come with a pepperoni mushroom pie at suppertime. He even come'd upstairs to see my new little pussies. Wanna see 'em?" He babbled on.

"I seen a picture of that pretty little thing and I'd'a loved doing her, but cutting ain't my style. I paid long and hard for my hard-on. Don't need no more trouble with coppers or tight-assed girlies. Two days out of the pen and you assholes think I'm dumb 'nough to go and take out a security guard and young babe. Man, 'em guards kep' me alive in the pen. I'd nev'r kill one of my keepers, no way no how."

Duffy responded. "Nice, Billy, nice. I can see you're a completely rehabilitated citizen. No, I don't think you did these murders, but you are going to be one busy man from here on out always having to explain your whereabouts. The dicks will never go away, Billy.

"I'd like the telephone number of your pizza delivery store. We just want to make sure your pie arrived nice and hot and on time. I'm sure your momma here will back your story all the way. We'll be seeing you again. That's the bonus of being so famous Billy, no one will ever forget you."

Smith responded with a smile. "You wanna see my pussies before you go? I need to find 'em good decent homes. I don't wanna put 'em out on the street. Some maniac could come along and slice 'em up. You go make Decatur a safer place for my pussies. You hear?"

CHAPTER 45

ADDING IT ALL UP

DUFFY GRUMBLED as they walked back to the car. Billy Smith was a total waste of time. They would confirm Smith's story with the pizza parlor, but expected this was most likely another dead end. They headed back to the station to have a meeting of the minds.

Duffy instructed Lombardi, "Let's get our team over here. Check out Barlow's availability, too."

They needed to brainstorm as a group. It was time. The case was slipping through their fingers.

POLICE HEADQUARTERS – 6 P.M.

Everyone was seated when Duffy and Lombardi walked in. Duffy went to the front, Lombardi sat down.

"Thanks for coming, men. We need to pool our collective info and punch this thing around. Carl, what does the lab have for us? I need reports on everything."

Carl stood up. "Nothing of consequence beyond what we already know with Melanie's prints. The blood on Melanie's shoes and duffel bag matched up with Jennifer's blood, no surprise. This butcher left us squat."

"Shit." Duffy felt battle fatigue.

Hank took over. "The prints we lifted from the dumpsters were compared to employees and we have matches, but credible alibis. None were in our data base. Barlow was too far away to get back in time for this meeting. So far, he and his men have found no one suspicious at the slaughterhouses. Not all clean records, but no felonies. Locally, we've had all the meat packing plants checked out. No disgruntled employees, business as usual.

"Our informants said the hookers never saw Jennifer around or heard she was in the business. There's no rumble on the street and we've come up empty-handed with the gangs and motorcycle clubs. We went over to Eisenhower High School and checked around the property. No vandalism or questionable incidents. Jennifer's teachers were all at graduation and have alibis for afterward."

Carl took a deep breath, and reported. "It appears the killer was invisible, a damn phantom. All the other dumpsters in the area were searched. No weapons were found and no more body bags, fortunately. Jennifer's two shopping bags holding shoes and stockings are still missing. Background checks were done on all the kids' parents. Some are debt ridden, a couple owe the IRS.

"The investigation surrounding all those farmers and their pagan rituals will take a while to complete. No one's willing to talk about these people and their practices. The symbol they show on their medallions and display in rock patterns on their property is called a triskelion. It's historically linked with the Celts. The farmers use this symbol to protect their land and bring good harvest."

Hank spoke again. "A.J. Green turned in a list of all the employees of the mall who were working that night. I've got three men making the rounds. So far no leads. Every customer we snagged at our barricades has also been interviewed. Same results there.

The room went quiet.

"Mike, we're all dying to hear about your interview with Billy Smith." Some humor erupted. Hank hushed the group.

Duffy responded. "Well, it turns out he's got himself a new prison, his own neighborhood. He can't do anything without being monitored. Billy was busy helping birth a litter of kittens last night. His arms looks like the mother cat had a free-for-all mauling him. He'd been clawed so much there should have been blood evidence left somewhere on those body bags. Abbott would have recognized him a mile away and never got out of his car the way he did."

"Excuse me for the interruption, but I think you've been waiting for this warrant." Brenda handed Duffy the paperwork. She left quickly.

"Let's continue." Duffy put the warrant by his jacket.

"Mike, what's happening with the Grant girl in the hospital?" Joel asked.

"If she did it we may never know. She may or may not fully recover. Even if she does, Emily might be her alibi. We looked over the tapes and couldn't see Natalie's car pull in or out of the lot so we don't know when she got there, or if she was sitting in her car waiting for Emily. Surveillance showed Emily was in Miller's Convenience Store during the time Abbott was killed. Natalie walked into the store from the same direction she did. The scope of the camera was limited and they both came into view from a blind spot.

"It doesn't make sense Natalie would leave the car, take off across the shopping lot, kill Abbott and then run back to help Emily out with the packages. Besides that, Natalie looked way too coiffed to have been out committing murders. It was obvious these girls only had partying on their minds. The note Natalie left on the door didn't indicate whether Emily and Natalie rode to the store together. If Emily could have walked over there alone earlier with Natalie meeting later. Only Natalie Grant knows at this point."

"Mike, what about Jennifer's father?" Carl questioned this time.

"The Lawsons were all accounted for, except for Jennifer, from the time they left the high school until her parents showed up here panicked over her disappearance. Neighbors saw them arrive home, friends and family corroborated their story."

Carl added, "I have another hypothetical I've been toying with."

"What is it? We'd love to hear something new that makes sense and will move this case forward." Duffy was receptive.

"Jennifer Lawson was a beautiful girl. We all agree. Could one of her father's friends have taken a liking to her and tried a little hanky-panky? Maybe an affair was actually started and something went wrong, so she threatened him with exposure. Adultery is definitely a highly valid motive for murder."

"Maybe, you've hit on something there, Carl. It's definitely worth checking out. Let's move on to what we've found out. It turns out Maggie Grant was doing Declan O'Neill and we still don't know if she's been involved with John Callaghan. We were interrupted by the doctor. That shut us down for the time being. I think we'll wait a few more days until there's some improvement in her daughter.

"Tomorrow, Rick and I are going to get all spiffed up and make an appearance at the Manas funeral, the man that was killed in the accident on the expressway yesterday. It's at 1300 hours at the old cemetery. We'll get to see all the farmers and their families together. Brenda just gave me the search warrant for Whispering Lake. I plan to hand it over to O'Neill at the funeral.

"You guys get over to the lake first thing in the morning. You'll probably need several hours to check out everything. If there is any evidence, let's find it. It would be great if we could retrieve the murder weapon. We'll get there as soon as we can. Rick and I have an appointment with Russell Stuart tomorrow late afternoon. Can't wait for that get together.

"Well, men, I think that wraps this meeting up. We still aren't dead in the water."

Everyone got up and left. An exhausted Mike Duffy grabbed his jacket and the warrant. He walked out with Rick.

"I'll be by your place at 0900. Be ready to roll."

CHAPTER 46
SUNDAY COMES

MIKE DUFFY was in his Sunday best, a navy striped suit with white shirt and blue tie. His thick gray hair made him look distinguished. He pulled up promptly. Rick Lombardi was outside waiting. His young good looks were complimented by a light gray suit. He got in.

"You look like you're in pain," Duffy chuckled.

"When was the last time you wore a suit and tie, Mike?"

"Can't remember that far back. Had to take this suit out of mothballs."

"Yeah, it smells like it. We'll have to drive with the windows down." Lombardi joked.

"I thought we'd head over to Whispering Lake and see if the Loch Ness Monster tossed our murder weapon right into the boys' hands. That would definitely make my day." Mike was clearly in a better mood.

Since they were passing through Heaven's Door, they decided to take a short detour first. They wanted to have a look at the location where the clans meetings were held. It was unlikely Jennifer Lawson's murder could have been committed at the hall considering her body bags were found a distance away in Decatur. Yet, around that meeting hall might be an excellent place to do the dirty work, they concluded. Of course, with hypotheticals there were always holes.

Lombardi started poking. "Where is the car the killer used, Mike?"

"We need to check every vehicle on the clans' farms. An open bed truck would have made an excellent shuttle service. Completely appropriate in this area, no one would be suspect," Duffy responded.

"KT has a valid alibi during the time Abbott was killed. She was home with her family. We've already agreed the same person did both murders so that basically eliminates her," Lombardi reiterated.

"However, the accomplice theory is still not dead." Duffy pointed out.

"Declan O'Neill was adamant their practices did not include human sacrifice. The rituals surround preserving nature. Still sounds odd to me." The young detective shrugged.

"Look up your history on the sacrificial lamb. There's plenty to do with Irish lore," Duffy quipped.

"You think Jennifer might have been a sacrifice?" Lombardi was dumbstruck.

"Possibly, all options are still on the table." Duffy was unwavering.

"When do you find the time to read, Mike?"

"In the wee hours of the morning. If you want to be a good detective read as much as you can. That's where murderers find their genesis for crime."

They reached the main street of town and saw the old greeting sign.

"Welcome to Heaven's Door
Enjoy your stay"

They felt like they had gone back in time. The place seemed out of a history book.

"Over there, across the road. See the rust-colored building with that symbol? That's got to be it. Look at the date, built in 1848. Pull over. I'm sure the doors are locked, but maybe someone's inside, a maintenance man or a groundskeeper."

The two men got out of their car and walked over.

A very tall, tired looking man answered the door. "Hello, may I help you?"

"Yes, hopefully you can. I'm Detective Mike Duffy and this is my partner, Detective Rick Lombardi. We're investigating a couple homicides. We met with Declan O'Neill yesterday. He told us about this meeting hall. Would it be possible for us to come in and take a look around?" Duffy was cordial.

"Sure. My name is Finn Sullivan. My son is Colin. He was one of the kids interviewed. Everyone's heard about the murders. Please, come inside."

"Yes, we've met your son and his buddy, Dylan. I don't think they'll be partying for a while. He got quite a lecture from me on responsibility," Duffy admitted.

"Good, he needed it. I would have picked him up, but he asked me not to. Dylan drove him over to my farm when they got released. He's very concerned about that girl, Natalie Grant. I gave him my old pickup truck so he'd have transportation to and from the hospital. I thought it couldn't get any worse than the drought. That was before my headman Manas died on the expressway Friday and those other tragedies occurred. I came over here this morning to do some paperwork. We're paying for the funeral, and I'm in charge of handling all the finances."

"That's a nice gesture, Mr. Sullivan. In fact, we'll be attending that funeral. Would it be okay if we looked around a bit?"

"Actually, I just finished up and was going to leave, but you're more than welcome to stay. When you walk around, watch your step. Some of our ancestors chose to be buried here beneath the floor boards instead of over at the cemetery. Our archives and library are here on the first floor. We have complete family journals dating back to the time our clans originally moved to Macon County. Also watch your head going down to the cellar, the ceiling is quite low. Please lock the doors behind you when you leave. Good day, detectives."

"Finn Sullivan apparently trusts the cops," Lombardi commented.

They walked around the first floor taking it all in. Duffy was awestruck.

"Hey, Mike, check out all these symbols, I think they're Celtic."

"Don't know my Celtic symbols, sorry."

"Come look over here on this wall. What the heck are the Brehon Laws?"

Duffy walked up. "Appears to be some form of old Irish and a later English translation. Has the feel of a poem.

Kind of like the words in the Bible. This place is some kind of mystical shrine."

"I'm heading down to the basement." Lombardi disappeared.

"Can you hear me up there?" his voice echoed.

"Yeah, I'm ignoring you," Duffy was preoccupied.

"Hey, they buried people along the base of the walls. There are several tombs side by side dated 1853. All I can make out is the clan name, O'Flaherty. The floorboards are marked, but not legibly." Lombardi investigated further.

Duffy thought, *odd they chose not be buried in the cemetery with the rest of the clans. Too many questions and a century of dust in between. I don't think a murder took place here on Friday. Things are too settled. I think we're just digging up the past, a very distant past.*

"I don't see any evidence of foul play down here. No underground passageways. The walls all appear solid. There are old, dusty gardening tools and a rusty pitchfork heaped in a corner. Too many cobwebs on them to have been used recently. No chance a body could have been cut up here. Not enough time to clean up especially since there's no running water. Have you noticed that, Mike? No water pipes, sink or toilet. Are you listening?"

"Yeah, I'm disregarding you." Duffy was amazed. He felt like he was in the bowels of the Smithsonian Institution.

"These archives go back to when the original land owner, Richard Barrett, brought these immigrants back here from New York Harbor off of one of those coffin ships. The library is like a museum of Irish literature. This desk's gotta be at least 125 years old. Just like Sullivan said, bound journals hand written with all the clans names, dates of birth and death, just sitting here on the desk. It's a treasure trove of Irish history. It surprises me vandals haven't broken in and stolen everything." *Why hasn't this happened?* he wondered.

"I'm comin' back up. They put in lights but no can or sink, get that. Guess when they built this place, outside was where you did your business."

"Did you hear a word I said? They've chronicled everything and everyone. I could sit here for hours." Duffy was blown away.

"Mike, if you need an Irish history fix, go sit in the Decatur library. It's time to go." They left, locking the door behind them, and got back on the road.

"Make a right turn at Eagles Pass Road, then keep driving." Lombardi played navigator.

They reached the accident scene and slowed. There were remnants of the flares and tire tracks. The air still smelled of smoke. They drove on.

Passing the O'Neill farm they referred to the directions which indicated Whispering Lake was straight up the road past the cornfields on the left and behind the tree line.

Lombardi warned, "There's a hard to find turnout that cuts through the woods to the lake. Watch for it." They moved slowly.

"Where the hell is this lake? No wonder those boys couldn't find it at night," Duffy bitched.

"There it is, Mike."

"How Natalie managed to drive fast through this obstacle course I'll never know. Ironically, she makes it out of the woods and then gets derailed by a lone deer." Duffy shook his head.

They rolled up by the boys. Carl and Hank came over to the car.

"Carl, tell me it wasn't a waste of time driving through that crater riddled road to get out here."

"So far we've only come up with socks, underwear and condom wrappers. Plus, a can opener, balloons, and three spent bottles of Jameson. Those kids definitely knew how to party. We've searched around the lake. Joel found a pair of guy's underwear down the way in a hard to access cove. It probably belongs to one of our wonder studs. We didn't find any weapons or blood or anything else suspicious." Carl was sweating.

"Sex trumps everything. What else?" Duffy was unimpressed.

Carl continued, "There were girl's things scattered around, too. Nothing with any blood on it. We did find a wooden cross just past the tree line where a dog was buried. The leaves are ankle deep in all directions. Saw some shoeprints, big sizes zigzagging through the meadow. Apparently the lost travelers looking to find the party. It looks like our boys plopped down under that tree. There was a trail of kite string wrapped around trees obviously placed as markers to find their way back to their car. All in all nothing points to murder. Moved stuff around but only came up with worms and roots. Do you want us to send divers down?" Carl started scratching.

"Yeah, I guess we'd better."

"Damn mosquitoes are everywhere." Carl flinched.

"Lucky we're wearing suits or we'd be eaten alive." Duffy laughed.

"I knew not to wear aftershave. Don't you boys have bug spray?"

"Thanks a lot, Mike. You didn't mention we'd need it." Hank's face had been attacked.

"You've got to be kidding, Hank. Go to a lake without it and you're instantly the menu "Special of the Day!" You know better. Serves you right! Mosquitoes gotta eat, too."

"Mike, you really are an ass hole." Hank walked off.

"What else is new?" Duffy replied.

Duffy and Lombardi went down to the lake. They noted water marks on the rocks along the lake edge. The drought had really pushed the water level down. Both agreed it didn't make sense anyone would bury evidence in the ground with a handy lake sitting right there. They left the guys with instructions and took off for the funeral. Duffy had the search warrant in his jacket for O'Neill. He would keep everything all nice and legal.

MANAS AITMATOV'S FUNERAL

THEY SAW the Gothic Church sitting on the hill as they pulled up. Still early, they decided to walk out into the graveyard.

"Hey, Mike, come over here."

"Well, I'll be damned. Here's the original landowner, Richard Barrett. He's got the best view. Lucky guy. Looks like his wife Nora died way before him," Duffy observed.

Lombardi was checking out the grounds. There were white river rock patterns.

"Can you believe it? It's the same pattern we saw lining the driveways up to O'Neill's farm and Callaghan's," the young detective noted.

"It's probably that triskelion symbol O'Neill mentioned. Hey, look. Each gravestone has that symbol etched on it, too. We've got to check out what it means."

"We better get back, Mike. Cars are pulling up."

Behind them, at the base of the hill was a processional. Farm trucks and cars pulled up in sequence.

"There's Declan O'Neill and his family. Everyone's congregating around him. He really is the Irish Godfather to these people. Finn Sullivan's walking with John Callaghan and his wife Mary," Lombardi observed.

"That must be the widow and her family. Let's wait until they filter into the chapel. No need to cause a ruckus." Duffy and Lombardi faced away.

"Did you notice all the men are wearing those gold medallions around their necks? I've heard the Irish are really into their folklore, but not like this. This is deeper."

After all the mourners entered the chapel, the detectives slipped in unnoticed. Declan O'Neill spoke first.

"As you all know, Manas' family worked for the Sullivan Clan for over 35 years. His father, Seitek, came here from Kyrgyzstan speaking only Russian and his native Kyrgyz.

He worked hard learning English and taught his young son, Manas, the labor of the earth. Manas proved to be worthy in all respects. We watched him grow-up, marry and have children.

"The nine clans representing our farming community are present: Callaghan, McCloud, Avery, Graham, Kelly, Murphy, O'Flaherty, Sullivan, and O'Neill. I speak as representative for all, Sonja. You and your family have our deepest condolences. Manas was a fine human being and shall be dearly missed."

O'Neill sat down and Finn Sullivan went to the podium.

"Sonja, friends, family. I'd like to share some things about Manas you might not know. He was named after the legendary founder/hero of Kyrgyzstan. Their religion, Tengriism, existed long before Islam became the prominent religion for the Turkic people. Tengriists believed that wearing turquoise would protect them against the "evil eye". Periodically, I would find a piece of turquoise placed in one of the triskelion patterns on our property. Manas was protecting our land. We came to appreciate each other's heritage. His sense of humor lifted my spirits when things got difficult. I'll miss you."

Sullivan went over to the open coffin and placed a gold medallion on Manas. He prayed aloud. "May you know eternal peace. Amen."

O'Neill spoke up. "Will the pallbearers please come forward?"

The detectives took the cue and exited before anyone spotted them. They wanted to observe faces and behaviors.

"That was the shortest service I've ever attended," Lombardi commented.

"Keep walking. O'Neill doesn't waste time on anything including the dead. Where the heck was the priest?" Duffy wondered.

"They probably chose to spare the wife a heart-wrenching service. I don't know about the priest. Beats me. These farmers look like decent hard working people. Sullivan's eulogy was simple, but thoughtful. I need to read up on Irish mysticism. Looks like I'll be sitting in the library next to you," Lombardi declared.

"I've got this gnawing feeling something's staring us in the face, and we just aren't seeing it. I'm at a loss. Watch your step, or you'll land in that grave. The coffin is coming, bow your head." Duffy and Lombardi stepped back.

Declan O'Neill waited for everyone to assemble. He noticed the detectives.

"Friends, let's gather round and share a moment of silence as the casket is lowered. Sonja, I give you this piece of turquoise to toss into the grave. It will keep away the "evil eye". Each clan member will add one river rock from their farm. Finn Sullivan will be first and the rest of us will follow. Next, the shovel will be passed along.

"Manas, it's time to move on to your next home. Sleep peacefully, my friend. Lord, have mercy on this soul. Amen." O'Neill then glared at the detectives. The service had ended.

"Excuse me, Mrs. Aitmatov, we came to pay our respects. My name is Mike Duffy and this is Rick Lombardi. We're from the Decatur Police Department. I see you have a good support group, and I'm sure they'll help you through your time of need. We're deeply sorry for your loss."

"Thank you for coming. Did you know my husband? I don't understand…"

"Excuse us, Sonja. Patrick, take your brothers and sisters away. Right now, that's an order! Detectives, what on earth are you doing here?" O'Neill was steaming.

"Mr. O'Neill, we were in the neighborhood and thought it only right to come pay our respects. Nice to meet you, Mrs. O'Neill, I'm Detective Duffy and this is my partner, Detective Lombardi." Duffy nodded.

"I heard you came to our meeting hall earlier today snooping around, but Finn and I got interrupted and he never did give me the whole story. I sure hope you didn't turn our ancestral place upside down. There's a lot of history in there and as custodians we are responsible for keeping our traditions and that includes our sanctuary. What did you mean you were in the area?" O'Neill was noticeably shaken.

"First of all, we left your hall intact and treated it with respect. What we were looking for wasn't there. We have a team working over at Whispering Lake. They've been there since seven this morning. We didn't want to disturb you before the funeral. Here's the search warrant. We're not ignoring anything, Mr. O'Neill. How shall I phrase it, turning over every river rock. We have divers in the lake right now." Duffy was unwavering.

"Search all you want. The most you'll come up with will be fish hooks and tackle. Anything else down there will be older than you. I understand you've got murders to solve, but unless someone happened onto my property independent of my kids and their friends, you're digging in the wrong direction. If one of them did it they'd have to be a damn good liar. Then again, we've all taken your polygraph and passed, so what do you say about that, detectives?

"We have a widow in mourning. You've served your search warrant so leave now and show some decency."

"Good day, Mr. and Mrs. O'Neill. We'll be off your property once the divers have checked every square inch of that lake. That is unless we find something." Duffy wouldn't be thwarted.

Siobhan O'Neill spoke. "Don't you men realize we're mourning more than the man we just buried? Natalie Grant is lying in the ICU. Emily Martin is dead, as well as Jennifer Lawson. When you catch the man that did this we will expect an apology." Siobhan's eyes bore deep.

"I hope that day comes, Mrs. O'Neill. We'll be going now."

EAGER FOR A BREAK, Duffy and Lombardi arrived back at the lake. Carl saw them first.

"The boys won't be done exploring the lake for at least two to three hours," Carl figured.

"What happened at the funeral?" he asked.

"The farmers were shocked when they saw us graveside. John Callaghan almost fell into the grave. We'll need to wait a while before we interview any of them. Just bad timing all around. Maybe, Russell Stuart is available for an earlier talk," Duffy hoped.

Duffy and Lombardi headed back to Decatur. They decided to go to the library and check out Irish mysticism and the significance of the triskelion symbol. Their late afternoon appointment with Russell Stuart gave them some leeway.

They pulled up to the Stuart's home right on time. They couldn't wait for this appointment.

"Well, detectives, come on in. I got to thinking about this case. I guess I was pretty hard on you boys and want to apologize. How about a beer?" Stuart was hospitable.

"Thanks, Mr. Stuart, but we're working. A tall glass of water would be appreciated."

"Call me, Russell. I'll get you a pitcher. Please go sit in the living room. I'll be right back." Stuart placed the water pitcher and glasses on the table and sat down.

"Mr. Stuart, we do appreciate the apology. We had our doubts your girls were involved in the murders. There were too many inconsistencies. A million possible screw-ups, but not one print or speck of evidence that would incriminate anyone. Now we know it was an unfortunate coincidence." Duffy was conciliatory.

"I doubt seriously if either one of my daughters will ever be walking in a dark parking lot again. Rachel is taking them over to the hospital to see Natalie. The peace around here is appreciably refreshing. On Sunday, if I don't go to church, my wife has the "honey do" list waiting in hand to destroy my relaxation. So I go to church. Do either of you have a family?"

"Nope. Haven't had that pleasure yet," Duffy smiled.

"Stay single. Can I show you my library? I'm pretty proud of all the signed books I have in there. The door's always locked; it's my only haven."

"As much as I would like to see your collection, unfortunately, we have a case to solve. Is there anything at all you can tell us that will further this investigation? You probably know a lot of secrets about the people in this town. Newspapers live off of daily gossip and loose lips—you guys often get tips sooner than the police."

"Any tips I receive will be directed immediately to the Decatur Police Department. I can assure you of that."

"Russell, did you and the Mrs. socialize with the Lawsons?"

"Our daughters introduced us at the school's Parents Night several years ago. We got together a few times. That was some time ago. Why do you ask?"

"We're simply trying to understand the relationships of the parents to one another," Duffy explained.

"Rachel wasn't friends with Sally Lawson or any of the other girls' mothers. She ran away from her own kids, so why be around mothers that always talked about their children? My wife spends a lot of time at that shopping center. She's a regular shopaholic. Rachel doesn't have many friends, has no patience. Ask Deidra and Melanie about that. My girls pretty much fend for themselves. Having twins was too much for her. My wife can't cope—it's as simple as that.

The detectives got up. They realized this interview was over.

"Russell, thank you for the interview. If you think of anything, give us a call." They shook hands.

"Good luck with the case, detectives." They walked out.

Outside, Lombardi chuckled. "Now I actually feel sorry for the guy. Is this what I have to look forward to?"

"Why do you think I'm so pessimistic, Rick? This is supposed to be the American dream. Yeah, right!" Duffy was the ultimate cynic.

It had been about three hours since they left the lake. Duffy wanted to get a hold of the boys to see if it had coughed up the murder weapon. The skeptic in him knew the answer would be no. Duffy's stomach grumbled. He suggested grabbing dinner. They chose O'Malley's Irish pub.

Their time in the library researching Irish folklore and mysticism had put the both of them in overload. Duffy figured a good old Irish bartender could explain all of this stuff to them in plain English. At least that was the plan.

CHAPTER 47
NATALIE'S BACK

SHE WAS BACK in the hospital lost in a world she no longer recognized. Yet, seeing things through her mind's eye allowed her to venture forward from the darkest of corridors into the realm of light. She could feel old memories waking up. Many were terrifying.

Natalie was still unconscious with a tube in her throat four days later. The charge nurse, Alice, tried to reassure Mrs. Grant that Natalie was doing fine. She explained that her body had been through a lot of trauma and needed to rest. Natalie's vitals and blood work were good. Nurse Alice suggested that Mrs. Grant take a little break for a while in the waiting room. The nurses would be changing shifts shortly and she had to give report.

An emotionally exhausted Maggie Grant walked back to the waiting room. She couldn't help but fixate on her daughter's uncertain future. Dr. King had mentioned the possibility of complications, but what kind of complications, she wondered? He said they would know more when Natalie regained consciousness. Would Natalie recognize her or would she be a total stranger? That thought haunted her every waking moment.

Nurse Alice poked her head in the waiting room. "Mrs. Grant, Dr. King has just arrived. He asked me to come get you. He wants to have a conversation with you about Natalie."

"Thank you." She walked back with the nurse.

"Mrs. Grant, nice to see you." The neurosurgeon was smiling.

"Dr. King, I'm so concerned. When will Natalie wake up?"

"You need to be patient. I've just checked Natalie's chart. Her ICPs are down so I pulled her catheter. I've written orders to decrease her sedation even more so we can get her breathing tube out. Natalie is making good progress and we expect her to wake up at any time.

"Let's go over what might occur when she does regain consciousness. I want you to be prepared. One of the most common complications after what your daughter has experienced is called Post Traumatic Amnesia. She may experience "islands of memory" in which she'll be able to recall only certain events. But, there are different types of amnesia, Mrs. Grant..."

He went on to give her a thorough explanation of each kind. But Maggie Grant never heard a word. All she heard was the possibility that her daughter could have amnesia and not recognize her or anyone else. She began to panic. Then the doctor's words echoed back in her head.

"...There is a small nuclei of cells the size of an almond, deep inside the temporal lobe of the brain called the Hippocampus. It is an important keeper of our memories. Hopefully, Natalie's injuries weren't severe enough to cause any permanent damage to this part of her brain. The edema is subsiding now. This is going to be a watch and wait situation. When Natalie awakes the nurses will notify me immediately. Do you have any questions?"

Maggie Grant was numb. "No, I guess we'll all know soon enough."

"We have every reason to be optimistic. I'm sorry to have to run off, but I do have other patients and families to see. Take care of yourself." He was gone.

Maggie retreated to the waiting room. When she arrived, a vaguely familiar young man was sitting there.

"Good morning, Mrs. Grant. How is Natalie doing?"

"The same I'm afraid. You are?"

"Colin Sullivan, Natalie's friend."

Her mind was so scattered it was hard for her to keep faces and names straight. She tried to be sociable.

"Yes, now I remember. You're the friend that rescued Natalie from Bernard's car. You haven't left here have you? Don't you have to go home? Aren't your parents concerned about you?"

Colin's physical and mental exhaustion was apparent. He had not left the hospital once since he arrived that Saturday afternoon. He spent the nights in his dad's pick up in the back parking lot. Finn Sullivan had brought essentials to keep Colin comfortable.

"Both my parents know where I am. I've explained the situation to them. They understand. I'm 6'4" and these chairs barely support me. I walk the halls a lot. I figured you needed your privacy anyway. I won't leave until I know Natalie is out of danger. Your daughter is a wonderful person. I got to know her well that night." Colin lowered his eyes.

"I see."

Colin wanted to explain himself to Natalie's mom. He felt a deep responsibility for Natalie's accident and Emily's overdose. He wanted to tell her how much he cared about her daughter. Colin had no idea what her reaction would be when she found out he was the one who had brought the alcohol. He cleared his throat

"I go to school at Notre Dame and live in South Bend, Indiana. Patrick O'Neill is a school buddy and invited me and another friend Dylan Maguire to come celebrate his sister's graduation. We drove down that afternoon after work. Dylan was here on Sunday, but had to return to South Bend. He asked me to tell you how badly he felt. Patrick and his brothers went back yesterday.

"We all work for the same body shop and the boss threatened if we didn't get back to work by today, he'd fire us. I called and told him I needed to stay and he could fire me if he had to. He did. Dylan was my ride back so I guess I'm planted here for a while. Mrs. Grant, I'm the one who brought the Jameson along."

He waited for a reaction. He didn't get one so he continued.

"I don't think I ever want to taste alcohol again. No one can believe what happened that night. It seems surreal. I haven't paid any attention to the news. Did they find the killer yet who murdered Natalie's friend and the security guard?" He took a deep breath.

"No, not yet. I can't even think about that. I'm happy we're getting a chance to talk, Colin. I've been so preoccupied worrying about Natalie I've pushed Jennifer and Emily's tragedies to the back of my mind."

"Mrs. Grant, when we found out Emily was in trouble Natalie ran to help her. I wanted to drive, but she wouldn't let me. If I could change places with Natalie right now I'd do it in a heartbeat. She doesn't even know that Emily and Jennifer are gone. How do you tell her?"

"We'll figure it out when the time comes."

"My dad is Finn Sullivan. His farm is down the road from the O'Neills. They're good friends. I grew up with my mom in Chicago. I've only been down here a few times over the years. It's difficult between my parents and I'm their only child.

"You were talking with the doctor when he came by on Saturday to get me settled. He sends his good wishes. He didn't stay long because he had to make arrangements for a funeral this past Sunday. The person that was killed in the expressway disaster was his headman."

"Friday night seems like a lifetime ago. I am John Callaghan's bookkeeper. Because of that freeway accident and the drought a meeting was called. Your dad was there. We had met before. It's ironic that so many tragedies happened on the same day and they all seem to be interconnected. Doesn't your boss understand people died here this weekend and that a girl is still fighting for her life?"

He didn't respond. She changed the subject.

"You say you just met Natalie? It sounds like you've known her a lifetime. She's fortunate to have met you, Colin. Sometimes it takes errors in judgment to find our true path. We can't bring Emily or Jennifer back, but I pray Natalie will come through this ordeal unharmed.

"KT and her family have been a Godsend. Siobhan O'Neill calls daily asking if there's anything they can do to help. You wouldn't have believed the way the two of us argued that dreadful night. What a turnaround. A crisis sure shows people's fiber. I feel badly for KT. Two girlfriends are dead and her best friend is in a coma. I think KT is worried that Natalie won't remember her."

All Colin could remember were the terrible arguments between the two girls. He unloaded ruthlessly on KT before they left. Maybe he was too harsh. They continued to small talk.

"You do remember the twins coming. Melanie and Deidra visited here a couple of times."

"Yes, they're such lovely girls." Maggie's mind started drifting.

"I talked with them in the cafeteria on Sunday. They sure love Natalie. They did say the police suspected they might have had something to do with Jennifer's murder. Those girls couldn't hurt a fly. What's with the Decatur Police Department anyway? They harassed us even knowing we all had legitimate excuses."

Colin thought about the detectives giving him and Dylan the third degree before they left. They never forced anyone to drink, yet no one could make him feel any worse than he already did. He needed to see Natalie. He had to ask.

"Would it be possible for me to go in and see Natalie for just a minute? I know I'm not family, but it would mean the world to me." He held his breath.

"Of course, I'll let the ICU nurse know you have my permission. I've always liked…."

Just then, Nurse Alice came running in.

"Excuse me, Mrs. Grant, Natalie is awake. We've pulled her breathing tube and she is breathing on her own. Dr. King has been called. He'll be here shortly. You can go in now."

Maggie jumped up, looked at Colin and muttered some niceties, than took off with the nurse. Her heart was pounding.

When she entered Natalie's room, she heard mumbling and saw her daughter's eyes were open.

"Natalie, you're back, you're back! It's me, Mom. You're going to be fine now. It'll just take time. Alice, she's closed her eyes again. Is she back in a coma?"

"No, I think Natalie just fell asleep. This is quite jolting for her. Her body needs to wake up slowly. She's just made her first breakthrough."

"Thank you, Alice, thank you! I've got to go make calls to my family."

Colin was pacing outside in the hallway.

"Mrs. Grant, how is she?"

"Natalie woke up. She looked at me for a minute, then fell back to sleep. I'm afraid she didn't recognize me, but the nurse assured me she's made a breakthrough. Thank you for helping my daughter. I left your name with the nurse. I need to go call my son and sister." She hurried down the hall.

"Excuse me, nurse, my name is Colin Sullivan. May I go in and see Natalie for just a minute. Mrs. Grant said I've got permission."

The nurse checked the guest list. She looked up at him and smiled.

"Your name was just added. You understand the rules, so please limit your stay. Room 22."

He tiptoed in. Natalie's head was bandaged. Multiple IV's were attached to her arms and neck. The love of his life was before him. He cried as he poured his heart out.

"Natalie, it's Colin. I'm so happy you've come back to us. I still don't understand it, but I fell in love with you the first time we kissed. They said the chance of you remembering the day of the accident is remote, but I hope you'll remember me. Your mom and I just had a great conversation. Now that I know you're okay, I can leave and take care of family matters. My life's in limbo. I'll be back soon, my love." He kissed her softly and slipped out of the room.

Maggie Grant had made her phone calls and went back to find Colin. He was gone. She approached the nurse.

"Excuse me, have you seen that young man, Colin, who was in the waiting room?"

The nurse answered, "He went in to visit with your daughter. Is there a problem?"

"No, he must have gone. All his belongings are gone from the waiting room. I'm just surprised that he didn't say goodbye."

"Mrs. Grant, you have a telephone call at the nurses' station." Another nurse handed her the phone. She thanked her.

"Hello, Mrs. Grant, Detective Duffy here. How is Natalie doing?"

She told him the good news.

"That's wonderful. You did mention last Saturday you'd continue our conversation. Is this a good time?"

"Yes. Where would you like to meet?"

"How about in the hospital cafeteria?"

"That would be fine."

"In 45 minutes?"

"I'll see you then."

EXCEPT FOR SOME staff members and a few visitors sitting around, the cafeteria was empty. Mike Duffy was the first to arrive. He had exhausted all his leads. Natalie Grant was still an unknown, but Maggie Grant could be the wildcard in his arsenal. He was sure of it. She walked in.

"Hello, Mrs. Grant, can I buy you a cup of coffee?"

"Coffee would be nice, thank you."

"We left off on your relationship with John Callaghan."

"Yes, we did."

"Detective, you're digging around in people's personal lives. I don't think you're going to find out who killed Jennifer Lawson there, but you could hurt a lot of people in this pursuit."

"Let me be the judge of that."

"Okay, here's my private closet of skeletons. After Declan and I broke up, my husband sensed a change in my attitude toward him. I was no longer the meek, abused wife I had been. One night Bernard was drunk. He went to hit me and I fought back. Sadly, Kevin witnessed everything. My ten year old son ran into our bedroom and started pounding on his father's chest. Bernard threw him across the room and a lamp shattered all over the place.

"The things he said to Kevin and me were horrible. Kevin started crying and screaming "wife beater" to his dad. I saw my family falling apart in front of my eyes. Bernard walked out on us and went down to his tool shed. It took me a long time to get Kevin settled down and back to bed. Apparently, this wasn't the first time Kevin had seen him hurt me. Things finally made sense to me about why he never wanted anything to do with his dad. Bernard was in the shed pretty late. I worried because he was supposed to take Natalie and Jennifer fishing with him the next morning.

"When he finally came up to bed his breath reeked of rye. I knew my marriage was over that night. The next morning he and Natalie left early. Natalie was the apple of his eye so I knew she would be safe. I felt relieved when he was gone. I picked up the telephone and called John Callaghan to get the name of a good divorce attorney.

"You were right about one thing. We weren't having an affair but had developed a close friendship. Life with Mary wasn't as smooth as he wanted everyone to believe. She never gave him any children and those farms need heirs to keep everything going. Well, when John answered, I told him I wanted to leave Bernard. He said he'd leave Mary and marry me. He said he'd fallen in love with me. That was Saturday morning at 11 a.m.

"When the police arrived at my home later on with Natalie and the news about the boating accident I was in a state of shock. They sat me down and told me Bernard had been killed. I was mortified and deeply guilt-ridden because I had tried all morning to figure out how to tell Bernard I wanted a divorce. Now he was dead.

"Natalie was traumatized beyond words. Jennifer was clearly in a state of shock, too. Both girls had to go down to the station and tell the police what happened. These girls were only 13 years old at the time, detective. Clearly they had nothing to do with the accident, but the cops still had to do their investigation. After that day I told John I couldn't ever consider marrying him. God paid me back for my sins. I couldn't destroy another marriage."

"Then why do you work for him?" Duffy asked.

"That's obvious. I said I wouldn't remarry, but I didn't say I wouldn't love again. Because of the accident, Mary had no suspicions about John buying Bernard's business or offering me the bookkeeping job. She felt sorry for me, everyone did."

"She isn't suspicious of the two of you?"

"I'm sure she has wondered through the years, but John and I agreed our love would never hurt any more people. You were right about something else, detective. I did race over to John's that night because he also told me Mary had threatened him with divorce when he told her how bad things had gotten. When she heard they needed to take out a loan on the farm she went wild. John desperately needed me.

"We'd both been through such misery and I thought finally we might have a chance at happiness. I didn't give it a second thought about leaving the girls unattended. Natalie has always been trustworthy. I never imagined those kids would run off and do what they did." Her eyes welled up.

"Are you satisfied, Detective Duffy?" Maggie had exposed her deepest secrets.

Her opening up had only given him more insight into their relationship, but how, or if it connected to the murders was still a mystery.

"Only if what you're telling me is the truth. In fact, let's eliminate the gray area and have you take a polygraph after we're done here. I'm not without feeling, but nothing you've told us thus far helps solve either murder. All this investigation has added up to is a big fat zero and that doesn't sit well with me.

"Even though this is a high profile case funds aren't enough to keep working indefinitely. In time, this case will lose its priority and land right next to the victims, cold and buried if we don't get a break."

It never occurred to Maggie Grant that she would be asked to take a lie detector test. Telling her painful truth should have been enough, but she agreed to go to the station. There was nothing else anyone could take from her at this point. Duffy interrupted her distraction.

"We've interviewed and investigated pretty much everyone but your daughter. We know she was with Emily that night and it would have been difficult for her to be involved, but she may be able to fill in gaps for us and clear herself completely."

"My skin crawls when you suggest Natalie could be implicated at all. It's preposterous."

He continued, "Natalie needs to get well first, we can appreciate that. Nevertheless, as soon as possible we'll need her statement. My job is to get to the bottom of these murders. We'll expect you later for the polygraph. Thank you again for having this chat with me. The personal stuff will be kept confidential."

CHAPTER 48

COLUMBIA UNIVERSITY GRADUATION

NATALIE COULD FEEL her lost memory melding with her active mind. There were still black holes, but things were coming into focus. Suddenly conscious of her surroundings she saw Liam walking up to the podium. He was a talker so she knew there was still a bit of time left to solve the mystery. She fast forwarded six years to the week before graduation from Columbia University.

Natalie had just been offered a full-time job at Matrix Publishing house where she had been interning during graduate school. Graduation was a couple of days off and her mom, brother, and KT were flying in from Illinois for the big event. Fortunately, her mother made the arrangements. All Natalie had to do was pick them up from LaGuardia Airport.

The plane arrived on time and the trio made their way to the passenger pick up area. In spite of the heavy traffic, Natalie caught their attention, pulled over and everyone piled into her white Honda Accord. Natalie spoke first.

"I'm so thrilled you're all here! Mom, have you eaten?"

"We had a small bite at the airport. Truthfully, I'm exhausted, Natalie. Please just drop Kevin and me off at the hotel. I'm going to bed early tonight. We'll catch up in the morning." Mrs. Grant laid her head back.

"KT, I hope you're not tired! I've got the sofa already made up for you. I can't wait to hear all the local gossip."

"I'm not tired at all. You look great, Natalie. I really like your hair short."

"Yeah, I got tired of blow drying long, curly hair. Between school and work, I'm lucky I get to eat and sleep. But that's changing now. I start full-time at Matrix Publishing one week after graduation. This is my company car. Got a pretty decent salary to start," Natalie boasted.

After an hour of driving through heavy New York traffic, they arrived at The Hotel Newton, a small hotel on the Upper West Side where Mrs. Grant and Kevin were staying. It was just a short drive to campus. They all got out, exchanged hugs, and KT jumped into the front seat.

"Kevin, please get the suitcases. Good night, girls. See you at 9 a.m."

"Good night, Mom. Please make sure Kevin doesn't oversleep." Maggie nodded and walked inside the hotel.

"Don't worry about me, sis. I have no intention of going to sleep at all. I'm planning on checking out the night life in the Big Apple." He had trouble written all over him.

"This is New York, Kevin; you just can't sneak into the clubs. Don't tell me you have one of those fake IDs."

"Stop mothering me, Natalie." Kevin rolled his eyes.

"Okay, go have fun." The girls took off.

A short time later they arrived in Morningside Heights. After squeezing into a tight parking spot, Natalie and KT walked for another ten minutes before they arrived at her place.

"This is where I live," she said smiling.

"Welcome to Villa Grant. Now we just have to climb the stairs to my unit. I'll take your suitcase, it's the least I can do."

KT protested, but Natalie wouldn't hear of it. They trudged up several flights of stairs and arrived at her front door. They walked inside.

"Wow, pretty nice, Nat." KT was impressed.

Natalie put down the suitcase and turned to her girlfriend.

"Okay, give me the scoop on what's going on with you."

KT looked around taking in everything.

"Well, my life isn't all that exciting. Guys come and go, no one stays long enough to develop a real relationship." She walked over to Natalie's extensive bookshelf.

Natalie followed her. "I'm sorry. I was hoping there was someone special. How are your brothers doing?"

"Patrick's still single. He just bought a full service body shop in Decatur. My parents aren't too thrilled that he ended up a mechanic after sending him to Notre Dame. Aidan is graduating from law school next week. His girlfriend Tracy is a keeper. Liam works with Dad on the farm handling all the day to day business. It seems like he dates a different girl every month. Mom and Dad finally explained to him why he was sent off to live with Aunt Brigit. He was speechless.

"I was shocked when I heard the truth. It appears my mom lost a baby girl in her seventh month of pregnancy. Only my dad and Aunt Brigit knew. She cried when she told me the baby was buried in the old cemetery.

"As for my parents, things were never the same after that drought hit. Dad and his friends were sure smart diverting water from Whispering Lake to their fields. It saved their crops. Three of the clans sold out to my dad. John Callaghan was one of them. He moved to Wisconsin with his wife, Mary. There were rumors about him having a girlfriend, but no one ever found out if that was true or just gossip.

"Daniel McCloud sold out, too. He got sick and couldn't manage his farm. Finn Sullivan, Colin's dad decided to go back to school and get a law degree. I heard Colin encouraged him to do it. My dad helped with the tuition and bought out the other farmers' interests in his land.

"Colin left Notre Dame and transferred to the University of New Mexico on a full scholarship. Patrick said Colin changed his whole life around because of you and that night out at Whispering Lake. That night sure changed a lot of people's lives. No memories ever came back for you?"

"No, not really." Natalie stared at her collection of books.

"Here I am rambling about people and places you don't even know. I guess I'm hoping something will trigger your memory. Is that okay?" KT looked for approval.

"Sure, I know you're trying to help. I do remember pieces of things, but the images blur and evaporate. Once in a while I see a face that makes me smile or want to cry, but I don't know why. Sometimes I sense danger and that's what scares me the most."

"There is something I never told you. Maybe now's the right time. The only time you slept over at my house, there were unorthodox practices going on with my family that I kept from you." Not seeing any reaction, KT continued.

"That night when we went to sleep, I saw you get up and go over to the window to let some air in. I had intentionally closed it when we first went to bed. I didn't want you to hear anything strange. The noises must have awoken you because you just stood there for a time looking out."

Natalie just stared at her friend. Splintered memories of that night always preyed upon her. Maybe now she'd understand why.

"Please go on, KT."

"Well, my parents were at odds because of religion. My mom held tight to her Catholicism while my dad kept to his pagan beliefs. Mom just couldn't accept the fact that her younger daughter's mental handicap was a hopeless condition. She ignored the doctors' diagnoses and turned to the church. Darcy was being exorcised the night you stayed over. It was my sister that you saw running in the cornfields. I heard her scream, too. I pretended I was asleep. The whole thing terrified me. You went back to bed and never mentioned it to me. Does any of this ring a bell in your memory?"

"Yeah, it does. I guess I'm running from something I can't see, too. Maybe that's why the image never left me."

Do you remember Colin at all, Natalie?"

"No. Whatever happened before, the memory is completely gone. I felt nothing when I looked at his picture. It's so weird looking at people that claim to know you and there's no recognition. I gave up on the doctors years ago. My yearly MRIs showed no permanent brain damage. Each doctor said to be patient and optimistic. As you can see, I have a lot of medical books. Unfortunately, doing my own research didn't help either. Go on, tell me more about Decatur."

"There are times I wish I could just wipe away my past. I'm not close with either one of my parents anymore. I'm still invited to family functions, but they got real cold toward me after the accident. I've tried to talk to them about it several times, but finally just gave up. I'll always have Darcy though. She's still pretty much the same." KT seemed unhappy.

"Natalie, I've got to say something to you." Tears filled her eyes.

"I'm really proud of you. I just want you to know that." The girls hugged.

"KT, you never abandoned me even though I didn't recognize you. That showed me your character. I read the newspapers and saw lots of pictures of us together. Whatever happened to Jennifer's family?"

"They moved away six months after her memorial. Once in a while I go out to the cemetery and visit with her. My life changed, too, when Jen died. The police watched me closely for weeks." KT walked over to a mirror, looked at herself, and continued.

"Then, there was sweet Emily. Her parents ended up getting a messy divorce. Their marriage unraveled soon after her death. We did find out why Em had panic attacks. It appears that her cousin Marco shoved her head under the water in a kiddie pool when they were little kids. Emily passed out and Marco's parents came running to the rescue after hearing his screaming. They felt responsible for not supervising properly and kept it a secret. After Emily's funeral Marco broke down and admitted what had happened. Every year on her birthday, I go out to her grave with flowers. I really miss her." KT looked at Natalie through the reflection.

"What about you, Natalie? Any love interests in your life?" KT turned to face her.

Natalie's facial expression changed.

"One night stands, yes, love interests, no. I don't trust men. I always think I've got to be one step ahead of them. I never said so, but after I left the hospital I worried about being killed. One of my best friends was murdered and I sensed someone was after me, but I could never figure out who my enemy was." Natalie caught KT's stare.

"I know what you mean. I was paralyzed with fear for months. I finally let it go."

"I've stopped trying to figure myself out, KT. I don't need a guy in my life to make me happy. I've just graduated from college and landed a wonderful job that I can't wait to start. Well, we need to get our beauty sleep. See you in the morning."

COLUMBIA GRADUATING CLASS
COMMENCEMENT DAY

THERE WAS A CRUSH of people milling around, visiting and taking pictures. The graduates stepped forward when their name was announced to receive their diploma. Every parent wanted that coveted shot.

Standing off to the side, far away, was Colin Sullivan. He had learned from Patrick O'Neill that Natalie was graduating. He needed to come even though he knew she wouldn't remember him. Here it was six years later and his heart still belonged to her. He'd been with many girls since, but none compared. Only the girl on the stage about to get her diploma could move him in every way. Colin's feelings possessed his every thought.

Natalie Grant, you sure have affected my life. It was that single night we spent together gazing at all those stars. Astronomy was the magic that brought us together and now I've made it my career. In August I'll finish my dissertation in Astrophysics. My beautiful Virgo, we made magic then. Maybe, one day you'll remember us and we'll make magic again.

CHAPTER 49

NEW YORK

NATALIE'S MEMORY was accelerating quickly now as she moved forward in time. She revisited herself at 29 years of age. Her journalism career was soaring and Colin Sullivan was in New York for the weekend. She was coming down the home stretch.

The State of the Planet Conference was about to get under way. Maxwell Wallace, the publisher of Matrix Advertising lined up the interviews he had scheduled for his magazine. Everyone in the business was jockeyed for coverage.

Phones rang off their hooks. Matrix Advertising was humming. Mr. Wallace's assistant, Ornella Peterson walked over to Natalie's desk.

"Excuse me, Ms. Grant, Mr. Wallace would like to see you. He said to just go in even if he's on the telephone."

"Thanks, Ornella. I'm on my way."

Her boss motioned with his hand to sit down.

"Senator, as I was saying we'd love to get your comments about your environmental concerns and how you feel the conference balances on global issues. Will you have time to do an interview with us when the conference takes a lunch break? Great, Natalie Grant will be your interviewer. She's my sharpest journalist on staff. You can count on us. We'll see you tomorrow."

Maxwell Wallace was up to his neck in commitments, meeting with dignitaries and arranging the social end of things.

"Natalie, we want you to cover the State of the Planet Conference. I won't be able to attend so I'm giving you the hottest assignment of the year. With the line-up of speakers it's the best seat in all of New York City. Gorbachev, Kofi Annan, Wallace Broecker, and Richard Lindzen, the list goes on and on of Who's Who. We've scheduled two interviews for you so far. You just heard my telephone call with Senator Moynihan. I have the utmost faith in you. Here's the information." She stood to receive the packet and sat back down, stunned.

Natalie wanted the assignment desperately, but had given up hope. She kept that to herself. The other journalists were jealous of her as it was.

"Thank you, Mr. Wallace. I promise I won't let you down." She shook his hand and hurried out. Her secretary, Tami Barger, caught up with her.

"Ms. Grant, a Mr. Colin Sullivan is waiting for you in the reception area."

"Please tell him I'll be out there shortly. Mr. Wallace just gave me the State of the Planet Conference assignment. I'm taking lunch and then we'll work on a list of things I need you to get ready."

"That's great you got the assignment. Everyone in the office will be envious for sure. Go enjoy yourself." Tami excelled at her job.

"I don't know what I'd do without you, Tami. I better get going."

Natalie decided to freshen up in the ladies room, add a bit of lipstick before going out to see Colin. *That man sure is persistent,* she thought. She walked out.

"Hello, Natalie."

"Hello, Colin."

They stood looking at one another. There was an undeniable mutual attraction.

"Thanks for agreeing to have lunch with me on such short notice." His excitement showed.

"You called at the right time. There's an exhibit in town I'm dying to see. What brought you to New York?"

"I'm here for The State of the Planet Conference."

"What a coincidence. I just got assigned to attend the conference and do some interviews. Why are you attending?"

"Richard Lindzen will be speaking and I'm quite a fan. I can't wait to hear what he has to say about climate change. I've read many of his papers on the subject."

"That's right. I heard you became an Astrophysicist. Pretty impressive, Colin."

"One night under the stars my future was decided." He probed for some recollection. He saw none.

"Let me grab my coat and we'll be on our way. It's an ideal day to walk in Manhattan. Do you know anything about Jackson Pollock?"

"Only that he was a major American painter who was involved with the Abstract Expressionist Movement." He opened the door and escorted Natalie.

Out on the street the awkward couple pushed through the throng of New York walkers. Colin had yearned for this reunion for years. He feared rejection so he only called periodically to say hello and share small talk. This weekend he was determined to seal their fate.

"I'm impressed. You do know your painters. I studied art history in school, but got quite an education on him at an upscale gallery that had a private collection of his on loan. His unorthodox methods of painting captivated me. I guess I like people who take chances and don't play it safe.

"Ironically, Pollock had a long struggle with alcoholism and died in a car accident. I was hoping I might find missing pieces of my life through his paintings. Am I talking too much?"

"No, Natalie, please go on. This is quite interesting actually."

"We're almost to the Museum of Modern Art. Okay, I'll continue. Pollock wasn't your conventional painter. He used inexpensive household paints instead of artist paints and developed a "drip" technique. He would pour and drip paints onto his canvases using a variety of methods and applicators. He used knives, hardened brushes, sticks, and even basting syringes to achieve different results.

"He was a free spirit and wouldn't be confined to a traditional easel or an upright canvas. Pollock preferred using his entire body to help create impression so having his canvasses on the floor allowed him the utmost freedom. He poured his own liquid brilliance onto those canvasses." Her knowledge was all-encompassing.

"You've really done your homework on this guy."

"Pollock understood the nature of chaos. You can literally reach inside his paintings for deeper levels of meaning. He wasn't hampered by beginnings and endings. He broke away from convention and chose to discontinue titling his works and just number them. Numbers wouldn't create images in people's minds and shut down their imagination.

"I've sat many a time just staring into his masterpieces. I try to let my mind wander hoping somewhere deep inside I can find the road back to my past. Maybe, my memory loss is just a blank canvas with a number on it. If I stare deeply enough I might find that reflection and the numbers will match up."

"That's a pretty amazing concept, Natalie." Colin was intrigued.

"Well, so far my road back to my inner canvas seems to be blocked. I can't get beyond certain points. Hopefully, one day that won't be the case. There's the hotdog vendor. Let's grab a hotdog and sit here on the steps of the museum."

Colin watched Natalie eat with delight. He could imagine her sexually. She stirred all his senses.

His stare didn't go unnoticed. She asked, "Why haven't you gotten married, Colin?"

"I made a commitment to a beautiful young girl that I would love her forever. I've kept my word. So why didn't you marry, Ms. Grant?"

"It's hard to live life and move forward when questions about your past prey on your psyche. You have your entire life to draw on. My life's recorded in other people's minds, not mine. I get to hear about who I was, what I did, and what a great person I've always been. It's like hearing about a character in a book and you say to yourself, could that possibly be me?

"Honestly, Colin other than you being a really nice guy and sticking by me all these years I have no recollection. I wish I could tell you otherwise, but I can't. I'm truly sorry."

Colin wouldn't fold. "Natalie, have dinner with me tonight. The sky will be clear and the stars will be bright. Just let them do their magic. You'll see, you'll remember, I promise."

"You're one determined man. Okay, meet me at 6:15 in front of my office building. I know a great Italian restaurant in Little Italy. We can walk along Christopher Street afterward. I live in the vicinity. If you like, I'll make you an Irish coffee at my place."

They finished eating and walked into the exhibition. Colin was already thinking about their evening.

At last, 6:15 p.m. arrived. Colin was there waiting. Natalie came through the door on time. She hugged him and said he'd better be good and hungry. Angelo's was known for giving large portions. They grabbed a cab.

A short time later they were sitting in a far corner of the restaurant enjoying food and wine. Talking came easily to the two of them. Colin fantasized during the entire meal. He couldn't wait to touch her.

"You were right," he said, "that was the best Italian food I've ever had. How far is Christopher Street from here?"

Natalie answered him, but her mind was elsewhere. She was thinking about having sex with him. He was very good looking, smart, and obviously into her. She thought, why not, she hadn't been with a man in some time. She had needs, too.

"It's a bit of a walk, but we can take a taxi if you like."

They decided to walk. The sexual tension between them intensified with every step. They arrived at Natalie's building a while later. She had already warned him about the marathon stair climb up to her apartment. For Colin, it would only be an appetite builder. He couldn't wait to taste her.

Natalie opened the door to her place. "Well, what do you think?"

"Impressive," he walked inside.

"That's quite an extensive library. You sure have a lot of medical books. Studying to be a doctor in your spare time?" He was bemused.

Natalie stood behind him. She responded.

"The doctors couldn't answer many of my questions so I resorted to researching the mystery of the brain on my own. I've learned quite a bit over the years about long-term and short-term memory loss."

"How about making me that Irish coffee you offered." He was aching inside.

"Colin, would you like to go with me up to the rooftop? The view should be amazing tonight."

Natalie couldn't help but notice Colin was aroused. It turned her on.

"I'd love to." He watched her every move.

Natalie explored the kitchen pantry. "Found the Jameson. Get ready for the best Irish coffee of your life."

Colin walked into the kitchen and took the bottle out of her hand.

"The coffee can wait. Let's do some swigs." Colin looked deep into Natalie's eyes.

"You go first, Colin." Her heart was pounding.

"Okay, I drink to you, this moment, and to new memories being made tonight."

He took a swig and handed her the bottle. "Your turn."

"I drink to windows being opened in my heart." She swallowed deeply.

"Want to do another or go upstairs?" Colin inched closer.

"Let's go up to the rooftop. We only have two flights of stairs to conquer." Her insides stirred.

"I'm sure it'll be worth it."

It was mental striptease walking up the stairwell. He grabbed her butt. She returned the gesture. They maneuvered the exit door open, then walked out.

"Close your eyes, Natalie. Now open them." Colin was in his glory.

Millions of stars glistened across the night sky. In spite of the city glow, they were visible everywhere.

"Amazing! Look at all those stars." Natalie was in awe.

He held her tightly. "I want tonight to be a night we'll both remember forever." Then he kissed her passionately.

She looked up at him. "Are you sure you want this?"

"Yes. I told you the stars have magic. Just let them open your heart. They did years ago. We were fantastic together; I know we can be again." He pressed against her.

Natalie pulled back. "Wait!"

She knew she would ultimately make love to him, but first she wanted to tease him, make him work for it. It always made the sex better. She unzipped his fly and released him.

Colin was hung like a horse. He knew he could satisfy her every need. He had before. Natalie liked what she saw. Just staring at him made her wet inside. She put her hand on him. He moaned in delight. Colin felt familiar in a strange way. That boggled her.

"You told me that night our short time together was just an appetizer. I've waited years to collect on your promise to appease my appetite. The hunger never left me, Natalie. Only you can satisfy it. So what do we do now?"

The time had come to finish what she started so many years ago. Colin was a total turn on, the complete package. If nothing else the evening would be memorable. They inched back kissing one another while she stroked him the entire way to the exit door. She would give him what he had been yearning for. Natalie would rock his universe again.

Back inside her apartment, she turned off all the lights and led him to her bed. Only soft light filtered into the bedroom from scented candles. Natalie emerged naked from the bathroom. Colin was waiting, stretched out across her bed, naked as well. He was the ultimate stud. She approached him with some rope and a scarf. He just stared.

"I want you as my sexual prisoner. I'm very good at tying knots. Being blindfolded has its sensual advantages," she purred.

Colin told her to do whatever she wanted. He was receptive. Natalie gave him a verbal picture of what he had coming. She had a jar of cream to tantalize and make his skin feel hot. Of course, she would be on top massaging it in. Together they would become a volcano, erupting simultaneously. When she was done, his appetite would be completely satisfied.

Done teasing, she said, "Lean back, it's time to feast."

She bound his hands and covered his eyes. Natalie was right. It definitely spiked his arousal. She put cream on her hands and breasts and some on his body, then massaged it in.

She whispered, "I can do amazing things with my tongue," as she slithered down.

"You want to know what I fantasize about…I'm visualizing it right now. Keep going." He loved every second.

"I'm just getting started, Colin." She then got on top of him.

"You feel so good to me, every hard inch of you. How could I have forgotten this? Let's lock ourselves up in the moment. I want us to be oblivious to everything beyond the present, is that okay?"

"Yes. Yes! You're driving me out of my mind. Don't stop!"

His skin was on fire. His whole being was tingling. Colin moaned as he arched in release.

"You deserve this from me, you've waited long enough. Maybe tonight we can paint our own canvas. OH, NO! Here it comes again. My head is throbbing. I'm getting a flashback, Colin, I'm remembering things, images, I'm remembering!"

2 A.M.

Colin couldn't sleep. All he could do was gaze at Natalie. He thought, *no wonder I've been obsessed with her forever. She's wild and kinky. That was erotic being tied up and blindfolded. Just feeling her hands and tongue was electrifying. I've got to stop thinking about her and get some sleep. The conference starts at 9 a.m.*

6:30 A.M.

Colin woke up. He turned to kiss Natalie, but she was gone. He got out of bed. On the nightstand was a note.

"Good Morning, Colin. I had to leave early. It's going to be a busy day doing interviews at the conference. Towels are in the bathroom. You'll find everything you need. Please lock up when you go. I had a great time last night. Call me when you come through New York again. Natalie."

What did you remember? he thought. *Whatever it was sure changed your mood. After last night I thought for sure you were mine. Maybe I was wrong.*

CHAPTER 50

KT'S SUICIDE

NATALIE DIDN'T UNDERSTAND the inner connections of the people in her life. She never saw Colin again after their fling in New York. It had been ten years since Natalie and Colin had their rendezvous. Her career took off and life moved on, yet she never felt settled. She didn't know what was driving her: the unsolved murders, KT's suicide, or the fear of the unknown? She simply had no choice but to push on.

The call from her mother the morning of October 31st telling her about KT's suicide was the turning point. They would be burying her on November 1st. Natalie made arrangements for her mom to pick her up at Decatur Airport at 9 p.m.

They talked on the way home from the airport. Natalie shared plans to write a book about the girls. She had written about everyone else's life, why not her own. She knew her boss wouldn't mind if she took a short sabbatical.

They arrived home. Natalie's bedroom hadn't changed since she was a little girl. As she entered, she was deluged by strange memories. She decided to take a sedative and go to sleep. Fortunately, the night passed without incident. Natalie and Maggie got up early and dressed in black. The funeral was scheduled for noon. Kevin would meet them at the cemetery. He, too, had never found a permanent relationship. Maggie worried about both her children.

CAITLIN O'NEILL'S FUNERAL

MOTHER AND DAUGHTER arrived at the cemetery by Heaven's Door. Kevin was waiting. They all walked into the chapel together and sat down in the back. Natalie couldn't believe it. Everything was in real time now. Liam had just finished and returned to his seat. It was finally her turn to speak. Yet, she still had missing pieces to the murder mysteries that surrounded her girlfriends. She reviewed her eulogy.

"Ms. Grant, would you like to say a few words about Caitlin?"

"Yes, certainly." Natalie stood up and approached the podium. She nodded to Mrs. O'Neill and her family.

"Hello. My name is Natalie Grant and I would like to tell all of you about the Caitlin O'Neill I knew. KT, as her friends called her, was a warm and compassionate person. I was lucky. I got to have her as a best friend twice. KT showed unwavering support of me. She didn't abandon me when I looked at her without a thread of recognition. KT was loyal and dependable and even flew to New York when I graduated from Columbia University. We shared our joys and sorrows and knew we could count on one another.

"When my world came crashing down and I almost died, KT wouldn't let me give up. She helped me start my life over again. I will always be grateful to her for that and keep her in my heart forever. Mrs. O'Neill, my heartfelt condolences go out to you and your family."

Natalie left the podium and started to walk back to her seat. Mrs. O'Neill touched her arm and whispered, "Natalie, your words were very touching. I'd like to speak with you in private right after the service. I have something to give you."

Patrick complained, "Mom, can't that wait until after we bury Caitlin?"

"I just need a moment alone with Natalie, Patrick, it won't take long." Siobhan was unyielding.

The priest took the podium. "The O'Neill family wishes to thank everyone for attending Caitlin's funeral today. Please join them at the burial site where final prayers will be offered. This portion of the service is now concluded."

The O'Neills filed out first. As Mrs. O'Neill approached Natalie, she motioned to meet her outside. Natalie slipped out.

"Natalie, over here quickly while I have a free moment. Caitlin left this letter for you. She sealed it with instructions to give to you after she was buried. I have no idea what's inside, but whatever it is please keep its contents confidential. Caitlin's past needs to stay private.

"My life hasn't been the same either these past 20 years. After losing my husband, I've felt so alone. Now with Caitlin's death I know I have to move on. I have my other children to think about. Maybe one day you'll come out to the farm and have lunch with me."

Natalie took the envelope and held her hand.

"Thank you, Mrs. O'Neill for the letter and the invitation to lunch. I will definitely come out and visit."

"KT was very troubled, but she did pick good friends like you. I've got to go now. God bless you." Siobhan was whisked away by her family.

"Natalie, are you coming?" Maggie Grant watched from the chapel steps.

"Mom, this is very difficult for me. I need to go back in and freshen up. Where's Kevin?"

"He left right after you said your eulogy. It was too depressing for him. I know this is taking a heavy toll on you."

Natalie's insides were shaking. The whole experience of reliving her past was coming down on her.

"I won't be long."

Staring at the restroom mirror, she wondered. *Why am I constantly paralyzed by the significance of things? Now three of my high school girlfriends are dead. That only leaves the twins and me alive. Why didn't Deidra and Melanie come?* Natalie splashed water on her face and fixed her hair. *Now my hair's perfect!*

She walked out of the restroom into the stare of a menacing familiar face. They were alone in the chapel.

"Ms. Grant, hello, remember me? I'm Detective Rick Lombardi, Decatur Police Department. I worked the Lawson case."

"Detective Lombardi, of course I remember you. I remember everything that's happened to me after my accident. What can I do for you here at my best friend's funeral?" She tried to move past, but he blocked her way. "Excuse me. My mother is waiting," she snarled.

The detective just stood there staring at her. Lombardi had aged rough. His face showed the ravages that stress and hard living create. Natalie was incensed at his presence.

"You think you're pretty slick, but I've seen you in New York watching me," she said accusingly. "Why have you been stalking me all these years? You know I couldn't possibly have been involved with those murders. What's your problem, still frustrated because you and your police department never solved Jennifer's murder or that security guard's? What was his name?" She was acerbic in tone.

"His name was James Abbott. You know that double murder case was my very first homicide assignment. If you recall, Mike Duffy was my partner back then. When the case went cold he told me to let it go. There would always be new homicides waiting on our desks to be solved. Well, I never could let that one go, maybe because of how gruesome the murder was or because you were still the wild card.

"After Mike retired five years ago, I thought long and hard about you. It seemed highly improbable that the murders would stop abruptly that night if the murderer wasn't one of you. That's when I came to New York just to see how you were getting along. I learned you had become quite a successful journalist. No marriage, no kids, no personal ties. You lived alone and kept to yourself. No problems with the law. You seemed to be living a respectable life."

"Detective, the murderer obviously ran. Any smart cop would have figured that out. The killer was probably three states away when you found Jennifer in that dumpster."

"I would sit up nights just trying to think like the killer, wondering where he or she had made a mistake. Killers always make mistakes, Ms. Grant. Call it gut instinct, but I believe crimes that go off too perfect in their methodology can also reveal flaws within their very perfection. People can actually get trapped by their own obsession to cover up every detail."

Natalie had enough. "I need to go now. Good bye."

"Ms. Grant. I'll make this brief. I guess you're probably in Decatur only a day or two for the funeral. I want to let you know you haven't fooled me. Out of six girls you were the brightest, the one who always stood out in front from academics to athletics. An exceptionally strong athlete who also knew how to be light on her feet is quite a winning combination. I guess all those years of ballet school paid off.

"Having that accident while taking poor Emily Martin to the hospital sure was convenient as things turned out. With brain surgery and amnesia, we figured you could never be convicted even if you did kill those people. But we didn't have anything to connect you to either of the murders. You were the only person who didn't have an airtight alibi, but you were very clever.

"Emily was in the convenience store during the time Abbott got his neck slashed. You were, supposedly, waiting patiently for over 20 minutes in your dad's car on the side parking area, beyond the field of the surveillance camera. Or, were you off across the parking lot doing murderous acts and then drove back undetected just in time to help Emily out with the grocery bags.

"With Emily dead there was no one to refute your story. Things were too coincidental for both murders not to have been committed by the same person. Our profilers agreed.

"You probably figured no one would believe a 17 year old girl could commit such horrific acts of murder. Dismemberment was way too grisly for a woman to do, especially a teenage girl. This case showed premeditation, meticulous planning, knowledge of dissection, and extreme physical agility. How could a girl do all of that? It baffled us.

"Obviously, the murderer wanted to send the police chasing in the wrong direction. There were blatant clues leading the investigators toward sex offenders and violent woman haters. If it was you, did you act alone? Had you met Mr. Sullivan before that night? Was he your accomplice? Even though his buddy Dylan swore for him and he passed the poly, we kept our eye on him for quite some time. Especially after we learned his father's farm was located in the same area."

"Stop this now! You're a wicked man. I have to go."

"When we did the background check on your family we learned that your dad had died five years earlier in a boating accident, ironically at Whispering Lake. The detectives on the case deemed it an unfortunate accident. It was judged an open and shut case, showing no evidence of foul play.

"Of course, the only two witnesses present were you and Jennifer Lawson who were only too happy to tell the police about the can of leaking gas that got all over your dad's clothes, his smoking, and of course, the alcohol he had consumed. You probably used the strong gas fumes as an excuse to get you and your girlfriend off the boat. Very cleaver staging for a 13 year old. It wasn't an accident, was it, Ms. Grant?

"When I first saw the picture of you and Jennifer in the newspaper article looking so pathetic I didn't notice anything unusual. It wasn't until I went back into the files years later that a light finally came on in my head. There was a subtle difference.

"Your hair is perfectly straight today, but you really have naturally curly hair, don't you? You have to blow dry it straight. I never noticed it before. Your hair was curly in that picture. I've seen many pictures of you, but that was the only time your hair was ever curly.

"Every hair in place, right, Ms. Grant--just one of those obsessive little details you always controlled. Ironically, this perfection was your undoing. The article mentioned neither of you went into the lake. So I asked myself, how did her hair get curly if she didn't go in the water? Because you DID, that's why! You killed your father. When your father put gas in the motor from the leaking gas can you saw your opportunity materialize.

"What really happened out there between you, your father, and Jennifer Lawson? When did you plan to kill him? Was Jen your accomplice in murdering your father or just a convenient scapegoat? Did Jennifer witness it? Did she finally confront you after all these years and threaten to tell all? Is that why you murdered her, Natalie Grant?"

"Stop saying these horrible lies! You're very sick and disturbed, you really are!" Natalie was visibly shaken.

"The only other time your hair was curly was after your own accident. Two times Whispering Lake told on you and no one noticed. One day after you were transferred to a regular hospital room I came by for a visit. Your bandages were off and your hair had been washed but left natural. You were asleep. I was oblivious to your curly hair then, but noticed several pierced holes in each earlobe. You weren't wearing earrings because of surgery so I let it slide. Having sisters I just gave you a pass with the French twist hairdo. I can't believe I missed it. Mike told me the clues were staring us in the face.

"Now it makes sense that on party night you turned Whispering Lake into one big bathtub. You got to thoroughly wash your hair and body eliminating any possible trace of blood you might have overlooked? All transgressions eliminated under the cloak of darkness, under the guise of fun and frivolity.

"How long did it take you to plan out Jennifer's murder? You were methodical, I'll give you that. You didn't leave any tracks. There were no prints or hard evidence despite the violence of the act. I remember Mike questioning your updo while watching the surveillance tape. How'd you keep it like that? It must have taken a whole lot of hairspray. Did that hairspray cause you to lose a small gold earring when you hurled the body bags over the dumpster?

"Was that what you went back to look for? James Abbott just got in your way so you killed him. What's a little collateral damage after what you had done?

"Unfortunately, we couldn't see anything incriminating on the surveillance tape with your black leotard and tights, no solo earring, no signs of anything odd. No one seemed to remember that. I guess with all that hair covering up your ears no one would be the wiser. Even with the tape enhanced we were outfoxed. What did Jennifer Lawson do to make you slaughter her?" His words bore venom.

"I've never killed anyone. I was investigated and cleared, detective. As for my hair, it's very curly and gets frizzy with humidity. My father's boating accident took place in summer. August gets very humid around here. You should know that.

"I've gone over all the newspaper clippings looking for answers to my own questions. I saw my hair. That day must have been very hot and sticky out there by the lake. That's the only explanation. Are you satisfied now?" Her expression was icy.

"Ms. Grant. I know we can't arrest you. We never did find a murder weapon or any evidence linking you to either one of the murders. But I know in my gut you murdered both of them."

"Good day, detective. Don't ever come around me again. You're despicable coming to this cemetery with your false accusations. Now get the hell out of my way!" Natalie's face contorted.

"Goodbye, Ms. Grant. If your memory ever does decide to return, please be sure to look me up. We could have a very interesting conversation."

"Go, NOW!" Natalie demanded.

Lombardi turned and walked out of the chapel. He was gone.

"Natalie, I'm over here. We need to get out to gravesite quickly. You're trembling, dear, who was that man you were talking to?" Maggie took Natalie's hand while they walked.

"That was Detective Lombardi. Remember the younger detective on Jennifer Lawson's case? He's been stalking me for years. I've seen him. He said some terrible things to me." They arrived at the gravesite.

"Lower your voice, Natalie. They're giving the blessing."

"We honor your memory and the love you leave behind, we offer your spirit this traditional Irish blessing:

May the road rise to meet you.
May the wind be always at your back
May the sun shine warm upon your face,
The rains fall soft upon your fields. Until we meet again,
May God hold you in the palm of his hand.
Amen."

The priest was finished.

"Goodbye, KT, I'll really miss you." Natalie whispered, "Mom, I can't handle any more. I need to get out of here."

"Okay, we'll go." They slipped away quietly.

"Have you ever let the authorities know he was stalking you?"

"Up until today he never approached me, let alone lay blame on me of anything. Mom, he just accused me of murder!"

"You've got to be kidding me! These detectives are insane. Let it go, Natalie. I don't want you getting all worked up. This day is difficult enough. That nice fellow, Colin Sullivan came up to me while I was waiting for you. He didn't want to bother you now, but asked if he could call on you later. I told him he could. Is that okay?"

"Sure. He seems to always turn up when my life goes through monumental challenges. I've got to start writing my book as soon as I can. I'm going to call my boss first thing Monday morning and request a sabbatical. There's the car."

CHAPTER 51
FACING INNER DEMONS

THE DRIVE HOME from the cemetery was disheartening. Natalie stared out the window numb. Maggie relived the cruel interrogations she had endured with Mike Duffy in the hospital. They were still vivid in her mind. She finally spoke.

"These cops are heartless. You have to ignore them." Natalie kept quiet.

They pulled into the driveway.

"Natalie, why don't you go upstairs and rest. I need to go to the market and pick up some things for dinner. You've had an emotionally trying day. Please disregard that vengeful man. He's just like his old partner who kept bothering me while you were struggling for your life.

"Those detectives pried into my past where they had no right going. I'm not surprised in the least he showed up today. The police know you weren't involved with those murders. You and Emily were together. You have nothing to worry about." Maggie tried her best to comfort her daughter.

"Thanks for everything, Mom. I have something I need to read first, then I'll take a nap. See you at dinnertime."

She went upstairs, sat on her bed and opened KT's letter.

Dear Natalie:

I'm writing this letter to you because I can't do what I'm about to without purging my soul. It's my agonizing torment that underlies why you'll be receiving this letter after I'm buried. Two months ago, as you know, my father passed away. At his gravesite, my mom confronted me with some horrible accusations.

My dad went to Whispering Lake the day after our party and stumbled onto a partially buried garbage bag out where we buried our dog five years before. When he pulled it out of the ground the weight tore open the bag and a bloody cleaver, knife and cutters fell out. They were the murder weapons used on Jennifer. The girls, my brothers, and their friends all had alibis, I didn't. So, my dad assumed I buried the murder weapons which made me Jennifer's killer. Especially considering it was out by our dog's grave.

Natalie, my parents believed I committed both murders. They felt I had the motive, opportunity, and time. My mom told me my father took the bag and its contents directly over to the cemetery. The gravediggers had dug out Manas' grave. My father crawled into it, dug it a little deeper and hid the stuff. When Manas was buried the next day he was buried above the evidence bag!

I never killed anyone, Nat! I need you to believe me. I can't go on living knowing my mother thinks I am a murderer. I'm sure the evidence would clear me, but I just can't handle life anymore. I know you've had a tough road and I don't want to make things any worse. But, I'm leaving the decision to you, if the past should be dug up. I don't know what good it would serve now, but you always had the brains in the group, you decide. Goodbye, KT

CHAPTER 52

COMING TOGETHER

SITTING HERE in my childhood bedroom, I am reflecting on all the unanswered questions that have plagued my life and the inner truth about my friendships with the girls. I'm still mentally stalked by flashbacks and sense an evil force lurking in my past. Should I awaken the terrifying things that torment me and threaten my very life? I've seen his vulgar, lascivious form in the darkness lusting after me, beckoning me. Why can't I see his face?

That unrelenting detective really upset me today. He seemed so cocky and sure of himself. What if he was right? What if I really did kill Jennifer and that security guard? What if? OH, NO…here comes another flashback! I've got to lock my bedroom door. There, now I'm safe. I must start writing while the gateway to the past is open.

TIMELINE

FRIDAY, JUNE 10, 1988

The day my life changed forever, graduation day and the day Jennifer Lawson and James Abbott were murdered. My instinct right now is to panic, but I must stay calm and focused.

5:02 P.M. Commencement is over. Jennifer and I exchange glances. We excuse ourselves from our families and head toward the girls' restroom. Alone now, we argue about a secret we have been harboring for years. Jennifer wants to get it off her chest, tell her parents. I say we should discuss it more, but not at school. We agree to meet later and have this thing out once and for all.

5:09 P.M. I leave the restroom and catch up with Mom and Kevin who are heading toward the parking lot.

Jennifer's very anxious even though she knows her parents have a graduation dinner planned and a big surprise. Jennifer thinks when our meeting is over, she will finally tell her parents what really happened regardless of the consequences. They would have to understand how things just got out of hand. With school finally over and this issue out of the way, she could get on with her life.

Truth was I made her think she was responsible for my dad's murder. He tried to rape her that day in the boat and she had to fight him off. She ended up witnessing his murder, becoming my ill-fated accomplice. I, alone, killed him.

We made a pledge, sworn with blood, that our secret would never be revealed. But five years of silence must have preyed on her, the pathetic weakling!

5:12 P.M. Jennifer left the restroom a few minutes after me. She's very upset and decides she just can't go home, so instead goes to the shopping center to buy new shoes for our party tonight. Our pledge of silence was no longer her priority, salvation was.

5:25 P.M. My family arrives home.

5:45 P.M. Mom leaves for the Callaghans.

6:05 P.M. Alone now, I figure out how to keep Jennifer from exposing my father's murder, and my hand in his killing. With Billy Smith being released, it will divert suspicion. It's not what I want to do, but it has become necessary. I must protect myself. All the pieces are coalescing into an orchestrated sequence of events now. I'm remembering everything. My father is responsible for what he got.

6:15 P.M. The telephone rings. I don't answer. There is no time to speak with anyone. I must stay absolutely focused. I go into my mother's bathroom and get some latex gloves from the bottom cabinet next to her hair dye. I put one pair on and shove the others in my pockets.

I enter my father's tool shed and pull out the box which contains my grandfather's collection of butcher knives. I take his favorite meat cleaver. There is a faded picture hanging crooked on the pegboard wall. It's of Dad posing with me showing off a giant fish he caught. Sitting defiantly on the shelf right below is a half empty, dusty bottle of his cheap rye. It makes me squirm inside. I snatch it up.

I must sidestep bad images so I can continue writing. I grab some old girlie magazines Dad kept hidden behind his workbench and an unopened box of Trojans he had stashed there, too. An extra set of car keys was taped beneath his workbench just the way he had left them five years before. I peel them away. Staring at the dusty floor, images of repeated assaults with a knife at my throat come crashing through my mind.

I had studied Dad's adept ability at handling knives, even as a child, while spying on him. It was part of my defense mechanism. Constant fear kept me always alert, thinking, planning, so I'd be one step ahead of him. Maybe I knew someday the knowledge would serve me well. Bernard Grant was always thinking about contingencies so I had to as well. Never knowing when the next attack would come necessitated my constant vigilance. There was simply no other choice.

Next I grab a spool of nylon rope and a pair of cutters. There was always a stack of towels around. I yanked a couple from the top of the heap. Dad liked his tool shed kept neat and clean. With so many knives, no one would miss one. Nothing else I take will be noticed either. I deposit the items outside, behind a bush next to the garage.

I wonder if Mom ever knew. I shudder at the thought! I will not allow injustice to make me a victim by an inadvertent oversight. I am a master of details, internally working off some primal sense of survival.

I pulled eleven large, heavy duty, plastic trash bags from the cabinet, take eight and double them. I use his portable fan to blow and resettle the five years of accumulated dust. Then I use his mini-vac on the floor eliminating any path of conspiracy. Fortunately, it is located on the wall next to the door. Confident things appear undisturbed, I winked at his picture and exit for the last time replacing the hide-a-key.

The final stretch. I unlock the garage door, retrieve the stashed items and put everything into Dad's trunk. There's paper toweling still stuffed inside the side pocket of the door panel remembering Dad's obsession for keeping the car immaculate. I remove my gloves and carefully put them on some paper toweling next to the driver's seat. Only thing left is to cleanup and dress. I take a two minute hot shower being careful to not get my hair wet. I take no chances. I wonder how all of this was going to play out.

I put my hair up in a French twist and spray it heavily with extra-hold Aqua Net hairspray so nothing moves. I put the remaining gloves into a side pocket of an oversized reinforced nylon gym bag. I take a navy running suit from the closet, and pull out Mother's new navy shoes which I had snatched two weeks before. They match my running suit perfectly. I know my mom has forgotten she bought them months back because she's still wearing her old ones. She'll never miss them. I quickly get dressed and throw a pair of black running shoes into the gym bag along with a black leotard and tights. I add an extra towel and take one final look before leaving.

I mentally review everywhere I've been and everything I've done. My adrenalin is pumping at top speed as I lock up the house and head back to the garage. Once inside, I lean into the front seat and don the gloves that were on the paper toweling. I then head back to the trunk and put all the assembled articles into the waiting gym bag, less three bags to line the trunk. So far so good! I slip behind the wheel, take a deep breath and pull Dad's car out of the garage.

6:40 P.M. I pull up to the curb in front of the vacant house. I open the gym bag, remove some gloves, and push a few into my left pocket. I'll have only minutes to put the body bags into the trunk so I must be totally prepared. I do a preliminary walk around and return to the car for my tools.

6:48 P.M. Jennifer is coming up the street carrying two shopping bags. She's tense, not smiling. I'm triggered by body language, a residual effect from years of sexual abuse. We greet and walk around to the backyard to have our private talk. The large drainage ditch was a gift from Heaven. Jennifer comments on my unusual attire and the gym bag. I give her an excuse and the matter is dropped.

WHISPERING LAKE FISHING TRIP
AUGUST 13, 1983

We begin our conversation by going back over the details of that fateful day five years earlier at Whispering Lake. It was going to be a wonderful outing, a fishing trip with my father. I made everything sound so fantastic that Jennifer was eager to join in.

I slept over at Jen's the night before so her mom drove us to the lake in the morning. Fortunately, we were the first to arrive. I was worried Dad would be hung over like he usually was after a night of boozing and would be in a nasty mood. No way did I want Mrs. Lawson meeting him like that.

Mrs. Lawson had a dental appointment so she left, cautioning us not to venture off. Since we were on private property there was no cause to worry. What I didn't know was my father was still pretty agitated from a fight with Mom. He desperately needed to let off some steam and some sexual frustration.

He kept a bottle of rye hidden behind the tackle box. What better way to spend a day than soaking a worm, leaning back, and sucking down some refreshment and having a little fun on the side. Dad was a simple man with simple pleasures and a healthy sexual appetite that couldn't be fulfilled by Mom alone. He never went whoring around. Nope, he kept everything close to home. After all, he had a daughter. Dad could manage that. Family was family.

Today, he meets Jennifer for the first time. I didn't want to be alone with him anymore. Maybe, he will take a liking to her instead. She is tall, blond, beautiful--everything I'm not.

Even if he doesn't like her, she could help me figure out what to do about the situation. I will be turning 13 in a few weeks and just got my period. I'm scared to death I'll get pregnant.

We walk down to the landing. I tell Jennifer how much I value our friendship. I want her to make a pledge that no matter what we share we'll be bound by a code of silence. Then I pull out a pocketknife from my duffel bag and we take turns making a small cut on our finger. We swear touching fingers, mixing our blood, to keep our pledge of secrecy the rest of our lives.

The morning air is already oppressive, indicating a sticky humid day ahead. Just like I had feared, my father shows up in a foul mood. When he sees Jennifer, he can't believe his eyes or his luck. At 13, she has the breasts of an 18 year old woman. He watches as her long blond hair sweeps across areas of exposed flesh, hugging her tiny halter top. It was in this awkward moment I see that all too familiar leer revealing his self-serving intentions.

His thoughts are transparent. Dad wonders if maybe I brought her along for another reason. That hope throbbed through his mind, chest and groin. His heart starts racing as he imagines himself entering her tight virgin body. Just watching her climb into the boat gives him an erection he almost can't hide.

We motor into the middle of the lake and begin fishing. Dad puts his arms around Jennifer from the back to show her how to hook the bait. He could smell her skin and the scent of her freshly washed hair. His hands graze her butt. She turns around abruptly staring at him with those piercing blue eyes. He hoped she wouldn't fight much. This lovely mermaid would definitely be the catch of the day.

I tell Dad I need to use the lavatory. We aren't far from the dock. He begrudgingly turns the boat around and heads back. He drops me off at the dock.

I watch from the corner of the restroom my perverted father. He immediately dug around for that bottle of rye he had hidden under his gear. Maybe a little swig would help shake off the jitters. With Jennifer just sitting there in front of him looking out toward the lake, he fantasizes about everything he wants to do to her. It's written all over his face. *Man, would I like to be the one to introduce her to womanhood and fuck her brains out.*

"Hey, Jennifer, would you like a taste of this rye? It's very refreshing, tastes like cola. It sure is sticky out here and getting warmer by the minute."

"I don't drink alcohol, Mr. Grant. My parents don't allow it. They say I'm too young."

"Well, honey, your parents aren't here and the way you look tells me you're not too young. Natalie never mentioned anything about you to me before. You sure are one hot babe!"

"Thank you, Mr. Grant. Where is Natalie? Why is she taking so long?"

"Call me, Bernie. I don't feel that old when pretty girls call me by my first name. Why don't you come sit next to me? Take a sip, it'll make you feel alive inside. Come on, sweetheart, just one little taste won't hurt anything."

"Mr. Grant, please, you're making me nervous. Where's Natalie?"

"Don't worry about her. The way I see it Natalie brought you along for me. Kind of a gift, you might say. She knows what I like. Natalie knows what pleases me. After all, she is my daughter. You really are quite a sexy thing. I want to show you something I've got for you."

He moves closer to Jennifer, grabs her and tries to fondle her firm breasts--she screams and pulls away fighting his clambering hands. He shoves Jennifer down to the bottom of the boat pulling her pants and underwear down as he does.

"Natalie, help me! Where are you? Get him off. Help me!!!"

I watch the entire scene unfold. I can't turn away. I pray Jennifer will let him have his way, this might be my freedom.

Finally, I yell, "I know you're scared, Jen. I was, too, my first time. It won't last long. It never does. Forgive me."

"Jennifer, stop squirming around. Hey you little bitch, you bit me! You sure are one frisky young thing. Not like Natalie, she just lays there like a corpse."

In her panic, Jennifer grabs the bottle of rye and slams it over his head. Realizing things are out of control I call out, "Jennifer, Jennifer, I'm coming."

"Natalie, why wouldn't you help me? Your father was trying to rape me. I hit him with that bottle of liquor. He was hurting me. I didn't know what else to do. He's not moving."

"Jennifer, be quiet! I have to think."

"I'm scared, Natalie. Is he dead? There's blood on his head."

"Stop talking, Jennifer! Can't you keep your mouth closed for just a minute? He's dead, that's for sure."

"We've got to get help, Natalie; we've got to call the police!"

"What are you going to tell them, Jennifer? That you've killed my father? Did he actually rape you? What proof do you have? I don't see a mark on you. That's murder, Jen!"

"I didn't do it on purpose, Natalie. I swear I didn't. You believe me, don't you?" Jennifer sobbed.

"Stop that damn crying. You were teasing him. That's what they'll think. You've been caught around older guys with marijuana before and the cops will know that. They'll think you're a troublemaker, a tease, and this wasn't so innocent." I try to sound convincing.

"What do we do?" Jennifer trembled.

"I've got a plan. The only thing to do is blow up the boat."

"Natalie, we can't do that! He's your father!"

"If we don't you might go to jail for murder. We'll tell the cops Dad put us on shore because you got sick to your stomach from the smell of the leaky gas can. He was going to fish alone for a while, then come back to get us. We'll need to row the boat into the middle of the lake and swim back to shore. But first we have to strip off our clothes. That way they won't know we went into the water. It's pretty hot so our hair will dry before we go for help."

"How can we blow it up?" Jennifer became my accomplice.

"We'll prop him up against the side of the boat and put the gas can right next to him and make a leak in the bottom. Then I'll light a cigarette and put it in his mouth. You'll jump out and I'll do the rest. Don't worry, Jen, the fire will make all our troubles go away, I promise."

"Natalie, I'm really scared!"

"I'm very sorry for what my father did to you, but he's been doing that to me since I was in fourth grade. I wasn't thinking right when I left you alone with him. I owe you. Remember our blood pledge. This is our secret for the rest of our lives. No one can ever know the truth."

"Oh, Natalie, I had no idea. Maybe the police will understand if we tell them the whole story."

"No, trust me. We can't take that chance. We have something we need to do and timing is everything. Let's get going."

We row the boat out with Dad sprawled on the bottom.

"Jen, it's time for you to get over the side of the boat. It won't take me long, but I need to be sure."

"Okay, Nat." Jen jumps into the water and begs me to hurry.

"I'm going as fast as I can."

"Natalie, what the fuck! What the hell are you doing? My head throbs like a son of a bitch. Help me get up."

"Dad, you're a sick bastard. You just tried to rape my best friend! You don't deserve to live." I raise my arm.

"Natalie, DON'T!"

The thick glass bottle of rye was stubborn like my dad, but this time lands a blow he wouldn't recover from. I continue to talk to him while he's lying there unconscious or dead, it didn't matter.

"It won't take long, Dad. That's what I used to say to myself when you raped me over and over. It won't take long. I was never warm when you touched me like that. I was cold as ice. Just like the carcasses that hung in Grandpa's meat locker. That painful icy stinging sensation still clings to my back where you pushed me up against the wall, remember that, Dad?"

Staring at him I say with conviction, "This will look like an accident. All I need to do is punch a hole in the gas can, pour some in the bottom of the boat and on you. This match will take you straight to hell where you belong. Bye, Dad." The torture was over.

"Jennifer, I'm coming. Swim to shore fast, the boat's gonna blow!"

"Natalie, you were yelling at your dad. Then you hit him again. Didn't I kill him?"

"No, you just knocked him out. I had to finish it. I didn't have a choice."

EXPLOSION, EXPLOSION!!

"It's over. Jennifer, go get your watch from the duffel bag and tell me exactly what time it is. We need to be careful what we tell the police. We can't make any mistakes, Jen. Do you understand? We're in this together, now and forever."

Jennifer just stood there stunned.

"What did we just do? Your dad is dead. I think I'm gonna barf."

"Listen to me, Jen, dry off. Then get us both a drink of the lemonade your mom packed. Part of me is scared, too, but another part is relieved he's dead. He was a monster. I could never tell anyone what he did to me. I had to keep my family safe from him."

We get dressed, drink the lemonade, and discuss the timeline. I have to make sure Jennifer understands how vital it is that our version of what happened be identical and believable.

11:51 A.M. "This time is important."

"Why?" Jennifer asks.

"Because our stories have to match. So let's get it straight now."

10:00 A.M. "Your mom dropped us off here and twenty minutes later my dad arrived."

10:20 A.M. "Okay, then what?" Jennifer is anxious.

"We got into his rickety old boat and he went to put the gas in the motor. The can was leaking on the bottom and it got all over him and the boat. The fumes were really strong. We went a little ways into the lake and you got queasy. My dad said he would bring us back to shore.

11:15 A.M. "He said he'd be back for us in about an hour. He wanted to relax, fish, and enjoy his day off. He hadn't caught any fish yet and didn't want to get skunked. We figured he'd return by **12:30 P.M.**

"We'll say we were behind the restroom by the picnic tables talking when we heard the explosions. We couldn't see him from where we were sitting. We ran to the lake and saw a lot of smoke and pieces of the boat floating in the water. Besides the leaky gas can, we knew he was smoking cigarettes and had a bottle of alcohol with him.

"We panicked and raced to the road to find someone that could help us. Let the police figure the rest out for themselves. What else can they think other than this was a terrible accident. I'm almost 13 and you just turned 13. Keep the story simple and we'll be fine." I feel optimistic.

"The story sounds believable, but I'm still scared. How do I lie to my parents? I'm not a very good liar."

"Maybe I should have just let my father rape you. Then this would be easy."

CHAPTER 53
THE FIRST TIME

NATALIE'S MIND is compelled to revisit the beginning of her emotional carnage. She ventured back in time, it was **December, 1980** when it all began. **December 22th**, three days before Christmas, that was the day she was raped the very first time. Natalie needed to remember. It would embolden her to face what she had to do.

You had taken me along to Minnesota to see Grandma and Grandpa. Mom and Kevin stayed behind to prepare for the holidays. We'd be back by Christmas Eve. When we arrived, I asked Grandpa to show me everything he knew about how to butcher an animal. I watched in awe as he disemboweled and dismembered a cow…the saws, knives, and blood. Most girls would squirm at the very thought but not me. I couldn't explain my fascination then, maybe now I can. Being with those carcasses in the meat locker I smelled death. I, too, felt like a carcass. I still do. Yes, I can still smell the blood.

You took me into the meat locker that first time when no one was around and you hurt me. Grandfather had no idea what you did to me after he left us alone to watch his butcher shop and went to make deliveries. We had only been out minutes before Grandpa came back. Embarrassed and confused, I hurt with a strange burning pain inside. **I was only 10. How could you?…** But you taught me well, Dad, to be numb to pain, both physical and emotional.

I stared at Jennifer, processing, calculating, and coming to final terms. There was no question. Jennifer was now a growing liability and needed to be eliminated. But how could I do it and not get caught? I needed to do something so grotesque, so aberrant, no one would ever suspect a girl. It must be something repulsive…I remembered the slaughterhouses so prevalent in Illinois. Men did these types of things, not women and surely not girls. Yes, this was the perfect idea. I would butcher Jennifer. She would be just another carcass to carve up. I knew I could do it.

CHAPTER 54

BEYOND REASON AND PAIN

NATALIE RATIONALIZED her actions. She had suffered silently through years of being raped. Natalie would never forget his foul breath, the sweaty smell of his body, or his dirty fingers probing her. She was beyond pain; nothing could touch her soul at this point.

Natalie wasn't a murderer by nature; she was just protecting herself and her family. It would destroy her mother if she ever found out the husband she still mourned had molested his very own daughter. Natalie would not allow her father to continue his abuse from the grave. She could pull this off if she was very, very careful about all the details. After all, she was a perfectionist.

Natalie guessed she knew all along things would come to this. Jennifer just couldn't keep her mouth shut. The whole town would know Natalie Grant's father was a rapist. Death wasn't so final, after all, if secrets were exposed. Natalie would have to remedy that, now and forever. The time had come. She had suffered far worse at the hand of her father. Fifteen minutes had past. It was Showtime.

7:05 P.M. Natalie simply stopped talking. Her eyes glazed over. She pictured the dismemberment. Everything she had learned from her grandfather would now pay off.

Jennifer just stared at her incredulously. She didn't even try to scream. Their blood pledge five years earlier was simply a self-serving ploy. The realization came over her that she was just a pawn. Jennifer never noticed Natalie's subtle movements.

Natalie slid her hands behind herself and put on a pair of gloves. She effortlessly took the switchblade out of her pocket and with one swift motion slashed Jennifer across the throat slicing straight through her left jugular. Then she stabbed her repeatedly in the chest without the slightest bit of hesitation or remorse. She stopped counting when Jennifer slumped to the ground. An internal clock started ticking.

It was all about the timing now. She worked fast and efficiently knowing she needed to be as methodical as possible. She set the knife down on the ground next to Jennifer, then removed the gloves, flipped them inside out and laid them alongside the knife. She put on a fresh pair, then opened the gym bag and grabbed the nylon rope and cutters.

Fortunately, Jennifer's body fell near the drainage ditch. Jennifer had on a cotton two-piece sleeveless summer outfit which presented no problem for the work at hand. Natalie tied a piece of rope around the upper portion of each of Jennifer's arms at the shoulder to stem blood flow from gushing too quickly when she dissected. She repeated this process on each leg at the groin. Several ropes were wrapped around Jennifer's torso acting as both tourniquets and carriers.

The ropes were doing their job well as there was very little blood spillage. Now, she pulled out the condoms, opened up one and stretched it over Jennifer's tongue pushing it to the back of her throat. There would be no mistaking that only a man could be this brutal. She got the bottle of rye, unscrewed it, and poured some alcohol across Jennifer's bloodied chest.

Calculating Jennifer's weight at about 125 lbs., Natalie grabbed the meat cleaver and proceeded to cut the body into manageable sections. Natalie had to use all her skill and strength. This was her greatest test. She felt close to the finish line and knew she wouldn't falter.

After Jennifer's body parts had been successfully transferred into the waiting bags, Natalie threw a girlie magazine and a few opened condoms into each one as well. She tied each bag carefully with rope using a sailor's knot.

Natalie meticulously washed off the knife, the cleaver, and the cutters. She completely hosed down the bags. The blood that had spilled despite her precautions washed easily into the open ditch and down the drain. She let the water run until it was clear. She also rinsed the area free of shoeprints.

Natalie stripped off her running suit and removed her shoes. She put it into the fourth bag along with the towel wrapped cleaver, cutters, rye, rope, gloves and remaining condom box and wrappers. Naked, but for her gloves, she went over to the ditch and hosed herself off just to be extra thorough. Memories of scrubbing herself repeatedly after attacks from her father still clung to her skin no matter how much she washed. She kept the knife out available for the unexpected.

Grabbing a shovel that was leaning up against the house she heaped dirt over the entire drainage area. A medicinal odor filled the air. Confident that everything was cleaned up and covered properly, she returned the shovel to the wall and put the hose back exactly as it was found. Natalie dried herself off with the paper toweling from the car. She slipped on her black tights and leotard and put on her clean black running shoes. She tucked the switchblade inside her leotard leg. Her hair was still sprayed up stiff. Natalie glanced around and smiled, time to go.

She left the three body bags slumped up against the side of the house like they were leaves and walked back around to the side grabbing Jennifer's two shopping bags on the way.

The now empty gym bag received both bags easily. She strolled toward the car nonchalantly. The street was quiet. Nothing had changed in the past 72 minutes. Even the air hung still.

She slipped inside and looked at her reflection in the rearview mirror to make sure no blood had gotten on her face, neck or hair. She'd learned early on that attention to details and timing was often the difference between success and failure. Jennifer's remains would hold in the double bags until she was ready to dispose of them. She only needed 30-45 minutes at the most. It would be dark by then. Pleased with herself she pulled away.

8:00 P.M. Natalie drove down the street reviewing the details and final preparations. It was still too light out to transfer the bags into the trunk. This would be nature's call. She could wait.

She had noticed the dumpsters in the parking lot on her initial drive-by. They were situated next to an exit in the shopping center's back parking lot. She could literally pull right up to them and dump the body bags in no time at all. Her plan was finalized. She'd use the third dumpster, the one closest to the street and the emptiest. That would be the most time-sensitive challenge and her most vulnerable point. It must be done before the shopping center's security guard makes his 9:00 P.M. rounds.

8:05 P.M. The center was unusually slow for a Friday night due to graduation parties. As Natalie waits for nightfall and that perfect moment, she decides to get a rocky road ice cream cone at the ice cream parlor, a well-deserved reward. An exhilaration filled her. While there, she placed everything from the trunk in the fourth bag and hid it behind the spare tire. She threw Jennifer's shopping bags, including a receipt and credit card, in two separate trash containers in the ice cream parlor parking lot.

8:30 P.M. The night descended into a charcoal black. Natalie eased her car into the driveway of the vacant house. This is where her physical strength would show. Donning gloves she moved swiftly, like a panther in the night, feeling stronger than ever been before. She moved the bags in less than 45 seconds into the waiting trunk.

Jennifer was cooperating at last. It took her dying to finally understand what the meaning of being a true blood sister was all about. Natalie let the car roll backward in neutral toward the street, then started the engine just as it reached the end of the driveway.

8:45 P.M. In less than five minutes she hoisted the three body bags into the dumpster and got out of there. The deed now done, it was surprisingly easy. Clearly, she had obsessed and fretted unnecessarily.

8:49 P.M. Shaking from exhilaration, excitement, and power she drove down the street a short distance, pulled over to the curb, and looked at herself in the rearview mirror. Something is definitely wrong, but what?

8:51 P.M. Suddenly, she realizes what it is. Her gold earring was missing. The thick layer of hairspray was meant to hold her hair in place so strands wouldn't fall out and incriminate her. But she didn't figure on it affecting the tiny back of her earring. Where was it? She started to panic.

Natalie grabbed the flashlight, got out of the car, and walked back to the parking lot. She didn't expect to find it, but couldn't leave without checking. Her plan had been flawless until now. As she approached the dumpsters Natalie saw the security guard making his rounds. So as not to look suspicious she decided to just walk over to his car and tell him the truth, that she'd lost an earring.

Suddenly, fear set in when she realized Jennifer's parents would tell the police that Jen was supposed to be at her house for a sleepover. Eventually everyone would know Jennifer was missing and the security guard would remember seeing her in the parking lot.

Abbott shined his flashlight on her as she approached his vehicle. He had been trying to converse over his two-way radio, but was only receiving static. He recognized Natalie immediately, which sent a chill through her. He put his head out the opened window and said,

"Hey, I know you!"

He said something else, but she didn't hear. Her panic was now skyrocketing. She told him about the earring. He offered to help look for it. That's when she knew she had no choice. Abbott would eventually finger her and she couldn't afford that.

He got out of his car and shined his light on the ground. Just as he does, Natalie hit him over his head with her flashlight. He managed to stammer, "What the hell!"

It was then that she slashed him across his left jugular just like she did to Jennifer. She was surprised how easy it was the second time. His vacant stare as he fell, and the unnatural twist of his head when he landed told her she had succeeded.

No time now to look for the earring. She got in the car and returned to the vacant house to wash off the knife for the final time. The flashlight was inspected carefully. No blood. The knife would go with the rest of the items.

9:13 P.M. Time to get to Miller's Convenience Store. Emily would be wondering where she was. Natalie parked and entered the store. Emily was at the counter receiving change from the cashier. Natalie took a bag from her. Emily asked what all the commotion was about in the back parking lot. She said she'd heard sirens, too, but didn't have a clue. The truth was she never heard a thing, but the pounding in her chest.

Her mind was already contemplating her final move. Dumping the fourth bag would be easy. Natalie had the perfect place. It was at Whispering Lake. There was a pet grave and a cross with a dog's name. It would be an excellent hiding place. Having KT bring an outfit for Natalie was a great idea. It would give her a reason to split from the group.

Here's where she stopped her timeline. Everything before the accident was now part of her active memory. No longer was her canvas blank, but a palate of living color. She had found her way home through the nightmares and flashbacks. Natalie opened her eyes and stared around her bedroom. The monster inside that had fought for dominion was now dead and gone. But she did have sorrow.

IT WAS UNFORTUNATE I had to kill that security guard. I couldn't leave that possibility open. Besides, it wasn't my fault. You made me do this, Dad! You used to hold that switchblade to my neck while you raped me. You threatened to slit my throat if I ever told anyone. No one ever knew what you did except for Jennifer. Now look where it led.

"Natalie, can you hear me? You've been up there for hours. That nice young man, Colin Sullivan, just called and said he was dropping by for a quick visit. He didn't want you to turn him down so he's just coming over. Please give him another chance, honey. He sees you for who you really are--a beautiful person inside and out."

"That's fine, Mom. I just finished the timeline for my book and I'm feeling ravenous. I think when Colin arrives I'll ask him to take me down to get a rocky road ice cream. Writing has triggered my appetite. I wonder if that ice cream parlor down by the Decatur Shopping Center is still open. It's been over twenty years since I've stepped foot inside."

EPILOGUE

NATALIE KNEW THE DAY would come when the past would catch up with the present. She did wonder how her life would have turned out had she not been faced with having to protect her family name. Yet, Natalie played the hand she was dealt.

She decided to bury KT's letter. Not simply destroy it as it was the only physical evidence beyond the grave that proved what had happened to them. It would be hidden in a safe location where no one would ever look. Now, standing in the cemetery where her dad was buried, she stared at his grave.

Natalie wanted to tell him how he had destroyed so many lives, but figured the secret buried close to his bones would suffice. The plot next to his was reserved for her mom, but she had changed her mind and wanted to be buried by her parents in Duluth. The decision to keep or sell the plot was Natalie's. Family was still family and she might like to be buried next to her dad. She had placed the note in an army surplus water proof container figuring it was good for a lifetime.

November was particularly cold this year. The dark clouds in the sky were ominous and the wind was kicking up. She knew the cemetery would be vacant with the harsh weather conditions. Funerals would have already been held and mourners long gone.

She watched the groundskeeper make his rounds crunched up in his heavy woolen coat trying to shield his face from the piercing cold. Soon he was gone, too, and she was alone.

The cloak of night was descending. Natalie dug a deep hole and placed the container inside. This time she wouldn't be discovered and details wouldn't be neglected. The irony of it all. Here she was burying the past again. She giggled as she finished.

"Some secrets need to stay buried."